The Political Theory of Recognition

The Political Theory of Recognition

A Critical Introduction

Simon Thompson

Polity

First published in 2006 by Polity Press

Polity Press
65 Bridge Street
Cambridge CB2 1UR, UK.

Polity Press
350 Main Street
Malden, MA 02148, USA

ISBN-10: 0-7456-2761-7
ISBN-13: 978-07456-2761-7
ISBN-10: 0-7456-2762-5 (pb)
ISBN-13: 978-07456-2762-5 (pb)

A catalogue record for this book is available from the British Library.

Typeset in 10.5 on 12 pt Sabon
by Planman I:TES India Ltd.
Printed and bound in Great Britain by MPG Books Ltd, Bodmin, Cornwall

For further information on Polity, visit our website: www.polity.co.uk

Contents

Acknowledgements

Discussions with many friends and colleagues have helped me to form my views on recognition. Among these are Chris Armstrong, Alison Assiter, Michael Bacon, Richard Bellamy, John Bird, David Boucher, Bob Brecher, Gary Browning, Kerstin Budde, Nick Buttle, Simon Clarke, Anthony Elliott, Alan Finlayson, Nancy Fraser, Steve Garner, Alan Greer, Paul Hoggett, Donald Horowitz, Heikki Ikäheimo, Susan James, Peter Jowers, Paul Kelly, Arto Laitinen, Adrian Little, Patchen Markell, Matt Matravers, Chris May, Cillian McBride, Tariq Modood, Monica Mookherjee, Anthony Moran, Jamie Munn, Mairead nic Craith, Shane O'Neill, David Owen, Carole Pateman, Alan Patten, Graham Smith, Judith Squires, Adam Swift, Charles Taylor, Jem Thomas, Jules Townshend, Sean Watson and Christopher Zurn. I hope those I've overlooked will forgive me.

I've also presented the ideas which have found their way into this book in a variety of different places over the last several years, including seminars at the universities of Brighton, Bristol, Cardiff, Queen's University Belfast, Southampton and UWE, and conferences organized by the UK Political Studies Association, the American Political Science Association and the European Consortium for Political Research. I've received invaluable feedback at all of these events.

John B. Thompson, my editor at Polity, has shown great patience with this project. Ellen McKinlay, my editorial assistant, has helped chivvy me along just when I needed to be. Two anonymous readers at Polity provided invaluable advice. Rose West, research administrator at the Centre for Critical Theory, helped prevent me from being overwhelmed by other responsibilities. Special thanks also to Pete Wiltshire, who helped make the final week bearable.

Throughout the period in which I've been writing this book I've received generous support for my research from what was the Faculty of Economics and Social Sciences and what is now the Faculty of Humanities, Languages and Social Sciences at the University of the West of England, Bristol. In particular, a period of research leave at the beginning of 2005 was invaluable.

When I first met her, I told Lucy I was finishing a book on recognition. Now I can honestly say that I've just finished it. It wouldn't have been possible without her.

This book is dedicated to the memory of my parents.

1

Introduction

1.1 The Rise of Recognition

In recent times, there has been a significant transformation of the landscape of politics. For at least two decades after the end of the Second World War, the politics of Western societies were characterized by what has been called the 'social democratic consensus'. As a result, these societies had a number of distinctive features. They were liberal in the sense that they had constitutions which protected citizens' basic rights and freedoms. They were democratic, since people could vote for political parties to represent them in the legislative institutions of the state. They were more specifically *social* democratic, since they engaged in a degree of income redistribution, welfare provision and economic planning. Finally, such societies were based on the assumption that nations and states should coincide, so that each nation should be governed by a single, unified political authority. In the societies which were governed by this social democratic consensus, politics took a familiar form. Citizens' public identities were defined by their identification with particular social classes and occupational groups. This sense of identity then strongly influenced their allegiances to particular political parties. These parties were distinguished primarily by their emphases on different elements of this consensus. In particular, while some parties were supportive of an extensive welfare state and strong management of the economy, others favoured a smaller state and a greater role for the free market. Thus politics was distributed along a familiar left–right spectrum, centring on a struggle in which different groups competed for as large a share of society's resources as possible (Gamble and Wright 1999; Sassoon 1997).

Since the late 1960s, however, the social democratic consensus has faced a number of challenges. On one side, the New Left criticized the liberal element of the consensus by suggesting that a regime of 'repressive tolerance' granted a merely illusory freedom. It also condemned the democratic element by arguing that the system was controlled by a political class which prevented genuine popular democracy. On the other side of the political divide, the New Right focused on the social democratic element of the consensus, arguing that the welfare state damaged economic efficiency and undermined personal freedom (Klatch 1999; Lyons 1996). As a result of the collapse of the consensus, citizens' experience of politics has changed considerably. Identification with classes or occupational groups has become a much less important element of individuals' sense of identity. Into this vacated space, so-called new social movements have emerged to present a novel sort of challenge to the politics of social democracy. The women's movement, peace movement and green movement, which appeared in the late 1960s, followed by many others later on, were associated with new types of political identity which did not fit on the traditional political spectrum. A series of challenges has also emerged to the nation-state itself. These have included the politics of nationalist and sub-nationalist movements, movements of indigenous peoples, and struggles against colonialism. As a result, a new politics of multiculturalism has emerged, which has attacked the assumption that there can and should be a simple coincidence of national identity and political authority (Modood 2005; Parekh 2000).

A number of political commentators have suggested that this transformation of the political landscape can best be understood by using the idea of recognition. 'A number of strands of contemporary politics', Charles Taylor argues, 'turn on the need, sometimes the demand, for recognition.' He says that today this 'demand comes to the fore . . . on behalf of minority or "subaltern" groups, in some forms of feminism, and in what is called the politics of multiculturalism' (1995b: 225). In a similar vein, Nancy Fraser reflects on 'the new salience of struggles for recognition, their decoupling from struggles for redistribution, and the relative decline of the latter, at least in their class-centered egalitarian form'. Her illustrations of this phenomenon range 'from battles around multiculturalism to struggles over gender and sexuality, from campaigns for national sovereignty and subnational autonomy to newly energized movements for international human rights' (2003: 88–9). Axel Honneth agrees with Fraser that 'a great many contemporary social movements can only be properly under-stood from a normative point of view if their motivating demands are interpreted along the lines of a "politics of identity" – a demand for the cultural recognition of their collective identity'. He gives the examples of 'feminism, ethnic minorities, gay and lesbian subcultures' (2003: 111).

As we can see, these three commentators all believe that contemporary politics has seen a shift away from ideas of class, equality, economy and nation towards those of identity, difference, culture and ethnicity. They also believe that it is possible to understand this political transformation as the result of the rise of the politics of recognition. They believe, moreover, that the characteristic form taken by such a politics is a struggle in which a particular group demands that other groups give it public acknowledgement for some feature it possesses, for which it thinks that it deserves recognition. Taylor, Fraser and Honneth do not just think that the idea of recognition can help us to understand the recent transformation of the political landscape. They also think that it can enable us to formulate an appropriate response to this transformation. They contend that the idea of recognition not only holds the key to understanding contemporary politics, but that it is also at the heart of what justice means today. For this reason, each of them articulates a political theory of recognition which is based on the premiss that a just society would be one in which everyone gets due recognition. In such a society, in other words, all individuals and groups would enjoy the practical acknowledgement that they deserve.

In this book, my aim is to compare and contrast the political theories of recognition formulated by Taylor, Fraser and Honneth, in order to determine which theory – or which combination of elements from different theories – is the most coherent and convincing. I believe that this is an important and worthwhile exercise since, if these theorists are right, then studying their accounts of recognition will help us to understand the shape of the contemporary political landscape, and will also give us invaluable guidance in matters of social justice today. For one thing, consideration of these theories could help us to under-stand the significance of debates such as that currently raging about the legitimacy of the project of multiculturalism. For another, it could help us to decide what we should do in response to demands for the protection of rights, the preservation of cultures, the redistribution of resources, and so on.

In this chapter, I shall begin my defence of these ambitious claims by introducing the principal themes of the book. I begin by outlining a number of examples of the politics of recognition in practice. I use these examples in order to construct a generic model of the politics of recognition (1.2). Following this, I sketch the three political theories of recognition on which I shall focus, concentrating in particular on the principal points of agreement and disagreement between them (1.3). In the final section, I summarize each of the chapters that are to follow. This provides an account of the principal lines of argument which I shall develop in this book (1.4).

1.2 The Politics of Recognition

On 1 December 1955 in Montgomery, Alabama, Rosa Parks was taking a bus home from work. She sat in the part of the bus which was reserved for whites, and ignored the driver's demand that she give up her seat. She was subsequently arrested and charged with disorderly conduct. Parks's individual protest against segregation was quickly taken up by a variety of civil rights groups. Together they set up the Montgomery Improvement Association in order to co-ordinate a bus boycott that lasted for over a year. The boycott ended in total victory for the protestors. In 1956 the US Supreme Court upheld a lower court's decision that the segregation of public buses was unconstitutional. On 21 December of that year the leaders of the boycott travelled together on the first desegregated bus (Cook 1998: 98–109). The Montgomery bus boycott was one of the seminal events of the American civil rights movement. A wide range of protests over the following decade led, amongst other things, to the passage of the Civil Rights Act in 1964 and the Voting Rights Act in 1965. Many years after the event, Parks reflected on her experience: 'What I learned best was that I was a person with dignity and self-respect, and should not set my sights lower than anybody else just because I was black' (cited in Fairclough 2002: 228). Martin Luther King echoed Parks's feelings when, in a speech about the boycott, he said that people were 'tired of being plunged into the abyss of humiliation'. As he declared, 'we are American citizens, and we are determined to acquire our citizenship to the fullness of its meaning' (cited in Fairclough 2002: 230).

On 30 October 1995, Quebec held a referendum that could have marked the end of the Canadian federation. The rather confusing question on the ballot paper was this: 'Do you agree that Quebec should become sovereign after having made a formal offer to Canada for a new economic and political partnership within the scope of the bill respecting the future of Quebec and of the agreement signed on

June 12, 1995, Yes or No?' At stake was the relationship of Quebec to the rest of Canada. A Yes vote would have meant the predominantly francophone province declaring its independence from the federation. In the event, the bill was very narrowly defeated by a margin of just 54,288 (0.06 per cent) votes in favour of the defenders of federalism. The political crisis symbolized by the 1995 referendum marked one particularly low point in the difficult relationship between Quebec and the rest of Canada. Some commentators have argued that the problems of the last two decades or so have been the result of Pierre Trudeau's strategy of 'national unity' that was encapsulated by the 1982 Charter of Rights and Freedoms. The Charter asserts that '[e]very individual is equal before and under the law and has the right to the equal protection and equal benefit of the law without discrimination' (§15.1). However, although the Charter appeared to meet all of the demands that the civil rights movement made of the American political system, many people rejected it on the grounds that it took no account of Canada's deep diversity. Some Quebeckers in particular felt that their distinctive collective identity was being ignored. As a result, they supported an opposing strategy that aimed to secure acknowledgement for the distinctiveness of Quebec within the federation. For instance, the Meech Lake Accord of 1987 proposed to amend the Canadian Constitution in order to recognize 'that Quebec constitutes within Canada a distinct society' (§2.1b).

In France, a law that banned the wearing of conspicuous religious symbols in state-funded schools came into effect on 2 September 2004. Although the law officially banned all religious symbols, it was widely understood that it was directed primarily against Muslim headscarves. The French government's policy appeared to enjoy the support of a substantial majority of French citizens (up to 70 per cent in various polls). It also brought together an unlikely coalition of supporters, from feminists who believed that the headscarf was a symbol of women's oppression, to members of the far right who wished to protect what they saw as the integrity of French culture against alien influence. The reason that was officially given for the ban was to preserve the secularity of the French state. As Jacques Chirac, the French President at the time, declared in a speech on 17 December 2003: 'In all conscience, I consider that the wearing of clothes or signs which conspicuously denote a religious affiliation must be prohibited at school. The Islamic veil, regardless of the name you give it, the Kippa or a Cross of a clearly excessive size, have no place in State schools. State schools will remain secular.'[1] Understandably, the headscarf ban was not welcomed by most French Muslims. The most frequent complaint was that the ban was clearly unfair, singling out Muslims for discriminatory treatment. Since other religious symbols such as Christian crosses were unlikely to be 'clearly excessive' in size, it was apparent that the policy was targeted at headscarves. This objection was accompanied by the demand that Muslims be treated in the same way as all other French citizens. In this particular case, this could mean either that all religious symbols should be permitted or, alternatively, that all should be banned.

In recent years, there has been an ongoing controversy in the United States about same-sex marriage. The most recent phase of the controversy broke out in November 2003 when the Massachusetts Supreme Court ruled that preventing gay people from marrying was unconstitutional. Then, as the *Guardian* reported, on 12 February of the following year, the Democratic mayor of San Francisco declared that marriage licences could be issued to gay couples. However, California's Supreme Court disagreed with the legal decision made in Massachusetts. On 12 March 2004, it 'ordered officials in San Francisco to immediately stop granting same-sex marriage licences, delivering a blow to gay rights advocates in the United States'.[2] Since 2004 was a Presidential election year, this issue became a matter of national importance. In his State of the Union address on 20 January 2004 President George W. Bush gave his support for the statute which 'protects marriage under federal law as a union of a man and a woman'. He went on to declare: 'Our nation must defend the sanctity of marriage.'[3] This argument against the legalization of same-sex marriage appeared to assume that the Constitution can and should embody certain fundamental moral values which are vital to the survival of American society. John Kerry, Bush's Democratic challenger in the Presidential election, declared himself in favour of civil union – but not marriage – between same-sex couples. Here the case for the legalization of same-sex partnerships also referred to the American Constitution, but in this case it is assumed that differences between individuals should be ignored in order to guarantee them all exactly the same freedoms.

There are very significant differences between these four cases. The first concerns the struggles of African-Americans for equality. These struggles took place in a social and political context that was quite unique. In the 1950s and 1960s, the experience of slavery was still a living memory for black Americans. It is worth calling to mind the fact that the Civil Rights Act of 1965 was passed exactly 100 years after the abolition of slavery. In these circumstances, one part of black Americans' struggle was to overcome a highly racialized account of their identity. The second case-study concerns a national minority which defines itself first and foremost in terms of its language.

This minority then seeks to have its distinctive identity recognized in the federation of which it is part. I focused on the case of Quebec and Canada. But the same issues arise wherever a national minority struggles for acknowledgement from the state in which it is located. The relationships of Scotland and Wales to the UK, and of Catalonia and the Basque country to Spain, present similar problems. In the third case-study, I examined a group which invokes its religious identity in order to challenge the political identity of the state. I focused on the particular case of the French government's ban on Muslim headscarves. But similar issues arise wherever a religious group finds itself at odds with the laws of its state. Other examples could include Sikhs, whose wearing of turbans puts them at odds with laws demanding that crash-helmets be worn on motorcycles, and the Amish in the USA, who have made a case for educating their children outside mainstream schools. In the final case-study, it is the relationship between people's sexual identities and the legal and political institutions of the state that is at stake. I described the controversy concerning same-sex marriage in the USA, but I could have looked at a number of other states in which the same issue is presently high on the political agenda, including France and the UK.

In spite of the important differences between these cases, I want to argue that, since they are all instances of the politics of recognition, they have a number of features in common. Three features are of particular salience. The first of these is a focus on the idea of identity or difference. The conceptions of 'race', language, religion and sexuality invoked in these various cases are all markers of identity: they point to certain features which make some people different from others. Thus black Americans are contrasted with white Americans, francophone Canadians with anglophone Canadians, French Muslims with French non-Muslims, and gay people with straights. It is its identity that marks out a particular object – be it an individual, a group or an institution – for public acknowledgement. Some French Muslims, for instance, believe that they should receive recognition in virtue of their distinct religious identity. A second characteristic shared by a number of these instances of the politics of recognition is a concern with equality and inclusion. Often the group demanding recognition feels inaudible and invisible. It has a strong sense of being marginalized and excluded, left out and ignored. Hence the demand for recognition is a demand to be seen and heard, to count for something, to be included. Here a group will characteristically argue that, since it is the same as others, it wants to be treated no differently from them. The first phase of the American civil rights movement can be associated with this sort of demand. A third feature of the politics of recognition may appear to be in tension with the previous feature. A group seeking recognition may feel overlooked, unvalued and even denigrated. As a consequence, it may demand that its distinctive contribution be valued and its unique identity affirmed. Rather than wanting to be treated the same as others, in this case the group places emphasis on its difference from those others. The claim that French Muslim schoolgirls should be allowed to wear the veil can be seen as a demand of this kind.

Although a number of other features of the politics of recognition are not unique to it, since they are nearly always present in specific cases, they are worth mentioning here. One of these is a concern not just with equality or difference, but also with resources. The group demanding recognition may believe that it is not receiving a fair share of society's assets. It may point to higher levels of unemployment experienced by its members or to the way in which the central state unfairly appropriates the resources found in its region. For example, this has been a complaint made by Scottish nationalists about the UK government's use of the oil resources to be found in the North Sea. Another of these additional features is a concern not just with individual rights or cultural survival, but also with democracy. A group may feel that the structure of the electoral system denies it fair representation, or that its minority status means that it is permanently excluded from power. The case made for reserved seats for the Maori in the New Zealand parliament is based on a concern of this kind. A final feature of the politics of recognition is that it is often characterized by struggle. For instance, one group may struggle to be incorporated in a polity from which it is presently excluded. Another may struggle for its distinctive identity to be given appropriate acknowledgement – by, for example, having its cultural works included in the literary canon of that society. Other groups may resist these demands for recognition, seeking permanently to exclude a group from citizenship, or to preserve the canon in its present form. With these rival groups joining the battle, the struggle for recognition is well and truly on.

1.3   Three Theories of Recognition

As I said in section 1.1, my principal aim in this book is to conduct a critical comparison of several political theories of recognition. For this reason I shall use the term 'political theory' interchangeably with that of 'theory of justice' or sometimes 'theory of social justice'. The *raison d'être* of a political theory is not primarily to understand or explain its object. Such tasks fall within the domain of political science. Rather, its aim is to explicate and justify a set of principles that can be used to structure political institutions, guide political practices, and inform political policies. Such a theory may, for instance, recommend the maximization of individual freedom, the achievement of equality, the reinvigoration of community, or indeed some mixture of all these goals. Having said this, a political theory will nevertheless depend on empirical theories of politics. It is no use recommending a principle of justice if certain ineliminable features of the world make the realization of that principle utterly impossible. Thus a political theory will rely on the findings of political science to demonstrate that its principles are feasible. For example, a communitarian theory must rely on a plausible account of the nature of community, and a libertarian theory must show that the degree of freedom it recommends will not result in anarchy. However, since many different sets of principles of justice are likely to be feasible, the purpose of a political theory is to persuade us that one of these sets of feasible principles is also the most desirable. Such a theory, in other words, aims to convince us that the principles of justice which it expounds are those by which we should live our common life.

Political theories of recognition are a subspecies of all political theories. These particular theories contend that, although other ideas such as freedom, equality and community may have a role to play, it is the idea of recognition which holds the key to determining the nature of justice. The principal aim of such a theory, then, is to justify a set of political principles which are derived from a particular conception of recognition. To be specific, it seeks to show how a society should be organized so that everyone enjoys the recognition which is due to them. As with any political theory, it will of course have to rely on – or, at the very least, tacitly assume – certain findings of political science. Such findings may include a psychological theory which explains why people strive for recognition, or an empirical account of the character of status orders in contemporary societies. However, at the risk of repetition, it must be emphasized that the interpretation and explanation of particular political phenomena are not the central aims of such a theory. Instead, its primary concern is to explicate and defend the ideal of a society in which everyone enjoys due recognition. Of course, theorists of recognition do not always agree about the form that such an ideal society should take. Each of them provides their own account of the idea of recognition, of the politics characteristically associated with this idea, and therefore of the shape of the ideal society in which complete recognition can be achieved. Since there is more than one political theory of recognition, it is the aim of each particular theory to persuade us that the principles of recognition which it recommends are superior to those of its rivals.

In this book, I intend to concentrate most of my attention on three particular political theories of recognition. I have several reasons for focusing on the theories offered by Charles Taylor, Axel Honneth and Nancy Fraser. First, all of these theories provide rich and complex accounts of the politics of recognition. They offer subtle and nuanced expositions of their normative principles, and they demonstrate a serious and sophisticated engagement with the world of practical politics. Second, these three theories cover a wide cross-section of the field as a whole. Political theories of recognition differ on a range of issues which are fundamental to them. These three particular theories, when considered together, cover much of this range. Third, these theories can be meaningfully compared and contrasted. They have enough in common to make it possible and worthwhile to weigh them up against each other. At the same time, they are sufficiently divergent to make a critical contrast between them interesting and revealing. While Taylor, Honneth and Fraser are participants in the same conversation, they make quite different contributions to it. It should also be noted that, although I focus on these three theories for the reasons just indicated, I do not overlook other accounts. Many other political theorists at work today – including Will Kymlicka, James Tully and Iris Marion Young – have interesting things to say about recognition, and I mention their ideas where appropriate below.

I now want to say a little more about the three theorists on whom I focus particular attention. In this book, it would be impossible to ignore the work of the Canadian philosopher Charles Taylor. His essay 'The Politics of Recognition', first published in 1992, began the contemporary revival of interest in this subject. Indeed, it remains the single most influential work on the politics of recognition in modern political theory. In this essay, Taylor suggests that one form of recognition can be found in what he calls the 'intimate sphere'. Here recognition, in the form of the love of significant others, is crucial to the formation of identity. For the most part, Taylor concentrates on the public sphere. Here he develops a distinction between two forms of public recognition: a 'politics of universalism' protects individuals' autonomy by guaranteeing their rights, while a 'politics of difference' protects individuals' identity by allowing them to protect their culture.

The second theorist of especial interest to me is Axel Honneth, one of the most important contemporary representatives of the tradition of German Critical Theory. Honneth's engagement with the idea of recognition took off in the early 1990s, and culminated in the publication of his book entitled *The Struggle for Recognition* in 1995 (first published in German as *Kampf um Anerkennung* in 1992). Honneth argues that a distinction must be made between three modes of recognition. Love is the strong affective attachment between specific family members, lovers and friends, the experience of which is vital for the development of personal identity. Respect for rational autonomy is a universalist mode of recognition which should be enjoyed by all human beings. Esteem is a feeling of solidarity which individuals can have with particular others who share their values.

The third and final theorist on whom I concentrate is the American Critical Theorist Nancy Fraser. Her interest in the politics of recognition began in earnest with her 1995 article entitled 'From Redistribution to Recognition?', and this interest has resulted in *Redistribution or Recognition?*, the book she co-authored with Honneth in 2003. The titles of both her article and the jointly authored book reveal Fraser's concern with the relationship between a 'politics of equality', or 'class politics', oriented around issues of redistribution, and a 'politics of difference', or 'identity politics', based on the idea of recognition. Her aim is to formulate a political theory in which redistribution and recognition play equal parts. To this end, she places a normative principle of 'parity of participation' at heart of her theory, and argues that redistribution and recognition may both be necessary to secure such parity.

One reason why these three theories exhibit a number of significant similarities but also a number of important differences is that they share some of the same intellectual sources but are deeply divided about others. The most profound influence on Taylor's thinking about recognition is the German Idealist philosopher G. W. F. Hegel. In his *Phenomenology of Mind* of 1807, Hegel sets out an account of the development of human consciousness in which the idea of recognition plays a central role. This process passes through a number of distinct stages of conflict, including the famous dialectic of lordship and bondage,[4] until reaching a final state of harmony in which all demands for recognition are reconciled. Hegel's account has influenced Taylor in a number of ways. Perhaps of most importance, he follows Hegel in arguing that the identity of the self is entirely dependent on its recognition by others. There is no doubt that Hegel's philosophical Idealism is also the single most important source for Honneth in his thinking about recognition. It is important to note, however, that Honneth's inspiration comes not from the *Pheno-menology*, but rather from earlier works such as the *System der Sittlichkeit* of 1802 and the *Realphilosophie* of 1803–4 (Honneth 1995: pt 1). This preference for Hegel's pre-Jena writings stems from Honneth's belief that in these earlier writings we find an insightful theory of human inter-subjectivity, rather than an overly speculative philosophy of con-sciousness. At the same time, Honneth believes that even Hegel's early theory is formulated within a metaphysical framework that cannot now be defended. Hence his ambition is the same as that which he attributes to G. H. Mead: namely, to produce a '"materialist" refor-mulation' (1995: 92) of Hegel's theory in which the indefensible meta-physical aspects are removed from the still valuable core of the system. From Hegel, Honneth derives not just an intersubjective theory of the self, but also an account of human history according to which it is nec-essary to pass through a series of conflicts before it is possible to reach a final state of reconciliation. By contrast, as we shall see, Fraser stands strongly opposed to the Hegelian tradition.

If Taylor and Honneth are united by their debt to Hegel, Honneth is linked to Fraser by their shared commitment to the tradition of Critical Theory. The origins of Critical Theory lie in the establish-ment of the Frankfurt School – or, more properly, the Institute for Social Research – in 1923. Prominent members of the School includ-ed Theodor Adorno, Max Horkheimer, Herbert Marcuse and Walter Benjamin. Drawing on Marx, Freud and Weber, as well as a variety of other philosophical and theoretical influences, members of the School produced a range of distinctive critiques of contemporary capitalist society.[5] For Fraser and Honneth, Critical Theory is distin-guished from other ways of understanding the world by what Fraser calls 'its distinctive dialectic of immanence and transcendence' (2003: 202). In other words, it contends that the perspective from which the world is criticized (and may thus be *transcended*) must be rooted (or *immanent*) in that world itself. Thus Honneth, for his part, hopes to demonstrate that there are certain structures which are both essential to the reproduction of the existing social order, and which at the same time contain within them the seeds of a better future order. His conviction, as we shall see, is that relations of mutual recognition can fulfil such a role. Fraser, by contrast, argues that, if widely accepted principles of justice – and in particular the principle of moral equa-lity – are interpreted in the right way, this will help to effect a pro-found transformation of contemporary societies. The quasi-religious hope which they both express is that, in the impure and imperfect world we know all too well, it is possible to catch glimpses of a bet-ter and fairer world to come.

Although the work of these three theorists will form the core of this book, I do not focus exclusively on them. I mention other ways of thinking about recognition, as well as a number of important crit-icisms of the very idea of the politics of recognition. In the first of these camps, we find commentators who are generally sympathetic to the project of the politics of recognition, but who nevertheless reject both the Hegelian and Critical Theory approaches to it. James Tully, for instance, repudiates those interpretations of Hegel's philosophy which suggest that we can aim to achieve an 'end-state' in which all parties enjoy perfect mutual recognition (1999: 175). Instead, he draws on a very different set of intellectual sources – including Arendt, Foucault and Wittgenstein – in order to argue for what might be called an 'agonic' conception of recognition. He suggests that, rather than seeking to achieve a final state of complete recognition, our primary aim should be to ensure that 'agonic democratic games', including struggles for recognition, can continue to be played as freely as possible (2000: 469). For him, struggles for recognition should be regarded as practices of freedom (2001: 22). Patchen Markell, another relatively sympathetic critic, argues that the currently dominant conception of recognition focuses too heavily on identity. As a consequence, he argues, this normative form of recognition colludes with a deeper ontological form of misrecognition. In other words, by seeking to recognize another's identity, we fail to acknowledge the unavoidable circumstances of our own existence (2003: 10). In his *Bound by Recognition*, Markell develops the idea of a 'politics of acknowledgement' as an alternative way of responding to demands for recognition which does not fall into the same traps as recognition. To be specific, acknowledgement is directed in the first instance to our own condition, it accepts our finitude, and it 'involves coming to terms with, rather than vainly attempting to overcome, the risk of conflict, hostility, misunderstanding, and alienation that characterizes life among others' (2003: 38).

As I have suggested, other political theorists reject the idea of recognition *tout court*. Brian Barry, for instance, defends his version of egalitarian liberalism against all versions of the politics of recognition. When exponents of recognition argue that liberalism is wrong to overlook important cultural differences, his robust reply is that it is right to ignore them. To his mind, the politics of recognition's focus on cultural differences means that it neglects much more important differences in individuals' opportunities and advantages (2001: 63–4). Against this stark opposition of liberalism to recognition, I shall argue that egalitarian liberalism is in fact a form of the politics of recognition – but one which focuses almost exclusively on one aspect of that politics. I shall argue, furthermore, that even egalitarian liberals are able to defend a range of measures associated with the politics of recognition. For example, Barry himself accepts that in some circumstances there may be good cases to be made for the creation of equal public spaces for all religions (2001: 29) and for the provision of bilingual education (2001: 65). Other critics of the politics of recognition take a very different tack. While Barry reasserts the need to protect the rights and freedoms of individuals against the claims of cultures, others argue that, by focusing on differences between groups, the politics of recognition overlooks what all of them have in common. Some of these critics reject multiculturalism itself, arguing that a focus on differences corrodes the ties which bind a nation together (e.g. Schlesinger 1992). Other critics, who are located within the recognition camp itself, nevertheless argue that we need to balance our concern with difference with a concern with commonality. For example, Tariq Modood contends that all British citizens must be shown due acknowledgement, where this means giving them a secure place in the public life of the polity. At the same time, he calls for a 'plural Britishness', a new national identity which emerges from a dialogue between all groups in society (2005). Both the debate between Taylor, Honneth and Fraser, and that between them and their various critics, will form the subject-matter of this book.

1.4   A Plan of the Argument

In the next three chapters, I examine the three principal modes of recognition that were identified in the previous section. Chapter 2 focuses on love, which, involving deep feelings of empathy with the needs and desires of a specific individual, is to be found in primary relationships between infants and their caretakers. As Hegelians, both Honneth and Taylor support the idea that love should be considered a form of recognition. They both offer an account of individual psychology in which affective recognition in loving relationships plays a vital role in the formation of human identity. Honneth, in particular, draws on the work of psychoanalytic theorists in order to make the case that struggles for recognition occur even in intimate relationships (e.g. Benjamin 1988). Fraser, since she is strongly opposed to the Hegelian tradition, rejects any psychological account of the subject. She argues that such accounts have no part to play in the political theory of recognition. Indeed, she believes that attempts to reach political conclusions directly from an account of the individual subject are profoundly mistaken. As we have seen, other critics also reject the broader focus on identity. For very different reasons, both Barry and Markell deny that identity can be a legitimate object of recognition. My aim in chapter 2 is to determine whether an analysis of love has any part to play in a political theory of recognition.

Chapter 3 examines the second mode of recognition that was identified above. It is commonly argued that respect is a universal form of recognition due to humans, for features that they have in common with all of their fellows. The American civil rights movement is a telling example of the politics of respect in practice. African-Americans demanded to be treated with respect, so that they could regain their dignity. Hence they struggled to win the rights and opportunities that their fellow Americans already enjoyed. What Taylor calls the 'politics of universalism' is his version of the politics of respect. Such a politics is founded on the idea that all individuals must enjoy the same fundamental rights, in order to protect their autonomy. Honneth also argues for a close correlation between respect as a mode of recognition and a system of individual rights. Like Taylor, he believes that respect for autonomy is expressed by attributing certain basic rights to individuals. An idea of equal respect also underlies Fraser's principle of parity of participation, and she argues that individual rights may be an important means of achieving such parity. Yet, in spite of these similarities, there are a number of significant differences between these three theorists' accounts of respect. These include disagreements about the grounds for respect, and about how closely respect should be tied to rights. My task in chapter 3, then, is to evaluate the key strengths and weaknesses of these three accounts. By doing so, I shall be able to determine the character of respect as a mode of recognition, and to identify the sort of politics that may be associated with it.

In chapter 4, I turn to the third of the three modes of recognition already distinguished. Esteem is the positive acknowledgement of a particular type of person in light of the distinct characteristics that they possess. It may refer, for instance, to ideas of identity or difference, culture or community. One particular example of the politics of esteem in practice would be the campaign for Quebec's French identity to be acknowledged as a distinct part of the Canadian multicultural mosaic. In this case, a group feels that its characteristics and values do not receive appropriate acknowledgement. Hence it seeks at the very least an end to denigration, and it is also likely to demand positive affirmation from others in its society. What Taylor calls the 'politics of difference' focuses on this mode of recognition. He suggests that in some circumstances a particular group should be allowed to take measures to protect its culture. But he rejects the idea that it is necessary – or even logically coherent – to attribute equal value to different cultures. Honneth deals with esteem in his discussion of the politics of solidarity. According to him, esteem involves a feeling of solidarity with others. He argues that a society shows due esteem to all of its members if everyone's contribution to the social good has a fair chance of being appreciated. Fraser does not think that esteem can be associated with a distinct and separate type of politics. But she does argue that parity of participation may require the implementation of measures which involve the upward revaluation of devalued identities. Esteem, for her, is one means of achieving participatory parity. In chapter 4, my aim is to compare and contrast these accounts of esteem. In this way, I shall be able to establish the character of esteem as a form of recognition, and to specify the range of political practices that it may entail.

In the three chapters that follow this, I consider three other features of political theories of recognition.[6] Chapter 5 examines the relationship between recognition and redistribution. Here I focus in particular on the debate between Fraser and Honneth about the right relationship between these two concerns. Fraser is concerned that the rise of the politics of recognition has taken place at the cost of the politics of redistribution. According to her, for much of the post-war period, the overriding political objective of democratic states was to secure a fair distribution of society's opportunities and resources among its citizens. This was reflected in academic political theory, particularly in the accounts of egalitarian liberalism developed in the USA in the 1970s. She argues that in recent decades this concern with redistribution has been largely eclipsed by a relatively novel concern with the politics of recognition, as democratic states have responded to demands for the acknowledgement of specific group identities. Once again, this has been reflected within academia with the articulation of ever more sophisticated accounts of the politics of identity and difference. While Fraser certainly does not dispute the importance of recognition, her argument is that its rise to prominence has led to the unjustified relative neglect of redistribution. In an attempt to counter this tendency, she has developed a theory of social justice which has two analytically distinct, mutually irreducible, but practically interrelated dimensions: an economic dimension focusing on redistribution and a cultural dimension concerned with recognition. A number of critics have challenged various aspects of her theory. I focus in particular on Honneth's alternative account of the relationship between redistribution and recognition. In sharp contrast to Fraser, he believes that recognition should be the single master principle of a theory of social justice. For him, all matters concerned with the distribution of economic power and resources can be understood as matters of recognition. In contrast to both of their positions, a

sympathetic critic like Tully (2004) suggests that no systematic distinction between these two politics can be made, since all struggles
for recognition are simultaneously struggles for redistribution, and
vice-versa. My aim in chapter 5 is to determine whether Fraser or
Honneth gets the best of their argument.

In chapter 6, I examine the relationship between recognition and
democracy. I show why the theorists of recognition on whom I concentrate in this book believe that democracy – especially a version
which focuses on deliberation – must play a key part in determining
what recognition requires. They all believe that it is only through
political deliberation that a polity can determine how best to show
due recognition to all of its citizens. For this reason, Fraser, Honneth
and Taylor think that a just society must be, amongst other things, a
democratic society. Yet, although beginning from this common premiss, each of them articulates his or her own particular conception of
democracy as the political framework in which claims for recognition
can be adjudicated. Taylor defends a civic humanist model of democracy based on an ideal of participatory self-rule. Fraser believes that
the application of the principle of parity of participation must take
place in a deliberative democracy. According to Honneth, democracy
must be regarded as a system of 'reflexive co-operation'. In order to
assess the relative merits of these theories, I shall pay special attention to three features of these models of democracy: their accounts of
the character of political community, the nature of representation,
and the status of the values of democracy. Kymlicka and Young will
play an important part in this discussion as theorists who are sympathetic to the idea of recognition, and who consequently defend forms
of group representation. By the end of the chapter, I shall be able to
reach a conclusion about the character and cogency of the links that
each theory makes between democracy and recognition.

The final feature of the political theory of recognition that I wish to
consider is the idea of the 'struggle for recognition'. As we have seen,
the origins of this idea can be traced back at least as far as Hegel's
Phenomenology, in which he describes a struggle in which two individual consciousnesses battle for domination over each other. In contemporary commentaries on recognition, this idea of struggle is used
widely to describe any form of politics which involves issues of identity and difference. Having said this, one of my three theorists of
recognition uses the idea of struggle in full awareness of its Hegelian
connotations. At the risk of over-simplification, it could be said that,
for Honneth, struggles for recognition serve the purpose of history.
This is because they help to bring about a perfect state of mutual
recognition. For this reason, he believes that, by examining the

phenomenology of struggles, it is possible to discern glimpses of an ideal society in which recognition is fully achieved. Looking at it the other way round, Honneth also believes that the knowledge that struggles anticipate this ideal enables us better to understand the struggles themselves. In chapter 7, I shall examine Honneth's account of struggles for recognition. I focus on the three principal stages of his argument. The first suggests that hurt feelings lead to a sense of injustice, the second that this sense triggers struggles for recognition, and the third that such struggles lead to the moral development of society. As a counterpoint to Honneth's strongly Hegelian account, I shall use Tully's agonic account of recognition in which the open-ended and unpredictable character of struggles for recognition is emphasized. I shall end the chapter with a considered conclusion about the cogency of Honneth's account of struggles for recognition.

By the time I get to chapter 8, I shall be in a position to evaluate the key strengths and weaknesses of each of the three theories of recognition under investigation in this book. In particular, I shall be able to determine whether one theory stands head and shoulders above the rest, or whether it may be possible to synthesize the best elements from each in a single unified political theory of recognition.

Before turning to the first of these tasks, I want to make a couple of final remarks. First, it may be worth calling attention to the fact that most of the chapters which follow this have a similar general structure. A brief exposition of each thinker's views is followed by a critical comparison of them. I deviate from this structure to some extent in chapters 5 and 7. While the former focuses on Fraser's and Honneth's rival theories of redistribution, the latter focuses strongly on Honneth's account of struggles for recognition – although I do use Tully's alternative agonic account as a point of contrast. Second, it may also be worth pointing out that in this book I make repeated reference to a fairly limited number of examples of the politics of recognition in practice. One reason for doing so is that these are cases in which Taylor, Honneth and Fraser take a particular interest. Another reason is that, by considering the stance that each of them takes on the same issue, it is easier to conduct a critical comparison of these three theories. Third, I should say that there is a small amount of overlap between chapters. Occasionally, similar phrases or sentences pop up in different places. Although this might be noticed by someone who reads this book in a single sitting, I think it is justified in order to make each of the main chapters relatively independent of the others. My intention is that anyone who is interested in the topic discussed in a particular chapter will be able to turn directly to it and make sense of the discussion to be found there.

2

Recognition as Love

2.1 Introduction

During the Algerian struggle for independence from their French colonial masters, Frantz Fanon worked as a psychiatrist at the Blida-Joinville hospital in Algiers. In his book *The Wretched of the Earth*, he described 'the problem of mental disorders which arise from the war of national liberation which the Algerian people are carrying on' (1967: 200). One case that Fanon described concerns a 22-year-old man who had shown no interest in the political struggle, concentrating instead on his career as a 'multicopying-machine maker' (1967: 220). One day, however, this man suddenly had the idea that his family considered him a traitor, and he abruptly withdrew from them. A few days later, he believed that he heard someone in the street calling him a coward. This was the final straw, precipitating a complete mental breakdown. After a few days, locked away in his room and praying obsessively, he wandered out into the street and soon found himself in the European part of town. Here things got even worse. While his fellow Algerians were stopped and questioned by the police, he was ignored. This confirmed his delusion that everyone thought he was with the French. 'He went to the soldiers,' says Fanon, 'threw himself upon one of them and tried to snatch his machine-gun shouting "I am an Algerian".' The police arrested him, interrogated him, but released him a few days later when they realized 'that they were dealing with a sick man'. Later on, in hospital, talking about his experience, the man said: 'I was glad to be struck, for that showed me that they considered that I too was their enemy. I could no longer go on hearing those accusing voices without doing something. I am not a coward. I am not a woman. I am not a traitor' (1967: 221).

While this fascinating and horrifying case could bear a number of interpretations, one way to read it is in terms of recognition. Seen in this light, it reveals something of how complex the dynamics of recognition can be. In this particular case, the man appears to be acting on the assumption that he can only enjoy recognition from his fellow Algerians if he is actively involved in the struggle against the French. Failing this, he turns in desperation to the colonial oppressors in order to seek recognition from them instead. It is possible to draw a number of more general conclusions from this case. First of all, it suggests that recognition goes all the way down. In other words, the experience of recognition is essential to create and sustain human identity. As the psychologist R. D. Laing says, 'a necessary component in the development of the self is the experience of oneself as a person under the loving eye of the mother' (1965: 116). Furthermore, this case suggests that, if relations of recognition are broken, damaged or severely distorted, then psychological harm will result. Fanon, for one, was convinced that the psychological problems which he described were the direct result of the presence of the French colonial power in Algeria.

If recognition is vital to the constitution of human beings, and if its absence results in psychological damage, what cognizance should political theorists of recognition take of these facts? In this chapter, I shall show that the three thinkers of particular interest to me in this book give very different answers to this question. Both Axel Honneth and Charles Taylor, as thinkers who place themselves firmly in the Hegelian tradition of thinking about recognition, offer accounts of individual psychology in which the idea of recognition plays a crucial role. Both believe that the experience of such acknowledgement is vital for the formation of the human subject. Honneth takes this idea the furthest, regarding what he calls 'love' as one of the three primary modes of recognition. He believes, moreover, that this is the *first* mode, the one which must precede all others (see Benjamin 1988: 11). Without love, Honneth maintains, respect and esteem are impossible. For this reason, it could be argued that his entire political theory of recognition depends on his psychology of recognition. Taylor is rather more cautious about making such a direct connection between psychology and politics. He expresses considerable ambivalence about the place of a psychological account of human identity in a political theory. Generally, he wants to hold these two levels of analysis apart, although I shall argue that he fails to do so consistently. In marked contrast to both of these thinkers, Nancy Fraser, who sets herself firmly against the Hegelian tradition, rejects any form of what she calls 'psychologism' (1997: 157, 164), a term that she uses generally to refer to the practice of deducing political conclusions directly from accounts of the individual psyche. As we shall see, she believes that any theory of recognition which makes itself dependent upon a psychological explanation of the subject has a number of serious weaknesses. In place of a psychological account, Fraser defends a 'discursive' account of individual subjectivity (1997: 153).

In this chapter, my aim is to evaluate the very different positions taken by these three thinkers on this subject. I shall be guided by one principal question: namely, is Fraser right to argue that Taylor and Honneth are profoundly misguided in what she sees as their attempts to base their theories of justice on a psychology of recognition? Putting the question this way reveals one important limitation on the scope of my discussion. Rather than consider whether such a psychological account of the formation of the subject makes sense, I ask instead whether such an account should form an integral part of a political theory of recognition.

The chapter is organized as follows. First, I shall sketch Taylor's account of the formation of the subject (2.2). Then I shall do likewise with Honneth's account (2.3). Next I shall present Fraser's critique of these recognition-based psychological models, and I shall sketch the alternative discursive account of the subject which she offers in their stead (2.4). Following this, I shall assess the cogency of Fraser's critique of Taylor's and Honneth's positions, considering in turn each of the three principal criticisms that she makes of psychologism (2.5). In the final section, I shall reach a verdict about the place (if any) that a recognition-based psychology of the subject should have in a political theory of recognition (2.6).

2.2   Charles Taylor: The Dialogical Self

In this section, I want to focus on Taylor's claim that the idea of recognition has a vital role to play in the modern conception of identity. In order to appreciate the import of this claim, it is important to understand that he makes a distinction between two types of recognition that occur in different spheres. He contends that 'in the public sphere . . . a politics of equal recognition' has become increasingly influential. At the same time, there is also a second type of recognition

to be found in what he calls 'the intimate sphere'. Here 'we understand the formation of identity and the self as taking place in a continuing dialogue and struggle with significant others'. Having made
this distinction, for the rest of his essay on 'The Politics of Recognition',
Taylor focuses on public recognition. As he says, 'I want to concentrate here on the public sphere, and try to work out what a politics
of equal recognition has meant and could mean' (1995b: 233). I
shall refer to these two types of recognition simply as 'public recognition' and 'intimate recognition'. In chapters 3 and 4, I shall consider Taylor's account of public recognition in detail. My purpose in
this section is to examine his remarks on the nature of intimate
recognition.

Taylor contends that human identity is formed through dialogue.
As he says, the 'crucial feature of human life is its fundamentally dialogical character'. Even '[t]he genesis of the human mind is . . . dialogical' (1995b: 230). I cannot generate my own identity purely from
inside, as it were. Nor is it simply determined by my place in a social
structure. Rather, my identity is dialogical in the sense that my
account of who I am is shaped and sustained by my intercourse with
others. Hence Taylor says that to discover 'my own identity' is to
'negotiate it through dialogue, partly overt, partly internal, with others'. 'My own identity', he continues, 'crucially depends on my dialogical relations with others' (1995b: 231). Here we can see how he
explicitly forges a link between identity and recognition by emphasizing the essential role that others play in the formation of the self. But
who are these others? Taylor uses the sociological term 'significant
others' to describe those who play a crucial part in the formation of
personal identity. This term, originally used by Harry Stack Sullivan
(1953), refers to those people who have the most significant effect on
an individual's sense of self. To put this in terms of the current argument, my significant others are those to whom I am bound by relations of intimate recognition. It is worth emphasizing a couple of
features of Taylor's account. First, dialogue with one's significant others goes on without end. It is not an initial stage that, once passed,
need never be returned to. Not just infants and children, but fully
formed adults continue to have external and/or internal dialogues
with those who raised them. As Taylor says, 'through language we
remain related to partners of discourse, either in real, live exchanges,
or in indirect confrontations' (1989: 38). This does not mean that we
cannot *try* to define ourselves as much as possible on our own terms.
But it does mean that our relationships with others will continue to
form the backdrop to these attempts at self-definition (1995b: 230).
Second, Taylor emphasizes the inescapability of the fact that human

identity is formed in dialogue with others. He holds that even the hermit and the solitary artist have (virtual) partners in dialogue. This may be God in the case of the hermit, and perhaps a future audience in that of the artist (1995b: 231). Without such partners in dialogue, human beings would not be able to make sense of their lives.

Taylor suggests that this modern idea of the dialogical self is associated with a number of normative values and personal ideals. I would suggest that these values and ideals give ethical weight and significance to the connection between identity and recognition. Thus he argues that in late eighteenth century there emerged the idea of an 'individualized' identity, an identity which is peculiar to me, a way of being true to myself (1995b: 227). My identity is not one I acquired simply by occupying a particular position in the social hierarchy. Rather, I have an identity all my own, one that makes me unique and irreplaceable. This concept of individuality takes on a moral form by association with an 'ideal of authenticity'. According to this ideal, I must be in touch with my own feelings if I am to become a human being with inner depths (1995b: 227–8). In other words, I am under an imperative to discover my true identity, to discover what is special about me. Only in this way can I live an authentic life, one in which I am fully in touch with my own self. Finally, these ideas of individuality and authenticity are connected to those of self-realization and self-fulfilment (1995b: 229). According to these closely related notions, I become most fully myself by giving practical expression to my own unique way of being. Having discovered who I am, I have a duty to myself to become that person.[1]

Given the intimate and profound connection between identity and recognition, reinforced by the values of authenticity and self-realization, it follows – as we saw in the case Fanon describes – that the individual can be damaged by misrecognition and non-recognition. As Taylor puts it, failures of recognition or acts of misrecognition by others 'can inflict harm, can be a form of oppression, imprisoning someone in a false, distorted, and reduced mode of being' (1995b: 225). If I do not enjoy the right sort of acknowledgement from relevant others, then I am rendered unable to achieve my goal of self-realization. The harm caused by such failures of recognition occurs when the subject makes the other's negative attitude part of their own account of themselves. As Taylor says, '[t]he projection of an inferior or demeaning image on another can actually distort and oppress, to the extent that the image is internalized' (1995b: 232). In this way, misrecognition 'can inflict a grievous wound, saddling its victims with a crippling self-hatred' (1995b: 226). Since others despise me, I despise myself. Taylor suggests that this understanding of identity as formed – and sometimes malformed – in interchange with others has led to the emergence of a new category of second-class citizenship (1995b: 234). For example, proponents of feminism and multiculturalism regard misrecognition and non-recognition as forms of oppression (1995b: 232). They argue that women in patriarchal society and indigenous and colonized peoples find depreciatory images reflected back to them. These groups internalize such images, and hence suffer from low self-esteem, which can then act as an obstacle to their actions (1995b: 225–6). Thus Taylor suggests that, with the 'spread of the idea that we are formed by recognition', misrecognition has 'graduated to the rank of a harm' (1995b: 251).

It is worth pointing out a further implication of this analysis of the potential failures of recognition. While the idea that identity politics is often characterized by struggles for recognition is fairly familiar, the idea that struggles for recognition also take place in the intimate sphere may be less so. Yet Taylor takes pains to point out that this is the case. As he remarks, 'we understand the formation of identity and self as taking place in a continuing dialogue and struggle with significant others' (1995b: 233). Intimate recognition is not simply a harmonious process in which the loving attention of caretakers shapes infants' identities. Rather, this relationship between subjects and their significant others is fraught with tension. 'On the intimate level', Taylor comments, 'we can see how much an original identity needs and is vulnerable to the recognition given or withheld by significant others' (1995b: 232). When I do not receive recognition from my significant others, I can demand it and fight for it, or I can give up the struggle and try to survive without it. Either way, the outcome of this struggle will profoundly affect my sense of who I am. This implies that my identity is partly formed in struggles with and against my significant others. Perhaps one could say, by extension, that my identity is partly formed by misrecognition and non-recognition (Benjamin 1988).

2.3 Axel Honneth: A Philosophical Anthropology

Honneth places recognition as love at the centre of his psychology of the subject.[2] Without 'care and love', he argues, 'children's personalities cannot develop at all' (2003: 138). However, in contrast to Taylor's distinction between intimate recognition and public recognition, Honneth's analysis is based on a threefold distinction between love, respect and esteem. Despite this difference, I would suggest that their two accounts have a great deal in common. Of particular relevance in this chapter, Honneth's conception of love can be correlated with Taylor's idea of intimate recognition.[3] This close correlation notwithstanding, it is worth saying that Honneth would probably be unhappy with Taylor's assumption that this mode of recognition can be located in a particular 'sphere'. This is because he rejects the idea that each particular mode of recognition can be experienced only in a particular institutional location. For this reason, he argues that Hegel's identification of love with the bourgeois family is a case of 'misdirect-ed concretization' (1995: 176; and see 2003: 145–7). It may be that there is only an issue of language at stake here. If Taylor does indeed locate this form of recognition in a concrete institution, then I think that Honneth would have good grounds for criticism. If, however, Taylor intends the idea of the 'intimate sphere' to refer to a dimension of human experience which exists *wherever* there are relationships of love, then I think that Honneth could agree with Taylor's account. Putting this particular complication aside, my aim in this section is to examine Honneth's account of love as recognition, before turning to examine his accounts of respect and esteem in the next two chapters.

To begin with, let us consider how Honneth defines love. He characterizes it in a number of ways. To experience love is to feel the 'affectionate attention of concrete others' (1995: 87). It consists of 'strong emotional attachment among a small number of people' (1995: 95). It marks our 'primary affectional relationships' with each other (1995: 96). These various ways of describing love highlight two important characteristics. The first is the role played by affect, by the emotions. Love involves a 'strong emotional attachment' between the parties concerned.[4] In some formulations, Honneth stresses that this is 'positive' affect – that is to say, it is a matter of love, not hate; care, not cruelty; friendship, not enmity.[5] The second characteristic of love is its necessarily limited scope. Here Honneth's assumption seems to be that there is only enough space in a human life for relatively few other people to have a significant impact on one's sense of self. Love, he says, cannot be extended at will (1995: 107). It can be shown only to our significant others – children, lovers and friends – and not to all.[6] This final remark highlights an important element of Honneth's conception of love. For him, love encompasses a range of relation-ships, including those between infants and their caretakers, between lovers and between friends. These different forms of love are, of course, significantly different in a number of respects. In contrast to parental care, friendship should not be asymmetrical, friendship is necessarily a less intense feeling than romantic love, and so on. There remains, nevertheless, a common core to all of these forms of love: namely, positive emotional attachment to a necessarily restricted number of significant others.[7]

Given this account of love, it is now necessary to consider its significance. Honneth argues that love is the first mode of recognition. It is, he explains, 'conceptually and genetically prior' to respect and esteem (1995: 107). Here conceptual priority seems to mean that we can only conceive of the other two modes of recognition if we already know love. This mode of recognition is the template that we must use for understanding the other two. Genetic priority means that individual subjects must first experience love if they are to be able subsequently to experience respect and esteem. As Honneth says, love is 'basic requisite' for all further modes of recognition (1995: 176). In order to understand this idea of genetic priority, it is necessary to understand that for Honneth love, like respect and esteem, is not just a relationship between subjects but is also a type of 'practical relation-to-self'. By this he means that the experience of each of these forms of recognition leads subjects to relate to themselves in a particular way. As we shall see in the next two chapters, being respected makes self-respect possible, and being esteemed leads to self-esteem. In the case of love, infants responded to with loving concern by their primary caregivers will acquire a 'body-related *self-confidence*' (1992: 193). Honneth uses this idea of self-confidence in a very particular way. If I develop such self-confidence, I believe that my needs and feelings have value, and thus I am able to express those needs and feelings without embarrassment or shame (1995: 107, 129; 2003: 139).[8] More generally, it is possible to say that, if I have such self-confidence, I value myself and my life projects. For Honneth, it follows that this positive self-relation is the necessary precondition for the formation of all further positive relations to the self (1992: 193; 1995: 107, 176). Only if I have self-confidence will I be able to acquire self-respect, where this means regarding myself as a rationally autonomous agent. And only if I have self-confidence will I be able to esteem myself, where this means believing that I make a valuable contribution to society. On the basis of this analysis, Honneth concludes that experience of the three types of relation of recognition in combination is the condition of possibility of 'personal identity-formation' and therefore of 'individual self-realization' (2003: 174).

Up to this point, my sketch of Honneth's account of love as recognition has been entirely sunny in outlook. It appears as if infants who receive loving attention from their primary caretakers will become adults with body-related self-confidence, and thus they will have achieved one of the necessary conditions of self-realization. In order to counter this optimistic picture, it must be emphasized that, like Taylor, Honneth is aware of the threats to this aspect of self-realization. In his analysis, he refers to two types of threat. A first type is built into the primary relationship of recognition itself. Following the work of psychoanalytic theorists such as D. W. Winnicott (e.g. 1965), Honneth believes that the formation of the subject takes place when both mother and infant struggle against their initial symbiosis in order to achieve independence from each other. It should be noted that this is not a once-and-for-all event, so that as soon as mother and infant break free of each other, the struggle is over. This would mark the collapse of the relationship, not its maturation. It is necessary, rather, to retain a tension between connection and self-assertion. As Honneth puts it, primary relationships should be characterized by a 'precarious balance between independence and attachment' (1995: 96; cf. 98, 105; Benjamin 1988: 12).[9] Thus he agrees with Taylor that there can be struggles for recognition even in relationships of love. A second type of threat to self-confidence occurs in our public lives. Honneth does not think that self-confidence, once acquired, is an impregnable shell. There can be threats to its continued existence, which persist throughout an adult's life. Here Honneth focuses on violent actions directed against the body, which threaten its integrity. Physical injuries such as 'torture and rape' affect people's 'physical integrity,' and so undermine their bodily self-confidence (1992: 190; 1995: 132). If this analysis of the potential threats to self-confidence were to be accepted, it would follow that certain types of political activity have a strong bearing on this first mode of recognition. For example, Amnesty International's campaigns against torture can be understood as struggles to protect bodily self-confidence; hence they can be seen as political struggles over this first mode of recognition. In this sense, I would suggest, there can be what might be called a 'politics of love'.

2.4   Nancy Fraser: The Discursive Subject

As we have seen, both Taylor and Honneth believe that the idea of recognition can be used to describe our emotional relationships with significant others. However, while Taylor attempts to draw a distinction between intimate and public recognition, Honneth believes that recognition as love plays an integral part in a complete account of the politics of recognition. Fraser stands strongly opposed to both of these accounts. In general, she opposes what she calls her '*status model of recognition*' to what could be called their identity model (2003: 29). In particular, she is determined to distance herself from what she calls 'psychologization' (2001: 27; 2003: 31), a term which she uses specifically to refer to Taylor's and Honneth's tendency to claim that misrecognition is unjust since it causes psychological harm. It is important to understand that Fraser does not deny that failures of recognition can cause such harm. Her point is that, even if they are harmful, such failures are not in themselves unjust (2003: 32). As we shall see in detail in chapters 3 and 4, she argues instead that injustice is a property of status orders and economic systems that act as obstacles to parity of participation. Fraser believes that there are several good reasons why a political theory of recognition should make its critique of misrecognition independent of a psychological account of subjectivity. I shall examine the three principal reasons she gives, before turning briefly to consider the account of the subject which she offers as an alternative to the psychological accounts to be found in her two rivals' theories.

One reason for a theory of recognition to eschew psychologization is that by doing so it will avoid the risks attendant on reducing the injustice of misrecognition to a matter of individual attitudes. To be specific, it will avoid the danger that the blame for feelings of inadequacy can be laid at the victim's own door. As Fraser says, '[w]hen misrecognition is identified with internal distortions in the structure of the self-consciousness of the oppressed, it is but a short step to blaming the victim' (2003: 31). It is as if we say to the victim: 'since it is *you* who have these negative feelings about yourself, it is up to *you* to change them.' Shunning psychologization will also help us to avoid the suggestion that the remedy for injustices of recognition must involve regulating the minds of the perpetrators. In Fraser's words, 'when misrecognition is equated with prejudice in the minds of the oppressors, overcoming it seems to require policing their beliefs'. If the problem is caused by the oppressors' contemptuous attitudes, then it appears to follow that the only answer is to make sure that these attitudes are rooted out of their minds. This will involve 'illiberal and authoritarian' attempts to shape their attitudes and beliefs (2003: 31). I suppose that this could include a variety of practices, from mild forms of political correctness to severe Maoist re-education programmes.

Fraser argues that a second reason to avoid the psychologization of a theory of recognition is to make sure that the normative values endorsed by that theory are not dependent on the validity of the psychological account. 'When claims for recognition are premised on a psychological theory,' Fraser argues, 'they are made vulnerable to the vicissitudes of that theory' (2003: 32). If the empirical basis of the psychological account were to be called into question, then this would undermine the case for the normative values to which it is supposed to lend support. Honneth's account of love, for instance, draws on the work of the object-relations school of psychoanalysis. But if doubt were to be cast on the plausibility of this psychological theory, then the validity of his account of justice would also be undermined. For this reason, Fraser concludes, we should avoid 'mortgaging normative claims to matters of psychological fact' (2003: 32). It is better that the validity of claims for recognition does not depend on the credibility of an empirical psychology.

There is a third reason to steer clear of psychologization. Fraser observes that, in contemporary conditions of ethical pluralism, not every individual can be expected to endorse any particular 'conception of self-realization or of the good life' (2003: 30). In the modern world, there is widespread disagreement about what constitutes a fulfilling life. In these circumstances, all particular conceptions of self-realization will reasonably be rejected by some people. It follows, Fraser believes, that any theory of recognition based on such a conception could not be 'normatively binding on all who agree to abide by fair terms of interaction under conditions of value pluralism' (2003: 31). Even if we wanted to co-operate fairly together, we could not find a basis for co-operation in an account of the human psyche which at least some of us would find unacceptable. To take the example of Honneth's theory once more, his ideal society would be one in which all the necessary conditions would be in place for individuals to be able to achieve self-realization. As we shall see in later chapters, these several conditions are quite demanding in their requirements. Fraser's point is that the fact of ethical pluralism means that some citizens will not be able to accept Honneth's particular conception of self-realization. This means that his theory of justice is 'sectarian' (2003: 30), and is thus disqualified as a candidate to supply the fundamental terms of co-operation for society.

For all of these reasons, Fraser rejects the recognition-based accounts of subjectivity found in Taylor's and Honneth's theories. In fact, she believes that a political theory of recognition should not depend on any psychological model of the subject. This does not mean, however, that Fraser lacks any account of the subject at all. In some of her earlier essays, gathered together in *Justice Interruptus* (1997), she offers what I shall call a discursive account of the subject. According to this account, 'social identities are discursively constructed in historically specific social contexts; they are complex and plural; and they shift over time' (1997: 152). Let us consider each of these three elements in turn. First, Fraser emphasizes that the discourses out of which social identities can be forged vary from place to place and from time to time. The social identities that can be constructed in early twenty-first-century North America are very different from those that could be constructed in fifteenth-century Japan. Hence it is important to study 'the historically specific social practices' in question. Second, Fraser wants to stress that social identities are 'exceedingly complex . . . knit from a plurality of different descriptions arising from a plurality of different signifying practices'. One may be a man, French, homosexual and working class all at the same time. These different aspects of one's social identity become more or less pertinent in different contexts. Third, social identities are not 'constructed once and for all and definitively fixed. Rather, they alter over time, shifting with shifts in agents' practices and affiliations' (1997: 152). As we change what we do, and with whom we ally ourselves, then our social identities may change with us. By contrast, Fraser implies, psychological accounts of the subject overlook its historicity, complexity and mutability. It is important to emphasize that, for her, this discursive account of the subject does not imply that it is merely a fixed position within a stable linguistic structure. Rather, since discourse is struggled over and continually contested, it is possible to theorize the possibility of 'emancipatory social change' (1997: 152). That is to say, we can show that subjects are able to break free from the constraints that currently shape them in order to make themselves anew. As Fraser says, although subjectivity is 'culturally constructed', it is at the same time 'endowed with critical capacity' (1997: 219).[10]

I have shown that Fraser does have a conception of the subject, but it is a conception which is centred on an account of discourse rather than an account of psychology. It may be worth noting that, in the essays I have been considering, Fraser explicitly argues that her political purposes are served by her discursive account of the subject. She claims that it can 'contribute to' or 'help' what she calls 'feminist theorizing' (1997: 152–3). This is not to imply, of course, that Fraser has simply tailored her account of subjectivity to suit her political agenda. She has independently valid reasons for thinking that her discursive account of the subject is plausible. But she also thinks that conceptualizing the subject in this way can help to advance the cause of feminism. To the best of my knowledge, Fraser does not make the claim that such an account of subjectivity could also be used to support her account of recognition. But it is worth considering what she might say if asked this question. Would she accept that a discursive conception of the subject might complement not just her feminist theory but also her theory of recognition? I believe that she would – or at least should – accept this proposition. This is because, as I shall try to show in chapter 4, such a conception of subjectivity would complement in particular her account of the discursive nature of status orders. If this is right, then it would follow that Fraser's account of subjectivity could play an important role in her political theory of recognition.

2.5   The Critique of Psychologization

Having identified the principal differences between these three thinkers' accounts, I am now in a position to assess the relative strengths of their positions. If Fraser's critique succeeds, she will have provided several independently valid reasons for thinking that a political theory of recognition should not be based on a psychology of the subject. But if it fails, then Taylor's and Honneth's recognition-based psychologies may yet have a legitimate place in their political theories. My discussion of these issues will be structured around Fraser's three principal criticisms of psychologization, criticisms which – as we have seen – she directs explicitly towards Taylor and Honneth.

Reduction to Individual Attitudes

Fraser's first point is that, if misrecognition is reduced to a matter of individual attitudes, then there will be a temptation to blame the victims for their feelings of self-contempt, and a temptation to try to regulate the minds of the oppressors. For this reason, she argues that the injustice of misrecognition should not be understood in terms of the harm done to the individual psyche. I think that there are two ways in which Taylor and Honneth could defend themselves against this charge. First, they could try to show that they do not commit the sin of psychologism. That is to say, they could try to show that they do not attempt to infer social and political conclusions directly from psychological premises. In that case, they would not court the dangers that Fraser identifies. To be specific, if they do not argue that misrecognition is wrong because of the psychological damage that it causes, then they do not run the risk of blaming the victims and trying to police the oppressors' minds. Certainly, Fraser is able to point to passages in which Taylor and Honneth describe the psychological harm caused by failures of misrecognition (2003: 28). But do they believe that misrecognition is wrong precisely because it causes such harm? Or could it be argued that their accounts of the political dimensions of struggles for recognition are independent of their accounts of individual psychology? In order to answer these questions, let us look at each theorist in turn.

To begin with Taylor, it could be argued that nothing in his discussion of the politics of universalism and difference suggests that these forms of politics depend directly on his account of individual psychology. On this reading, he makes a clear distinction between what I referred to as intimate and public recognition. While he uses a psychological vocabulary to talk about the former, he does not employ it when talking about the latter. Consider the case of Quebec, with which Taylor is frequently concerned. His analysis in 'The Politics of Recognition' concerns the correct balance in the Canadian state between the defence of individual rights and the protection of culture. The question he addresses is whether Quebec should be able to take certain measures to protect its francophone culture, even when such measures require the limitation of individual rights.[11] This political debate, it could be argued, has little or nothing to do with the question of whether misrecognition does harm to the individual psyche. Indeed, there are points at which Taylor himself takes pains to emphasize the distinction between the personal and the political. In an interview with the author published in 2002, he discusses the relationship between 'group identities' and 'individual biographies'. His conclusion is that 'the two are really at some kind of structural distance from each other'. A little later in the same interview, referring to 'very strongly felt categorial identities' – such as 'African-American' – Taylor describes the need to make these 'liveable', to allow 'the maximum degree of space to breathe for real life human beings, with complex identities'.[12] In both of these passages, it could be argued, he seeks to separate questions of psychological identity from questions of political identity. To the extent to which he held consistently to this position, Taylor would be able to evade the general charge of psychologism, and hence also the specific charge that his account of recognition risks blaming the victims and being tempted to police the oppressors' minds. Recognition would be understood as a matter of enjoying rights and cultural protections, rather than being regarded positively by others.

There are, however, other points at which Taylor does seem to conflate the psychological and political levels of his analysis. Hence it may be disingenuous to argue that his political theory of recognition hangs completely free of his intersubjective psychology of recognition. To be specific, he does sometimes appear to use psychological vocabulary to describe collective political phenomena. For instance, at the beginning of his essay 'The Politics of Recognition',

RECOGNITION AS LOVE **33**

he refers to Fanon's writings on colonialism. According to Taylor, Fanon believes that '[d]ominant groups tend to entrench their hegemony by inculcating an image of inferiority in the subjugated'. 'The struggle for freedom and equality', he concludes, 'must therefore pass through a revision of these images' (1995b: 251–2). Of course, Taylor is here reporting another's views, but it may of some significance that he does not criticize them. For stronger evidence that he is on occasion tempted to commit the sin of psychologism, let me return once more to the 2002 interview. With reference to his fellow Quebeckers, he remarks that, 'like all moderns, we are in the process of working out our identity, fighting among ourselves over it; and this internal struggle is impacted upon by the stance of powerful, hegemonic outsiders, those higher on the hierarchy of successful communities'. Then, referring to American attitudes, he says that 'these responses of nonrecognition can be crucially important to us, because this kind of negative reaction can deeply disturb the internal debate'. Here Taylor suggests that others' contemptuous attitudes can shape a sense of national identity, and hence the pattern of political debate. If Taylor definitely wanted to evade the first charge that Fraser makes of psychologization, then he would be well advised to avoid the temptation to use the same psychological language of recognition as Fanon to describe the particular social and political processes. However, as I shall suggest in a moment, if the dangers Fraser highlights result only from the *misuse* of the psychological theory, then Taylor may be able to continue to use it.

In Honneth's case, it is even harder to argue that he does not seek to deduce political conclusions directly from psychological premises. As we shall see in chapters 3 and 4, he contends that recognition as respect requires the creation of a system of subjective rights, and that recognition as esteem requires the maintenance of a horizon of values in which all citizens have a chance to win esteem. In principle, it would be possible to argue for both these forms of recognition without any reference to individual psychology. But in fact Honneth insists that love, as a form of recognition, plays a crucial role in supporting the other two. To recapitulate, the experience of love underpins an individual's self-confidence, which is the essential precondition for the development of self-respect and self-esteem. These three modes of positive self-relation in combination make possible individual self-realization. 'The justice or well-being of a society', Honneth concludes, 'is proportionate to its ability to secure conditions of mutual recognition under which personal identity-formation, hence individual self-realization, can proceed adequately' (2003: 174). What this means is that the experience of recognition as love is essential if individuals are to be able to achieve the goal of self-realization. It could be said, therefore, that a just society is one in which individuals are able to experience love. While Honneth is not as explicit as he might be about the concrete implications of this argument, he does offer some suggestions about what it might involve in practice. He suggests, for example, that subjective rights can protect the 'radical egalitarianism' of love (1995: 176). That is to say, if individuals enjoy certain legal protections within intimate relationships, then this may enable them better to sustain balance and reciprocity within them. In this way, it is possible to make political decisions that are explicitly designed to affect the experience of love.

In light of these remarks, I conclude that Honneth cannot – and indeed, may not want to – evade Fraser's first charge by denying that he seeks to deduce political conclusions from psychological premisses. In this case, it is necessary to consider whether there is any other way in which he – and Taylor, to the extent to which he is guilty of psychologism – could defend themselves against her criticism. I want to argue that, even if a political theory of recognition did seek to deduce political conclusions about justice from a psychological account of the subject, it may yet remain innocent of the specific charge that Fraser brings against it. A second way in which such a theory could be defended against the accusation that it risks blaming victims for their own internalized attitudes and justifying the policing of oppressors' minds would be to argue that these dangers result only from a *misuse* of a psychological account. In other words, it may be possible to challenge Fraser's claim that the articulation of an account of the individual psyche, and specifically an account of the problems it faces through failures of recognition, will inevitably tempt us into the dangers that she identifies. Rather than being an inevitable consequence of articulating such accounts of the subject, it may be argued that such temptations result, rather, from a failure properly to understand the import of the psychological theory, and in particular its account of the mechanisms of misrecognition. To blame the victims or to want to police the oppressors' minds is to demonstrate a profound misunderstanding of the origin and impact of misrecognition. If this argument were to succeed, it would show that the problem is not with psychological accounts of the subject *per se*, but only with the misuse of those accounts.

To make this case, I shall consider each of the two dangers that Fraser identifies separately. I would suggest that the former danger – of blaming the victims – depends on a false inference from the recommendation that victims should root out the negative attitudes that they have internalized to the suggestion that they are at fault for internalizing these attitudes in the first place. It makes good sense for those suffering misrecognition to work to overcome the self-denigrating attitudes from which they suffer. The idea of 'queer' politics, for instance, can be seen to arise in part from a collective effort of gay men and lesbians to overturn, and indeed reverse, the terms of their discrimination. It is in this context that Michel Foucault formulates the idea of a 'reverse discourse,' in which homosexuality 'began to speak on its own behalf, to demand its legitimacy or "naturality" be acknowledged, often in the same vocabulary, using the same categories by which it was medically disqualified' (1976: 101). It does not follow from this, however, that these groups are in some sense to blame for internalizing such denigratory attitudes to begin with. To suggest that someone should change their circumstances does not imply that they are responsible for those circumstances. Thus a 'psychologized' account of recognition should not, and need not, involve blaming victims for the misrecognition from which they suffer.

The latter danger – of wanting to police oppressors' minds – depends on the plausibility of the idea that one could, by changing the oppressors' attitudes, in effect *force* them to recognize their victims. But this makes little sense: certainly at the level of individual attitudes, recognition cannot be compelled any more than faith can be. You cannot be forced to value me any more than you can be forced to believe in God.[13] Furthermore, to say that misrecognition occurs when victims internalize negative attitudes does not imply that misrecognition consists of nothing more than such attitudes. It would be possible, for instance, to endorse this account of the mechanism of misrecognition, and at the same time to endorse Fraser's claim that misrecognition is rooted in institutionalized patterns of value.[14] This makes it possible to undermine the link between a conception of misrecognition as internalized negative attitudes and the idea that the end of misrecognition will necessitate policing the perpetrators' minds. In other words, one can accept this conception of misrecognition, but conclude that the rooting out of misrecognition must focus on changing patterns of value rather than on subjective attitudes. In light of these reflections, I would conclude that Fraser's first objection does not justify the abandonment of psychological accounts of misrecognition, although it does give us good reason to make sure that we apply them in an appropriate and well-justified way. Indeed, such an application may involve, where necessary, showing that victims are *not* to blame for their internalized attitudes, and that the end of oppression does *not* require policing the oppressors'·minds.

Dependence on Empirical Theory

Fraser's second reason for rejecting the 'psychologization' of the theory of recognition is that it makes that theory dependent on the empirical worth of the psychological account of the subject which supports it. If this account were to be challenged, the normative theory would be undermined. It seems to me that there are two ways in which one could respond to this criticism. The first would be to argue that a psychology of the subject can be safe from empirical challenge. If this were the case, then a political theory of recognition could draw on psychological arguments without risk. The second response would be to argue that all normative theories – Fraser's included – necessarily depend on empirical accounts of various phenomena. Since all such theories require accounts not just of the subject, but also of society, the economy and so on, it follows that such dependence is not in itself sufficient reason to condemn them. Let me explore these two possible responses in greater detail.

One way to answer Fraser's charge is to argue that there are a number of things that one can say about the human psyche with which it would be very difficult to disagree. These could include the following propositions, each making a more specific claim than the last. First, humans are social creatures: they need others to become human; and in all usual circumstances, their lives are interwoven with the lives of others. Second, humans need others to meet their emotional needs: they need to be cared for, and to be loved. Third, humans are only able to value themselves, and thus to live fulfilling lives, if they are cared for and loved by others. These three propositions in combination could be said to form the core of an intersubjective account of the subject which emphasizes the importance of recognition for the integrity of that subject. According to this way of responding to Fraser's criticism, it is difficult to imagine how serious doubt could be cast on any of these propositions. How could one deny that humans are social creatures who need to enjoy others' care and love if they are to flourish? This is not to say that these are in any way transcendental truths about the human condition; they are simply empirical claims about human beings from which it would be difficult to dissent. In this case, it follows that such a psychological account could be utilized by a political theory of recognition without risk. Since these propositions are highly unlikely to face plausible empirical challenges, to rely on them would not risk holding a normative theory hostage to them. In reply, Fraser might claim that the mere possibility that such propositions could be challenged means that we should not rely on them.

The second way of responding to Fraser's charge that Taylor and Honneth make the validity of their normative theories dangerously dependent on the validity of their empirical psychologies is to accept that such dependence is in fact unavoidable. Her argument is that Taylor's and Honneth's claims about recognition are valid only if certain psychological facts about the human subject are true. If such facts are challenged, then the principles of recognition that they are intended to support are threatened. However, so far as I can see, there is no reason why this argument should be restricted to accounts of the individual psyche. If it is inadvisable for a normative theory to depend on the robustness of a psychological account of the subject, then it must be just as inadvisable for it to rely on other empirical accounts too. In this case, Fraser's own theory of justice is as vulnerable to her criticism as those of Taylor and Honneth. Although, as we have seen, she eschews reliance on a psychology of the subject, Fraser's theory does depend on other sorts of empirical theories. To anticipate my discussion in future chapters, her normative theory depends on a particular empirical social theory. This includes an account of the nature of status orders and economic structures, and an account of the interaction between these two systems. Without this empirical account, it would be impossible to identify what she calls the 'intersubjective' and 'objective' conditions necessary to guarantee parity of participation. Hence, if the empirical basis of her social theory were to be challenged, the validity of her normative claims would also be threatened. In short, Fraser's account of how particular systems of cultural representation or certain distributions of economic resources affect the ability to participate in social life is as vulnerable to empirical refutation as the psychological accounts of the subject which she believes support Taylor's and Honneth's accounts of justice.

Does it follow that a normative theory should seek to isolate itself from any kind of empirical theory? Should the defence of political principles be conducted without any reference to supposed facts about the world to which it is intended that such principles be applied?[15] I think that this would be the wrong inference to draw from my argument. It would push political theories towards arid abstraction, and it would do so for no good reason. This is because it is impossible for such normative theories to do without the support of empirical theories of politics. As I suggested in section 1.3, political theories must rely on the findings of political science to demonstrate that their recommendations are feasible. The validity of a theory of justice will have to depend on all sorts of empirical accounts of the world. Given this, Fraser's claim that Taylor and Honneth are wrong to make the validity of their theories of recognition dependent on the validity of their empirical psychologies carries no weight. Since dependence on empirical theory is unavoidable, it is not a criticism to point out such dependence.[16]

Sectarianism of Self-realization

The third and final criticism that Fraser makes of psychologization is that, since all conceptions 'of self-realization or of the good life' (2003: 30) are sectarian, to invoke them in a theory of justice renders that theory unable to identify fair terms of co-operation for the society in question. I would suggest that it may be possible to launch a partial defence of Taylor and Honneth by distinguishing between self-realization and the good life. On the basis of this distinction, it could be argued that, while conceptions of the good life are necessarily sectarian, conceptions of self-realization need not be. Let me begin with conceptions of the good life. I would argue that the way the debate is set up makes it inevitable that such conceptions are unable to play a part in a theory of justice. Such a theory, it is argued, is intended to apply to societies characterized by profound ethical pluralism. In other words, these societies contain individuals and groups with widely divergent conceptions of the good life. If the aim of a theory of justice is to identify principles which can serve as fair terms of co-operation for all citizens, then it follows that conceptions of the good life can play no part in such a theory. For a theory of justice to invoke a particular set of ethical values is to guarantee that some citizens will be able reasonably to reject that theory. This is true almost by definition.

Does the same argument necessarily apply to conceptions of self-realization? Fraser's assumption seems to be that all conceptions of self-realization express a particular ethical vision. They suggest, in other words, how the good life should be lived. But it could be argued that self-realization and the good life need not necessarily be yoked together. Indeed, it sometimes looks quite strange when they are. Consider, for instance, Fraser's admission that 'misrecognition can have the sort of ethical-psychological effects described by Taylor and Honneth' (2003: 32). I would suggest that 'ethical-psychological' is quite a peculiar coupling: while the former element refers to normative values, the latter refers to the nature of the individual psyche. It seems likely that Fraser makes such an intimate connection between them since she believes that Taylor and Honneth move directly from the 'psychological' to the 'ethical' – from an account of the individual psyche to normative conclusions. I have to concede, given my remarks earlier on in this section, that, while Taylor is somewhat ambivalent about the connection between the psychological and the normative, Honneth does indeed make a direct connection between the two. Yet, even in Honneth's case, I see no reason in principle why he could not start from psychological premises and get to *moral* rather than *ethical* conclusions. That is to say, I see no reason why a psychological theory could not be used to provide empirical support for a non-sectarian theory of justice, rather than for a sectarian conception of ethical life. Consider my claim made above that it may be possible to specify certain propositions about the psyche which are unlikely to suffer empirical refutation. I would suggest that these very same propositions could form part of a psychology which aims to identify certain universal conditions necessary for individuals to lead minimally decent lives – whatever their particular conception of the good. In this case, such a psychology could be invoked in a theory of justice which is intended to specify principles of justice that are normatively binding on all citizens. This argument would of course require much more work to be persuasive. But at least I have made a case for thinking that conceptions of self-realization may not necessarily be sectarian, and in this case it follows that they could play a part in a theory of justice.

2.6   Conclusions

In this chapter, I have shown that Honneth and Taylor propound intersubjective psychologies in which the idea of recognition occupies a central position. For them, the formation of the human subject and its continuing psychological health is dependent on the recognition that it receives from its significant others. I have also shown why Fraser rejects the psychological account of subjectivity and offers what she calls a discursive account in its stead. In my analysis of these rival positions, my aim was to determine whether Fraser is right to argue that Taylor and Honneth should not base their theories of justice on a psychology of recognition.

Overall, I offered a partial defence of their positions against her critique. First, I argued that the danger that victims will be blamed and the minds of oppressors policed results from a misuse of the psychological account. It must be admitted that this danger is real, especially for accounts of recognition which concentrate their attention on subjective attitudes. If misrecognition is regarded as nothing more than one party's attitude of contempt being internalized by another party, then this may well lead to the dangers that Fraser identifies. In light of this risk, I would suggest that political theorists of recognition would be well advised to pay heed to Fraser's claim – which will be discussed in detail in the next two chapters – that recognition and misrecognition are rooted in social and political institutions. Second, I argued that to point out the dependence of political theories of recognition on certain psychological premises is not in itself an effective criticism. Since all political theories must depend on some empirical accounts, condemning such dependence carries little weight. The implication is that, if it could be shown that a particular empirical account *is* faulty, then this *would* undermine the validity of the political theory which seeks to draw support from it.[17] In short, it is not dependence on psychology itself which is the problem, but only dependence on an unreliable psychology. Third, I contended that Fraser's conflation of psychology and ethics, accounts of the psyche and conceptions of the good, may be unwarranted. I suggested that, while conceptions of the good life are sectarian by definition, accounts of self-realization need not be. Of course, more would have to be done to prove this point. It would have to be shown that a particular conception of self-realization could serve as the basis for political agreement between all citizens in an ethically plural society. What I have shown is that Fraser is wrong simply to assume that a political theory which depends on a psychological account of the subject must, as a result of such dependence, necessarily be sectarian.

In making these arguments, I sought to undermine some of the reasons for denying a psychology of the subject a role in a political theory of recognition. It may be worth saying that there may be other reasons to avoid psychologism, other reasons why a political theory should be independent of a subjective psychology. But at least I have shown that the reasons proffered by Fraser are not decisive. It is also worth emphasizing that my assessment of Fraser's critique of the use of psychological accounts in political theories of recognition has no bearing on whether these accounts themselves are valid. In this chapter, in fact, I have suggested some reasons for thinking that an account of the formation of the individual subject in a network of relations of recognition is at least plausible. It may finally be worth stressing that, although the tone of my analysis has been negative in the sense that I have sought to undermine some reasons against using a psychology in a political theory, it is at the same time positive in the sense that it has laid down certain conditions that any such psychology must fulfil if it is to play a role in a political theory of recognition. First, such an account should not regard recognition and misrecognition simply in terms of subjective attitudes. Second, it should be clear about the nature of the empirical theses on which it depends, and it must be prepared when necessary to defend those theses. Third, if it wishes to be non-sectarian, it should try as far as possible not to be controversial.

3

Recognition as Respect

3.1   Introduction

In his book *Respect*, Richard Sennett combines autobiographical reflection and sociological analysis in an effort to understand the role that the idea of respec t plays in contemporary society. He recalls growing up in Chicago's Cabrini Green housing project in the 1940s. This project was part of an attempt by the Chicago Housing Authority to preserve at least some areas of racially mixed housing in the city. However, as Sennett points out, the whites who lived in the project were either too poor to leave, or 'wounded war veterans who could not work full-time', or 'mental patients not ill enough to remain in hospital' (2003: 7). Reflecting on his time living in the project half a century later, Sennett suggests that

> Cabrini posed two problems which could challenge its residents' sense of self-worth. One was adult dependence, a condition which American adults tends to fear as demeaning; "welfare-dependency" is a synonym for humiliation . . . The other problem was that the project denied people control over their own lives. They were rendered spectators to their own needs, mere consumers of care provided to them. It was here that they experienced that peculiar lack of respect which consists of not being seen, not being accounted as full human beings. (2003: 12–13)

Cabrini Green is, of course, a very particular case of a particular housing policy put into action in particular circumstances. Sennett's

reflections on it do nevertheless illustrate several themes highly pertinent to the subject-matter of this chapter. To begin with, he paints a
vivid picture of the experience of disrespect. To lack respect is to be
treated like a child long after one has left childhood behind. Closely
related to this is the experience of being overlooked, rendered invisible, even when it is the conditions of one's own life which are at
stake. This picture of disrespect also suggests what respect would be
like. To be respected is to be seen, to be taken into account in matters
in which one is directly affected. It is to be treated like an adult, to be
allowed to take important decisions about the course of one's life.

It is possible to see these same themes at play in each of the four
case-studies that I introduced in chapter 1. In the American civil
rights movement of the 1950s and 1960s, African-Americans
engaged in prolonged struggles in order to win their civil and political rights. A second example was the struggle over the Canadian
Charter of Rights and Freedoms of 1982, which aimed to guarantee all individuals legal equality. A third example was the political
conflict over the law passed by the French state in 2004 banning
the wearing of conspicuous religious symbols in state schools.
Another case was the struggle of gay men and lesbians to win the
right to marry. However various these cases may be, they nevertheless have a number of features in common. First, they all make
more or less explicit reference to the idea of the equal protection
of the laws, famously enshrined in the Fourteenth Amendment to
the US Constitution. The demand here is for inclusion – to be given
the same protections that all other citizens currently enjoy. Second,
there is a shared opposition to any form of discrimination. It is
often insisted that laws, policies and institutions must be 'difference-blind'. In other words, matters should be arranged so that no
particular individuals or groups are singled out for special treatment. This is why, despite initial appearances, the case of the headscarves fits with the others. Both defenders and critics of the ban
claim that only by following their recommendations will it be possible to ensure that Muslims are treated on a par with all other citizens. Third, in each case there is a more or less explicit reference
to the idea that the state should be impartial. Commenting on the
foulard affair, Jean-Pierre Raffarin, the French prime minister at
the time the ban on headscarves was passed, argued that France
'has made the separation of the church and the state one of the
foundation stones of its political system' (*Guardian*, 13 March
2004). The argument here is that only a state which is independent
of any religious affiliation can be impartial with regard to all of its
members.[1] Finally, there is the idea that what these difference-blind

laws protect is the freedom of citizens to live as they please, so long as their choices are compatible with the equal freedom of their fellows.

What I shall call a 'politics of respect' is a way of thinking about and acting in the political world which gives a prominent place to these themes of equal protection, difference-blindness, state impartiality and individual freedom. It is my contention in this chapter that all three of the theorists of particular concern to me engage with such a politics. Although in no case is their theory of recognition exhausted by the idea of respect, they all draw on it in different ways. Charles Taylor's discussion of recognition revolves around a distinction between what he calls the 'politics of universalism' and the 'politics of difference' (1995b: 233). It is the former, I shall argue, which is his version of the politics of respect. The politics of universalism places a strong emphasis on the role that fundamental rights play in protecting individuals' rational autonomy. It is by protecting individuals' autonomy that they are shown respect. Axel Honneth's account of recognition also draws a tight connection between respect and rights. He argues that, in order for individuals to be able to achieve self-realization, one thing that must be put in place is a system of rights which enables them to respect each other (and hence to respect themselves). The relationship of Nancy Fraser's theory of recognition to a politics of respect is somewhat more complex than that of either Taylor or Honneth. I shall argue that, at the level of moral philosophy, an idea of equal respect underlies her principle of parity of participation. At the level of political theory, she argues that individual rights may be one means of achieving such parity.

My aim in this chapter is to offer a critical assessment of these rival accounts of the politics of respect. My discussion will address four particular questions. First, what is distinctive about recognition as respect? In particular, how can it be analytically and practically distinguished from love and esteem? For Arto Laitinen, respect is directed to individuals in their 'universality' (2002: 470). But, as we shall see, there is more to it than this. Second, what is the object of respect? Can respect be appropriately shown only to individuals, or can it be shown to some sorts of collectivities too? All three of the theorists under consideration here focus on the individual. It will be interesting to consider why they think that collectivities cannot be respected. Third, does the practice of respect take a distinctive form? Can it, for instance, be associated with particular institutions? Or might it be expressed by specific policies? So far I have mentioned the role of rights in expressing respect. But later on I shall have reason to question how close that connection should be. Fourth, why should someone (or something) be respected? Is one justification of respect better than others? Or do different reasons apply to different cases? I have suggested that rational autonomy may be one ground for respect. Could there be others?

The chapter is organized in the following way. To begin with, I shall consider Taylor's account of the politics of universalism (3.2). In the section after that, I shall examine Honneth's account of recognition in which respect is closely correlated with rights (3.3). Next I shall consider Fraser's account, which is based on an idea of equal respect, and in which individual rights may be one means of achieving participatory parity (3.4). In the following section, by considering each of the four questions just listed, I shall offer an evaluation of the key strengths and weaknesses of each of these theories (3.5). In the final section, I reach a number of conclusions about the nature of respect as a mode of recognition, and about the sort of politics implied by this account (3.6).

3.2   Charles Taylor: The Politics of Universalism

Taylor suggests that a distinction can be made between two different forms of the 'politics of equal recognition', which he calls the 'politics of universalism' and the 'politics of difference' (1995b: 233). While both of these forms begin from the assumption that all citizens must be recognized equally, each has a very different understanding of what this entails.[2] It is the politics of universalism which is of particular interest to me in this chapter since I shall argue that this is Taylor's term for what I am calling the politics of respect. The politics of universalism is founded on the principle of the 'equal dignity of all citizens' (1995b: 233). It holds that human beings, by their very nature, deserve to be treated with respect, and it argues that such respect should be enjoyed equally. Only in these circumstances will people be able to experience equal dignity. Taylor suggests that, for proponents of the politics of universalism, respect is due to people in light of their *universal human potential* for autonomy. In this, the politics of universalism follows Kant's premiss that our dignity lies in what Taylor calls 'our status as rational agents'. That is to say, we should respect people since they are able to act on principles that they have made reasoned decisions to follow (1995b: 235). It is because people are able to exercise rational control over their lives that they should be treated with respect.

According to Taylor's account, the politics of universalism contends that, since all humans without exception possess the capacity for rational agency, they should be treated equally. There is no reason to single out any particular subset of individuals for treatment which is better or worse than that enjoyed by the rest. It is for this reason that exponents of this form of politics vigorously defend the 'equalization of rights and entitlements' against any attempt to create distinctions between first-class and second-class citizens. What this means in practice is that citizens are entitled to 'an identical basket of rights and immunities' (1995b: 233). Hence the exponents of the politics of universalism favour universal civil, political and perhaps also socio-economic rights.[3] Taylor suggests that the American civil rights movement is an exemplary form of this type of politics in practice. This movement was concerned to extend rights that were already enjoyed by most American citizens to a group that was at that time excluded from them (1995b: 233). To take another example, the first sentence of the preamble to the Universal Declaration of Human Rights adopted by the United Nations in 1948 reads as follows: 'Whereas recognition of the inherent dignity and of the equality and unalienable rights of all members of the human family is the foundation of freedom, justice and peace in the world.'[4]

Taylor would endorse most of the elements of the politics of universalism that I have enumerated so far. He believes that all citizens should enjoy equal dignity, and thinks that protecting citizens' fundamental rights is an important means of guaranteeing this dignity. Thus he says that some rights 'are so fundamental that we can more or less commit ourselves in advance to upholding them in all possible contexts. The rights to life, to personal liberty, to freedom of opinion, etc. are in this group' (cited in Abbey 2000: 128).[5] He does not, however, endorse the most prominent form which this politics now takes. For the sake of the current argument, I shall call this 'procedural liberalism'. Such a political theory may be associated with the dominant strand of contemporary Anglo-American liberalism, whose exponents include John Rawls, Ronald Dworkin and Brian Barry. According to procedural liberalism, a just society is one that is committed to resolving disagreements by means of procedures which are fair to all individual citizens. To guarantee such fairness, these procedures must be independent of any particular set of values held by the citizens of that polity. This same basic idea can be expressed in other ways. Procedural liberals may argue that the state's institutions and policies must be founded on neutral principles which do not show favour to any particular way of life within that polity. Or they may argue that the 'right' should be prior to the 'good', by which they mean that the principles of justice that govern the basic structure of society must be independent of any conceptions of the good life held by members of that society. Dworkin's essay on 'Liberalism' (1978) is a classic statement of this position.[6]

Put in terms of the current argument, I would suggest that this form of the politics of universalism is based on a particular interpretation of the idea of equal respect. According to this interpretation, the principle of equal respect entails a commitment to what Taylor calls a norm of 'nondiscrimination'. This norm says that all individuals and groups should be subject to identical treatment since any variation discriminates against some people (1995b: 234). On the basis of this norm, procedural liberals argue that it is necessary to found the state on 'universal, difference-blind principles' (1995b: 237). In other words, the laws which govern the basic structure of society must take no account of the particular characteristics that distinguish different groups of citizens. It is this commitment to difference-blindness, Taylor believes, which leads to the criticism that 'a liberalism of rights' is 'inhospitable to difference'. That is to say, since it is unwilling to take account of differences between individuals and groups, it creates a political environment which is inimical to the flourishing – and perhaps even the survival – of those differences. While Taylor contends that it would be 'absurd' to say that such a politics seeks to abolish difference, he nevertheless thinks that it is fair to say that it is 'inhospitable' to the goal of survival (1995b: 248).[7]

It is possible to see how these various issues play themselves out in practice by briefly considering the Canadian case with which Taylor is much concerned. For at least two decades, a schism has existed between two groups with very different conceptions of the Canadian federation. On the one side are those Canadians who align themselves with some form of procedural liberalism. Taylor suggests that this political stance is exemplified by Pierre Trudeau's strategy of 'national unity'. He believes that such a strategy seeks to impose a model of liberalism on Canadian society which pictures the state as the provider and guarantor of a neutral framework in which individual rights are protected (1993: 174–5). From this political perspective, Canada could only qualify as a liberal society if it were to remain 'neutral on the good life' (1995b: 246). On the other side of the divide are those Canadians – including Taylor himself – who believe that it is possible for a society to pursue collective goals while still showing equal respect for all. In particular, they argue that Canada can recognize the distinctiveness of Quebec while still remaining a liberal society.[8]

3.3   Axel Honneth: Legal Recognition

Respect is the second of the three principal modes of recognition that Honneth identifies. His account begins with an explanation of the grounds of respect. Here Honneth, like Taylor, follows Kant's lead. He states that, in this mode of recognition, other individuals are regarded as 'morally responsible' (1995: 114). Indeed, he regards 'moral responsibility as the respect-worthy core of the person' (1995: 119). In other words, people deserve respect as creatures who can appropriately be held to account for their actions. If, for instance, someone breaks the law, then they should stand trial and be given appropriate punishment. Honneth contends that it is because humans have a capacity for rational autonomy that they can have moral responsibility attributed to them. Hence he says that, when I respect others, I regard them as 'capable of acting autonomously on the basis of rational insight' (1995: 114). Humans are capable of using their powers of reason in order to decide how to act. This is why law-breakers should face justice: they knowingly and deliberately choose to break the law. This analysis of the grounds for respect can also be expressed negatively. If I fail to respect someone (or think them unworthy of respect), I do not accord them the 'same degree of moral responsibility' as others, and I may allow their personal autonomy to be restricted (1995: 133). A number of groups may be treated in this way, including children, the senile and the mad.

The picture painted so far suggests that respect is an attitude that one person can have to another. It is important to note, however, that for Honneth this mode of recognition is necessarily mutual, or reciprocal. That is to say, my attitude of respect for others is inevitably tied up with their attitude of respect to me. Following both Hegel and the American sociologist G. H. Mead, Honneth contends that we can only see ourselves as rights-bearers – that is, as worthy of respect – once we have understood the obligations that we have to others. In other words, I can only respect myself if I see why I should respect others. To acquire such an understanding of my obligations, I must adopt what Mead calls the perspective of the 'generalized other' (cited in Honneth 1995: 108). Rather than looking at the world from my own particular viewpoint, I must attempt to take up that of no particular person in my society. One could say that I try to assume the perspective of society as a whole. From this perspective, I can see that there is no reason to treat me differently from anyone else in my society. The reason why I should be respected is a reason for everyone else to be respected as well. Honneth believes that the legal systems found in modern society help to realize this idea of reciprocal respect. Thus he declares: 'In obeying the law, legal subjects recognize each other as persons capable of autonomously making reasonable decisions about moral norms' (1995: 109). When I obey the rules set down in my society, I acknowledge the rights of my fellow citizens, and I fulfil my obligations to them. In this way, I show them respect. When they obey the same rules, they acknowledge my rights and their obligations to me. In this way, they show me respect.

This account of the reciprocity of respect provides a strong indication about the form which Honneth believes the politics of respect must take in practice. Again like Taylor, he suggests that this mode of recognition can be associated with a politics that gives prominence to individual rights. Indeed, the relationship between these two is much stronger than an 'association': respect and rights are conceptually and practically inextricable. The language that Honneth uses reveals the strength of this connection. At one point, for instance, he describes the three modes of recognition as 'love, rights, and esteem' (1995: 1), simply substituting the expected 'respect' with 'rights'. At other points, he refers to respect as 'legal recognition' (1995: 94, 173); and he says that to respect others is to recognize them as legal persons (1995: 108). As his translator puts it, the positive self-relation of respect is 'mediated by patterns of interaction, those organized in terms of legal rights' (1995: p.xv). At the political level, then, respect as a mode of recognition is actualized in a system of individual rights. By acknowledging my fellow citizens' rights, I accept that they should be able to take all sorts of decisions about the way they wish to live their lives. In this way, I respect their moral responsibility and rational autonomy. To put it at its strongest, Honneth's thesis is that respect can only be shown to others by treating them as bearers of rights; where rights do not exist, no respect is possible. The connection between respect and rights could not be closer than this. Later on, I shall consider whether this thesis is justifiable.

So far, Honneth has suggested that respect is shown to others by acknowledging their rights. This raises an inevitable question about the nature and content of such rights. Which particular rights must be acknowledged in order to show others respect? In order to answer this question, it is necessary to ask another: what conditions must be in place if individuals are to be able to exercise their capacity for rational autonomy (1995: 114)? By answering the second question, it should be possible to answer the first: by identifying the conditions of autonomy, it should be possible to specify a set of essential rights. It is important to realize that, for Honneth, these conditions, and hence these rights, vary over time. This is not to say that they are simply relative, fluctuating according to time and place. Rather, he argues that respect, unlike love, has a developmental potential. That is to say, this mode of recognition contains within it the potential for ever more complete realization.[9] In fact, the development of respect, and its expression in a system of rights, moves along two distinct axes: the scope of a system of rights can be widened, and the content of that system can be deepened. The first process involves the inclusion of ever greater numbers of people in the system of rights. Workers' and women's successful struggles for the vote in the nineteenth and early twentieth centuries would be examples of this process in action. The American civil rights movement represents a more recent example of the same phenomenon (1995: 120–1). The second process occurs when the package of rights acquired through struggle becomes ever more extensive. Here Honneth refers to T. H. Marshall's well-known account of the evolution of citizenship, in which three phases are distinguished: civil rights in the eighteenth century, political rights in the nineteenth, and finally social rights in the twentieth (1995: 117–18). In contemporary society, it is widely understood that, even if citizens have certain opportunities and freedoms, a lack of resources may compromise their practical capacity to exercise their opportunities and freedoms – and hence to be rationally autonomous. For this reason, it is now generally accepted that, in order to gain recognition as a citizen, it is necessary to possess all three of these types of rights. Hence Honneth's ideal polity is one in which individual citizens enjoy not just civil and political but also social rights (1995: 116, 177).[10]

3.4   Nancy Fraser: Parity of Participation

At first blush, it may appear that the idea of respect has no distinct role to play in Fraser's theory of recognition. This impression is created in part by the way in which Fraser sets up the problem with which she is concerned. As I shall show in chapter 5, she argues that, in order to integrate redistribution and recognition, it is necessary to combine social equality and the recognition of difference (2003: 9, 26–7). In this formulation, equality is aligned with redistribution, and difference with recognition. This seems to exclude the possibility that recognition could serve equality, rather than difference. This impression is heightened by Fraser's emphasis on the cultural basis of recognition. She says that recognition focuses on cultural injustice (2003: 13), and that such injustice is rooted in the status order (2003: 18). In these passages, Fraser is describing everyday understandings of recognition, to be sure. Later on in the same essay, however, she makes the same connection between recognition and the status order herself (2003: 50). This focus on culture adds to the impression that recognition is concerned with distinctiveness, rather than similarity. Finally, many of the remedies that Fraser proposes for misrecognition also focus on cultural distinctiveness. They suggest that such distinctiveness should either be affirmed or deconstructed (2003: 12–13, 47, 73, 75). Given these features of Fraser's theory, and in particular its focus on humans' particular rather than universal features, it may seem that she thinks that recognition is concerned with the acknowledgement of particular cultural identities, rather than universal aspects of human nature. In spite of this impression, I want to argue that the idea of respect does play an important, if understated, role in her theory. First, at the level of moral philosophy, it helps to ground her principle of parity of participation. Second, at the level of political theory, individual rights are one sort of political means that can be used to achieve such parity. Let us consider each of these aspects of Fraser's theory in turn.

At the level of moral philosophy, Fraser avers that parity of participation – the founding principle of her theory – is universalist in two senses. First, it 'encompasses all (adult) partners to interaction'. Second, it 'presupposes the equal moral worth of human beings' (2003: 45; and see 1995: 89). Although Fraser does not explain the relationship between these two propositions, I would suggest that the first follows from the second: since all humans are of equal moral worth, all citizens of a particular society should be able to participate on a par with their fellows. To put it the other way round, her principle of parity assumes that equal respect must be shown to all persons. This commitment to equal moral worth of persons is the reason why Fraser is concerned to demonstrate that her theory of justice is moral rather than ethical, deontological rather than sectarian (2003: 30–1). That is to say, she intends to prove that her theory is founded on normative values which are independent of those associated with particular communities and ways of life. It is only in this way, she believes, that such a theory can form the basis of a principled agreement between all citizens in conditions of value pluralism (2003: 31). Thus the non-sectarian character of Fraser's theory can be seen as an expression of her commitment to the equal moral worth of persons. Since all persons must count equally, it would be unjust to base the fundamental structures of society on principles which favour some citizens over others.

At the level of political theory, Fraser's belief in the equal moral worth of persons manifests itself in her commitment to what she calls 'universalist recognition' (2003: 46). As I have said, the overall tone of her theory may suggest that recognition focuses on distinctiveness. In fact, she argues that there are occasions on which recognition should be given in virtue of features common to all humans. Fraser's commitment to both forms of recognition is revealed in her question: 'does justice require the recognition of what is distinctive about individuals, over and above the recognition of our common humanity?' (2003: 45; and see 48) The way in which this question is phrased captures the spirit of her argument. She assumes that recognition of common humanity is necessary, but then quickly moves on to the more controversial issue of what might be called 'particularist recognition'. Fraser's answer to her own question is clear enough: in those cases in which injustice is the result of the denial of common humanity, universalist recognition is the necessary remedy. To put this in the terms of the current discussion, where people are disrespected, the answer is to ensure that they get respect. If, for instance, their capacity for rational autonomy is not recognized, it is necessary to make sure that such recognition is secured. The example of universalist recognition that Fraser gives is that of non-racial citizenship in South Africa since the end of apartheid (2003: 46).[11] Such a political system makes no distinctions between citizens on the basis of racialized identities, since such identities provide no good reasons for differential treatment. I would argue that Fraser underplays the significance of universalist recognition, since she tends to take it for granted.[12] However, it is worth emphasizing that in many circumstances injustice is the result of the denial of common humanity. For this reason, universalist recognition will be very widely applicable. The case of the American civil rights movement is just one example amongst a myriad others in which the struggle for recognition focuses on the demand that all people be treated as equals.

Fraser's attitude to what I am calling a politics of respect can perhaps be most clearly seen by considering some of the cases with which she is concerned. She suggests that a range of different 'collectivities' can suffer injustices of recognition: groups defined by their sexuality can be presented as perverse (2003: 18); 'androcentrism' leads to the devaluation of 'everything coded as "feminine"' (2003: 20); groups defined by ideas of 'race' are damaged by the stigmatization of 'everything coded as "black", "brown", and "yellow"' (2003: 23). Amongst various potential injustices of misrecognition, such collectivities can experience the 'denial of the full rights and equal protections of citizenship' (2003: 18, 21, 23).[13] What does Fraser think should be done about this particular type of injustice of recognition? It might seem to follow from the account of universalist recognition which I have just

RECOGNITION AS RESPECT   **53**

provided that the remedy is straightforward. As Fraser says, where misrecognition denies common humanity, the remedy is to affirm it. In this particular case, then, the solution would be to provide all adult members of society with 'the full rights and equal protections of citizenship'. In practice, however, Fraser is more ambivalent about the rationale for such recognition. Consider the case of same-sex marriage. As we have just seen, Fraser argues that 'heteronormative value patterns' can 'construct heterosexuality as natural and normative, homosexuality as perverse and despised' (2003: 18). Laws that allow only different-sex marriage can be seen as a manifestation of such heteronormativity. Fraser argues, however, that the answer is not necessarily to reform the law so that same-sex couples can marry as well. Instead, she suggests that her theory of justice offers two possible solutions: either the legalization of same-sex marriage or the de-institutionalization of different-sex marriage.[14] Either measure, she maintains, 'would serve to foster parity of participation between gays and straights' (2003: 39).[15] What is not acceptable for Fraser is the compromise solution mentioned in section 1.2. Allowing civil unions for same-sex couples, while restricting marriage proper to different-sex couples, would perpetuate the inequality of status between these two sets of citizens (2003: 39–40).

Fraser provides more detailed guidance on how to assess the relative merits of different remedies for injustice in her discussion of what she refers to as *l'affaire foulard*. As we have seen, this case centres on the French state's ban on Muslim girls wearing headscarves at state-funded schools. In considering the justice of this ban, Fraser suggests that we must ask two questions. First, is the law as it presently stands an expression of dominant values which therefore acts as an obstacle to participatory parity? Second, would the proposed alternative – here simply lifting the ban – create new barriers to parity within the group in question (2003: 40–1)? With reference to the first question, Fraser argues that, since there is no ban on the wearing of crosses in French schools, outlawing the *foulard* is indeed an unjust expression of majoritarian values.[16] Regarding the second question, she considers the argument that allowing the wearing of the *foulard* would entrench gender inequalities within the French Muslim community. Here, she suggests, there seems to be evidence to support both sides of the argument (2003: 41–2).[17] Fraser's point is that the best remedy for a particular injustice depends on the specific circumstances of the case. In some instances, it may be best to take a right presently enjoyed by some and extend it to all. In other instances, it may be best to withdraw an existing right so that no one can exercise it. In the present case, then, either the ban is extended to all religious symbols, or it is lifted from all such symbols. Either crosses are banned as well as veils, or crosses and veils are both allowed. The right solution is the one that best promotes parity of participation.

3.5 A Critical Comparison

At the start of this chapter, I said that my discussion of the politics of respect would revolve around four general issues. These were the distinctiveness, the object, the mechanisms and the justification of respect. In what follows, I shall consider each of these issues in turn.

Distinctiveness of Respect

All three of the theorists under investigation here link respect to universal features of human beings. All contend that people deserve this type of recognition for qualities which they share with all of their fellows. Honneth, for one, is very clear that this is what makes respect a mode of recognition distinct from others. Taylor is much less explicit about the distinctiveness of respect. Indeed, in a moment I shall argue that, while he makes a distinction between the politics of universalism and the politics of difference, he does not overtly align this with a distinction between respect and esteem. At a couple of points, Fraser does refer to the distinction between respect and esteem. However, unlike the other two theorists, she does not make a corresponding distinction – either explicit or implicit – between forms of politics which correspond to respect and esteem. In marked contrast, she suggests that a pragmatic decision must be made in each particular case about what is required by justice. Since Honneth is very explicit about what makes respect distinctive, I shall say no more about his position on this issue. I do, however, have some critical comments to make about the other two theorists' positions.

Taylor does not use the words 'respect' and 'esteem' to refer to two distinct modes of recognition. At the beginning of his essay 'The Politics of Recognition', for instance, he makes reference to the argument that misrecognition can lead to women's 'low self-esteem'. But then he suggests that in this and other cases misrecognition involves a 'lack of due respect' (1995b: 225–6). This is just one instance in which he elides the distinction between these two modes of recognition. In fact, Taylor refers to 'esteem' very rarely, instead using 'recognition' and 'respect' pretty much interchangeably to talk about all forms of recognition. Thus the politics of universalism shows 'respect' for the human potential for rational agency, while the politics of difference shows 'respect' for 'the potential for forming and defining one's own identity' (1995b: 235–6). I want to argue, nevertheless, that the distinction between respect and esteem is implicit in Taylor's account. I want to argue, moreover, that his account would be strengthened if this distinction were to be made explicit. Consider once more the way in which he contrasts the politics of universalism and difference. The recognition of the capacity for rational agency on which the former is based is very different to the recognition of the capacity for identity formation on which the latter rests. As Taylor says, while the former involves recognition of a quality that makes us the same as each other, the latter involves recognition of a quality that makes us distinct from one another (1995b: 233–4). In the terms that I am using here, I would suggest that the first sort of recognition is best understood as respect for autonomy, and the second as esteem for identity. In the next chapter, I shall argue that Taylor's failure explicitly to distinguish between respect and esteem creates serious problems for his theory. To anticipate my argument there, I shall suggest that, as a result of the conflation of these two modes of recognition, the conflict between universalism and difference appears to be a zero-sum game. Any gain for the politics of universalism must be a loss for the politics of difference, and vice versa. As a result, Taylor's own *via media* – to protect fundamental rights while permitting some measures which aim to ensure cultural survival – is an unstable compromise between the two. If, by contrast, he were to accept that respect and esteem are two analytically distinct types of recognition, then a coherent and principled defence of his position would be possible.

For much of the time, Fraser treats recognition as a unitary substance: it is a quality of intersubjective relations that makes parity of participation possible. It is for this reason that she can say that victims of misrecognition get less 'respect, esteem, and prestige' than others (2003: 14), and why she refers more generally to a collectivity being 'distinguished by the relative respect, prestige, and esteem it enjoys vis-à-vis the others' (2003: 50). These formulations suggest that there is no pertinent distinction between respect, esteem and prestige. These terms can be used interchangeably to help specify the particular position which a group occupies in the status order. If this was all that Fraser said on this matter, she would be as guilty of conflating the distinction between respect and esteem as Taylor. At one point, however, she does make a very clear distinction between these two modes of recognition, referring to the contrast made in moral philosophy between respect, which is 'owed universally to every person in virtue of shared humanity', and esteem, which is 'accorded differentially on the basis of persons' specific traits, accomplishments, or contributions' (2003: 99 n. 32). Her reasons for invoking this contrast are primarily negative: she wishes to distance herself from the claim – which she believes Honneth is guilty of making – that there is 'an equal right to social esteem' (2003: 32). Since individuals' 'traits, accomplishments, or contributions' are clearly very different, it is illogical to demand equal esteem for them. By contrast, Fraser asserts, since all individuals are equally human, it makes sense to argue that they should have a right to equal respect. To bring the two points together, she says that, in order for parity to be achieved, all individuals must enjoy both 'equal respect' and 'equal opportunity for achieving social esteem' (2003: 36). Unlike Honneth, however, Fraser does not make much more of the distinction than this. In particular, as I have already suggested, it does not feature in the main body of her theory, where for the most part respect and esteem (and prestige) are treated as synonyms. Echoing my comments about Taylor, in the next chapter I shall argue that the failure systematically to incorporate this distinction into her analysis is an important weakness of Fraser's theory of recognition. Use of this distinction, I shall suggest, would make her 'pragmatic' account more rigorous. Instead of simply suggesting that recognition may require the acknowledgement or the neglect of specific identities, depending on the circumstances, this distinction would imply instead that a system of rights guaranteeing equal respect must sit alongside a value community in which all citizens have an opportunity to earn esteem.

Object of Respect

I have suggested that the three theorists of recognition of particular concern to me focus on the individual as the object of respect. As I shall show, although only Fraser explicitly rejects the possibility that collectivities could be the objects of respect, both Honneth and Taylor assume that it is individuals who are to be respected. This seems to make sense given that the ground for respect – at least for Honneth and Taylor – is rational autonomy. Whilst individuals are able to use their powers of reason to choose how to act, it is difficult to imagine how any kind of collectivity could behave in the same way. I shall now examine each of these theorists' accounts of the object of respect in a little more detail.

We have seen that Taylor defends individuals' fundamental rights. However, as I shall explain in chapter 4, he also believes that other purported rights may in some circumstances be overridden in the interest of collective survival. What he calls the 'politics of difference' (1995b: 233) holds that 'collective goals' can, in some cases, take priority over a wide range of 'privileges and immunities' (1995b: 247). Although the politics of difference is still a form of liberalism, contending that all individuals should enjoy the same basic rights, it nevertheless accepts that specific societies should be able to take measures to protect their own particular ways of life. To illustrate what this might mean in practice, consider Quebec's raft of policies which are designed to protect the French language in that province.[18] To those who argue that these measures constitute an unjust restriction on their rights, Taylor's reply is that, since they do not violate any *fundamental* rights, they can be justified as legitimate means with which to defend Quebec's cultural character (1995b: 247). Thus Taylor does not believe that a principle of respect entails the defence of every individual right that could conceivably be proposed. Although it does entail the defence of fundamental rights, demands for the creation of other non-fundamental rights must compete with demands for collective protection. This analysis of Taylor's position may appear to contradict my assertion that, for him, only individuals can be rights-holders. Indeed, as we shall see in the next chapter, a number of commentators have suggested that he defends at least one collective right – namely, the right of a collectivity to cultural survival. Against this suggestion, I shall argue that Taylor does not defend a collectively held right to survival. While a group may be permitted to take measures which aim to ensure its survival, such measures do not take the form of rights, and do not guarantee survival.

Although Honneth does not explicitly reject the idea that the instantiation of a collective right could be regarded as an expression of respect for a collectivity, his discussion of rights focuses exclusively on 'basic individual rights' (1995: 115). This is to be expected given that rights are founded on, and designed to protect, the individual's capacity for 'moral responsibility' (1995: 120). Having said this, Honneth's recent thoughts on recognition may suggest an opening for the idea of collective rights. Restricting the role of esteem to reward for individuals' contribution to the common good, he is led to consider the possibility that there is a 'fourth principle of recognition, which would revolve around mutual respect for the cultural particularities of groups or collectivities' (2003: 159). He discusses, in particular, the case for the 'legal protection of the continued existence of a cultural community' (2003: 165–6). As we shall see in the next chapter, this is very close to Taylor's concern with cultural survival. Honneth's tentative argument is that most of the demands that are made under the banner of identity politics can be met satisfactorily by measures which fall into the existing category of 'legal recognition'. What this means is that demands for the recognition of identity can be understood as demands for respect. By implication, then, such demands can be met by taking measures which focus on the individual rather the collective. He suggests, however, that there is one type of demand which goes beyond anything that could be dealt with by legal recognition: this is 'the demand that a minority communal culture be socially esteemed for its own sake' (2003: 167). Here it appears as if the collectivity itself is the object of recognition. Since at this point we enter the territory of the politics of esteem, I shall defer further discussion of this matter until chapter 4. There I shall argue that Honneth would be well advised to abandon the idea of a fourth principle of recognition, and should instead expand the scope of his proposed principle of contribution.

Of our three theorists, Fraser is the most explicit in her hostility to the idea that collectivities could be given rights. She is adamant that the rights justified by respect can be enjoyed only by individuals. Her reasons for rejecting collective rights appear to be consequentialist. In a discussion of political strategy, she argues that one objective of such a strategy should be to 'avoid constitutionalizing group rights or otherwise entrenching status distinctions in forms that are difficult to change' (2003: 82). The problem with group rights, in other words, is that they make it more difficult to eliminate unfair distinctions in status. Once such rights are granted, groups will vigorously defend them in order to hold on to the privileges that come with them. Without such rights, then, it is more likely that status equality can be achieved. In reply to Fraser, it could be argued that, in some circumstances, the creation of group rights may be the best way to overcome existing status inequalities. This argument might be analogous to that made in favour of positive discrimination: preferential treatment for a previously disadvantaged group is temporarily justified in order to create a level playing field. In the case now under consideration, then, the creation of a collective right might be the best way of overcoming an existing inequality of status. However, even if this argument worked in some cases, it would not be sufficient to overcome Fraser's objections to collective rights. This is because she also develops a broader critique of all 'affirmative' political strategies which approve of existing identities. Such strategies, she contends, are likely to lead to the reification of identities, the neglect of power imbalances within groups, and the deepening of political schisms between groups

(2003: 76). Thus, even if a group right does do an effective job of overcoming particular status inequalities, it would still have these other damaging effects. Again, I defer further discussion of these arguments until the next chapter.

Mechanisms of Respect

According to Hegel, respect is the mode of recognition which has a particular institutional location: 'in the state . . . man is recognized and treated as a *rational* being, as free, as a person' (cited in Honneth 1995: 108). By contrast, the three theorists of particular concern to me in the book reject the idea that this mode of recognition can be associated with a particular sphere of society. For all of them, I would suggest, such an association would be a case of what Honneth elsewhere calls 'misdirected concretization' (1995: 176). This does not, however, stop each of them from associating respect with particular political devices. On my reading of Taylor's theory, the politics of universalism – his version of the politics of respect – is centred on the protection of fundamental rights. Honneth makes a very strong connection between respect and rights. For him, indeed, rights are the only means by which this mode of recognition can be expressed. I have suggested that, by contrast, Fraser allows a wider range of remedies to serve the goal of parity of participation. There are two issues I would like to consider further here. First, should Honneth in particular make such a tight connection between respect and rights? Second, is Fraser correct to argue that, when people are denied rights, this can be explained by reference to cultural values?

In section 3.3, I showed why Honneth believes that modern systems of rights are the essential medium for the expression of respect. This is why he uses 'legal recognition' as a synonym for respect: in protecting individuals' rights, the law enables them to show each other respect. I do not want to challenge Honneth's general thesis. I agree with him that Joel Feinberg provides convincing proof that, in a society without rights, individuals cannot develop self-respect (1995: 119–20; Feinberg 1980). But I do want to suggest that there are specific circumstances in which it is possible to show respect by *removing* certain rights. To make this argument, I shall return to Fraser's account of the remedies for recognition. Let us consider two examples to which I have already made reference. Fraser objects to the ban on headscarves in publicly funded schools in France because she believes that this ban discriminates against Muslim schoolgirls. But it does not automatically follow that the appropriate remedy for this injustice is to lift the ban. In some circumstances, the best solution may be make sure that the ban covers not just headscarves but also crosses and other religious symbols as well. To take another case, there are circumstances in which the best remedy for the non-recognition of same-sex relationships would be 'to de-institutionalize heterosexual marriage' (2003: 39) so that same-sex and different-sex couples are placed on the same footing. In both cases, the type of strategy being deployed is the same: it is to eliminate privileges 'now reserved for advantaged groups' (2003: 73). The intended effect is also the same: it is to create a situation in which equal respect is shown to all. Although the group which was previously advantaged is not shown more respect than it was before that advantage is removed, the removal of this advantage may nevertheless be the best way of ensuring that all citizens enjoy *equal* respect. What this analysis shows is that in some cases it is possible to show equal respect by *removing* an existing right – to marry someone of the opposite sex or to wear religious symbols to school – rather than by extending that right to a hitherto neglected group. This, I would suggest, shows that Honneth is wrong to argue that respect can be expressed only through the medium of rights.[19]

Fraser argues that, in all cases in which a group is denied rights, this is the result of 'institutionalized patterns of cultural value' (2003: 18). There is, in other words, a cultural basis for all such misrecognition. This is how she describes the situation: 'the denial of rights and equal protections of citizenship' is one of the possible 'effects' of misrecognition 'rooted . . . in the status order of society' (2003: 18). To give two specific examples, the denial of rights may be one of the 'results' of the institutionalization of androcentric value patterns (2003: 20), or it may be 'generated' by Eurocentric value patterns (2003: 23). In short, whenever a collectivity is deprived of the equal rights or protections of citizenship, it is because of the low cultural valuation of that group. But is it true to say that all cases of political misrecognition have a cultural basis? It will be instructive here to anticipate my discussion in chapter 5 of the debate between Fraser and Honneth on the relationship between recognition and redistribution. While Honneth argues that all injustices of maldistribution are the result of misrecognition, Fraser rejects this argument, since she contends that some such injustices are entirely independent of misrecognition. A fall in wage levels in a particular economic sector, for instance, may be caused by a change in global capital flows, and have nothing to do with the cultural valuation placed on the jobs in question. I would suggest that it may be possible to make an analogous point here. In this case, the argument would be that legal recognition cannot always be explained by reference to institutionalized patterns of cultural value. There are occasions on which a group may be deprived of rights for reasons not reducible to cultural valuation. For instance, one group may find itself deprived of rights which others enjoy because another group has wielded its greater political power or has utilized its greater resources in order to achieve this result. Of course, it is likely that, in a situation in which rights are denied, a differential cultural valuation will also be found. My point, however, is that the group in question is not denied rights *as a result of* this valuation. Indeed, the cultural valuation may be a *post hoc* rationalization of the political injustice. That is to say, a powerful group which deprives a weaker group of a right may then denigrate that group in order to justify depriving it of that right. I would suggest, then, that some instances of political misrecognition are not cultural at root. Some such misrecognition has a political basis which is independent of culture. This argument chimes in with a broader charge made by a number of critics who suggest that Fraser fails to give sufficient attention to the role of the state in matters of justice (e.g. Feldman 2002; Yar 2001). I shall return to this criticism in chapter 5 in particular.

Justification of Respect

The fourth and final general theme which has run through this chapter concerns the justification of respect. Once more, there is a significant overlap between our three theorists' positions. Both Taylor and Honneth argue that respect is due to humans in light of their universal potential for rational agency. Fraser is not so explicit about the basis of respect. While, as we have seen, she is familiar with the idea that respect is 'owed universally to every person in virtue of shared humanity', she does not identify what specific quality humans possess in virtue of which they deserve respect. There are two issues concerning the justification for respect that need to be pursued further. The first concerns a lack of clarity in Honneth's account of the reasons for respect. The second calls into question the links made between the grounds for respect and the means of expressing respect in all of the theories under consideration here.

In section 3.3, I showed why Honneth believes that humans deserve respect. They have, he says, 'at least the capacity to make reasonable, autonomous decisions regarding moral questions' (1995: 114). It is because humans are morally responsible for their actions that they should be given individual rights. Such rights protect their ability to exercise their moral responsibility by enabling them to choose what principles to live by and what personal projects to pursue. What this means is that respect is shown to individuals by granting them rights which protect their personal freedom. There are, however, points in his analysis at which Honneth seems to offer a rather different account of the grounds for respect. When one is 'universally recognized as a morally responsible person', it is because 'one is able to view oneself as a person who shares with all other members of one's community the qualities that make participation in discursive will-formation possible' (1995: 120). Here the idea seems to be that the ground for respect is the ability to play a full part in deliberations about the direction that a political community should take. While the capacity for rational agency appears to play an important role in both instances, there nevertheless remains a significant difference between them. In the first case, reason guides our moral decisions; in the second, it guides our political decisions. It is certainly possible to imagine circumstances in which these two grounds for respect could come apart. In a liberal but undemocratic polity, respect would be shown for the capacity for moral responsibility but not for the capacity for political participation. In a democratic but illiberal polity, by contrast, respect would be shown for the capacity for political participation but not for the capacity for moral responsibility. This appears to present us with a choice. Should we respect others because they can make decisions about the rules to follow in their personal lives, or because they can take part in deliberations about the rules by which their political community should live? Should individuals be respected by granting them rights which protect their personal freedom, or by granting them rights which enable them to engage in democratic deliberation?

In order to understand why Honneth endorses what appear to be two rather different accounts of the grounds for respect, it will be useful to refer to Jürgen Habermas's distinction between what he refers to as 'private autonomy' and 'public autonomy'. The idea of private autonomy is at work in the liberal claim that 'the principle of equal respect for each person holds only in the form of a legally protected autonomy that every person can use to realize his or her personal life project' (1994: 112). This form of autonomy corresponds to Honneth's first account: it says that individuals are respected when they enjoy rights that secure their ability to live in the manner of their choosing. The idea of public autonomy is in play in the democratic claim that 'those to whom the law is addressed can acquire autonomy (in the Kantian sense) only to the extent that they understand themselves to be the authors of the laws to which they are subject as private legal persons' (1994: 112). This form of autonomy can be seen in Honneth's second account: it says that individuals are respected only when they are able jointly to exercise what Habermas calls 'their autonomy as citizens' (1994: 113). It is important to realize that, for Habermas, these two forms of autonomy are not rival grounds for respect. As he puts it, 'private and public autonomy are equiprimordial' (1994: 112–13). This is because he believes that citizens could not securely enjoy their capacity to formulate and pursue their own life projects unless they were able to regard themselves as the authors of the laws which protect that capacity. In other words, if citizens are to have the confidence that their fundamental rights are protected, they must actively participate in the democratic system which passes the laws protecting those rights. This means that there is an 'internal connection between democracy and the constitutional state' (1994: 113). 'In normative terms', Habermas concludes, 'there is no such thing as a constitutional state without democracy' (1994: 122).

I think that Honneth would agree with Habermas's analysis, and in particular his argument that personal freedom and political participation are conceptually and practically intertwined. This is why he argues that 'in order to be involved as morally responsible persons, individuals need not only legal protection from interference in their sphere of liberty, but also the legally assured opportunity for participation in the public process of will-formation' (1995: 117). That is to say, to acknowledge someone's moral responsibility means in practice to protect their personal freedom *and* to facilitate their participation in democratic deliberation. This is because 'participation in rational will-formation' is a necessary condition of moral responsibility (1995: 114). It follows that for Honneth, as for Habermas, a polity which shows respect to its members cannot simply be a constitutional state in which laws guarantee personal freedom. In such a state, the freedom that its citizens enjoy could be withdrawn at any time. Hence a polity which respects its members must also be a democratic state in which citizens have the opportunity to shape the laws which protect their freedom. I shall pursue this idea further in my analysis of Honneth's account of the relationship between recognition and democracy in chapter 6.

The second issue concerning the justification of respect calls into the question the connection between this mode of recognition, the capacity of rational autonomy, and systems of individual rights. I have shown why Taylor, Honneth and possibly Fraser believe that humans deserve respect in light of their capability to exercise rational control over their lives, and that they should therefore enjoy rights which protect this capability. But this chain of association may be called into question. It could be argued that humans possess other universal qualities which provide quite different reasons for respecting them, and that these other qualities do not need to be protected by guaranteeing individual rights. Consider, for instance, an account of respect which is based on an idea of neediness. This could begin with the proposition that, since all humans have the same basic needs, this neediness can be regarded as a universal characteristic. It could then introduce the further proposition that, if humans do not have their basic needs met, they will not be able to live a life of dignity. Without the fundamental necessities that make life bearable, self-respect is impossible. If these two propositions were accepted, it would follow that respect can be shown, not by giving humans rights which protect their personal freedoms, but by taking measures to ensure that their basic needs are met. In short, it would be possible to respect humans by meeting their needs. If this account of the connection between respect and needs were to be accepted, it would threaten the connection between respect and rights. It would imply that respect need not be correlated with a theory of justice based on rights, but that it could be correlated with an ethic of care centred on needs.

How might the three theorists under investigation here respond to this argument? Does it threaten to undermine their accounts of the links between recognition as respect, rational autonomy and individual rights? Is it a genuinely alternative account of the nature of respect? I would argue that these two accounts are not in fact as divergent as they may at first appear. This is because the first account can and does incorporate a concern with neediness. Consider how this works in Honneth's case. As I said in section 3.3, Honneth argues that, in modern societies, social rights are necessary if individuals are to be shown respect. If they are to be respected, individuals do not just require their personal freedoms and ability to participate in politics to be protected; they also require their basic needs to be met by the provision of social rights. Consider also how Fraser's account implicitly includes a concern with basic needs. I argued in section 3.4 that, for her, equal moral respect is shown to all individuals by guaranteeing parity of participation. This standard requires two conditions to be met. The 'objective' condition 'precludes forms and levels of economic dependence and inequality that impede parity of participation' (2003: 36). I would suggest that the provision of a system of welfare that meets basic needs would be one way in which to meet this condition. My conclusion is that this alternative account of the grounds for respect is not distinct from the original account. In fact, consideration of the requirement to meet basic needs simply enforces the idea – most explicit in Honneth's theory – that recognition as respect necessitates the provision of rights to welfare.

There is, however, a further complexity concerning this issue which will be worth bearing in mind. Sennett suggests that the inevitability of continuing inequality presents a serious problem for the practice of respect. As he puts it, 'the nub of the problem we face is how the strong can practice respect toward those destined to remain weak' (2003: 263). In his analysis of this problem, the role of welfare is of considerable importance. 'In the public realm', he points out, 'dependence appears shameful.' By contrast, 'self-sufficiency brings respect in the eyes of others and breeds self-respect' (2003: 101). In these cultural conditions, welfare can undermine self-respect by implying that its recipients are dependent, in particular by not allowing them 'to participate more actively in the conditions of their own care' (2003: 261). It follows that it is possible that practical efforts to show respect by, for instance, guaranteeing social rights or meeting the objective condition of participatory parity could backfire. The result of such measures could be that the self-respect of some individuals is undermined rather than supported. I shall return to this point in chapter 5.

3.6 Conclusions

In this chapter, I have offered a critical evaluation of the accounts of recognition as respect to be found in the three political theories on which I have chosen to focus in this book. In section 3.1, I said that my analysis would focus on four particular questions. In these concluding remarks I shall return briefly to each of them in turn. First, regarding the distinctiveness of respect, I have argued that the latent distinctions to be found in both Taylor's and Fraser's accounts between this mode of recognition and esteem need to be made explicit. In chapter 4, I shall explain why this is so by showing that a defensible theory of justice is one that regards respect and esteem as two complementary modes of recognition. Second, so far as the object of respect is concerned, I have suggested that on occasion Taylor and Honneth consider the possibility that not just individual citizens but also certain collectivities could be the objects of recognition. I would suggest that consideration of Fraser's vigorous critique of group rights could be used to help them resist this temptation. Third, with regard to the political mechanisms by which respect can be expressed, against

Honneth I argued that in some circumstances respect can be shown by withdrawing rights, and against Fraser I argued that not all injustices of disrespect are cultural at root. In later chapters I develop this latter claim into the thesis that Fraser needs to introduce a third category into her currently dichotomous theory. Fourth, on the justification of respect, I have contended that the idea of rational autonomy is more complex than it may at first appear. For one thing, it is necessary to appreciate the relationship between private and public autonomy. For another, it has been argued by some that social rights – which Honneth, for one, believes are a necessary condition of autonomy – may in some circumstances undermine such autonomy.

Finally, I should emphasize that my assessment of these three politics of respect in this chapter has necessarily been provisional. I believe that both Taylor's and Honneth's theories would be at their strongest if they placed respect and esteem side by side as two distinct modes of recognition. I have also argued that Fraser's theory makes best sense if respect-type means and esteem-type means of achieving parity of participation are considered alongside each other. In this case, it follows that it will not be until the end of the next chapter that I shall be able to determine how well these two politics might operate in conjunction. I should also emphasize that I shall return to some of the issues raised here in later chapters as well. For example, in chapter 6 on democracy I shall consider the suggestion that certain groups may suffer a lack of recognition by being excluded from deliberative bodies. In chapter 7, the language of disrespect and humiliation will be of considerable interest when I consider the motives behind struggles for recognition.

4

Recognition as Esteem

4.1 Introduction

In January 2001, the Institute of Ulster-Scots Studies was established at the University of Ulster. The mission of the Institute 'is to explore the history, heritage and legacy of the Ulster Scots people'. More specifically, its role 'is to promote the experience of the Ulster Scots as a mainstream academic concern'.[1] Initiatives such as the creation of the Institute emerge from what is most often referred to as the 'two traditions' approach to Northern Ireland. After the return of direct rule from Westminster in 1972, it was an ever-growing belief of successive British governments that culture had to play a significant role in the solution to what was seen as the 'problem' of Northern Ireland. One particular way of thinking about culture grew to dominate the approach of the British – and later the Irish – governments to this issue. This was the idea that there are two traditions in this region, both of which must be given due recognition in any successful political settlement. It was this way of thinking which led to the establishment of the Community Relations Commission and the Ministry for Community Relations in 1969, the Central Community Relations Unit in 1987, and the Cultural Traditions Group in the following year, which was then absorbed into the Community Relations Council in 1990 (Finlayson 1997: 76; Porter 1998: 46). This idea of two traditions was also increasingly incorporated into official government discourse. From the mid-eighties onwards, the two governments attempted to refer inclusively to both communities in all official documents, including the Anglo-Irish Agreement of 1985 and the Framework Documents of 1995 (O'Day 1997: 201–2). It could be argued that the two traditions approach reached its apogee in the Belfast Agreement of April 1998. In the agreement, the idea that there should be equal recognition between the Unionist and Nationalist communities is given a crucial role to play. Article 1 states that 'the power of the sovereign government . . . shall be founded on' the principle 'of parity of esteem'.[2] The agreement thus seeks to ensure that, in all of its structures, institutions, policies and practices, the government in Northern Ireland gives equal acknowledgement to the two national communities (O'Leary 1999: 90).[3] In this context, then, the establishment of the Institute of Ulster-Scots Studies takes its place as one part of the effort to give recognition to one of the two traditions of Northern Ireland.

In a couple of the case-studies that were introduced in section 1.2, it is possible to see elements of the same sort of politics in action. One example was the campaign to recognize Quebec as a distinct society within Canada. The phrase 'distinct society' first occurred in the Report of the Royal Commission on Bilingualism and Biculturalism in the 1960s (McRoberts 1997: 195). The Meech Lake Accord of 1987 repeated it, stating that the role of the Quebec government was 'to preserve and promote the distinct identity of Quebec' (§3). Thus the idea of Quebec as a distinct society has for a long time been at the centre of the campaign to get its French identity acknowledged as a unique part of Canada's multicultural 'mosaic'.[4] Another example of the politics of esteem was the opposition to the law passed by the French state in 2004 which banned the wearing of conspicuous religious symbols in public schools. I have argued that, for many critics of this ban, it seemed clear that this law was directed in the first instance at Muslim headscarves rather than at other religious symbols. For some of these critics, indeed, the headscarf ban amounted to an expression of 'Islamophobia'. In other words, it was a manifestation of a distinct pattern of prejudice against Islam and against Muslims.[5] These two examples of the politics of recognition have a number of features in common. First, they both make reference to collective identities. In these particular cases, these identities are based on national and religious affiliation, respectively. Second, there is an assumption that these collective identities mark some people out as different from others. Francophone Quebecois are contrasted with Anglophone Canadians. In some contexts, French Muslims are contrasted with French Christians, Jews and secularists. In others, they are contrasted with French citizens. Third, in each case it is argued that it is in virtue of having such a distinctive identity that recognition is deserved.

Fourth, in each case proposals are put forward to undo this injustice which share an underlying logic. Quebec should be able to take measures to protect its distinctive culture. French Muslim girls should be able to wear the veil in public schools. In both cases, the rationale is that the groups in question should be able to occupy a more secure and visible place in the public life of their society.

I shall refer to the distinctive pattern of political thought and action which gives a prominent place to these themes of identity, distinctness, value and visibility as a 'politics of esteem'. All three of the theorists of particular concern to me engage with such a politics, although they do so in different ways. Charles Taylor's influential essay on 'The Politics of Recognition' did much to stimulate the current debate on the recognition of identity. I shall argue that what he calls the 'politics of difference' engages with many of the issues that I wish to consider here. According to his account, a group may be allowed to take certain measures to protect its culture in order to try to ensure its survival. Taylor's essay also deals with a second theme, which I shall argue is quite distinct from the first. Considering the claim that all cultures are of equal value, he accepts that it is reasonable to *presume* that all enduring cultures have some value. But he insists that this presumption must be put to the test in a hermeneutic encounter with each culture in question. As we have seen, Axel Honneth considers esteem to be one of the three primary modes of recognition. He believes that, in modern societies, esteem is (or should be) determined by a principle of achievement: an individual earns esteem in virtue of what they contribute to their society. This principle informs Honneth's 'formal conception of ethical life'. He argues that, in a society shaped by such a conception, all individuals have equal opportunities to earn esteem. Unlike Taylor or Honneth, Nancy Fraser does not clearly divide the political field into a politics of respect and a politics of esteem. She does, however, contend that what I am calling esteem is one of the conditions necessary to achieve parity of participation. To be specific, she argues that, where prevailing 'structures of prestige' judge some people to be less worthy than others, the aim of a politics of recognition should be to combat such disesteem in whatever way is most appropriate in each particular case.

The aim of this chapter is critically to examine these three rival accounts of the politics of esteem. My analysis will revolve around four particular questions. First, what is distinctive about recognition as esteem? Why might it be important to distinguish it, in particular, from respect? Second, what is the context of esteem? What background conditions must be in place if the practice of esteem is to make sense? Third, why should someone (or something) be esteemed? For example, is esteem due in virtue of the value of a culture or an individual's contribution to their society? Fourth, what does the practice of esteem look like? Can it be associated with characteristic political mechanisms?

The chapter is organized in the following way. In the next section, I shall lay out the principal elements of Taylor's position, clearly distinguishing his arguments about cultural value and cultural survival (4.2). Then I shall consider Honneth's alternative account of esteem, focusing in particular on his idea of the principle of achievement (4.3). After this, I shall turn to Fraser's account of esteem, concentrating on those remedies for misrecognition which follow the logic of esteem (4.4). In the following section, by considering each of the four questions I have just raised, I shall present a critical comparison of these three versions of the politics of esteem (4.5). By the end of the chapter, I hope to be able to determine which theory – or which combination of theories – offers the most defensible account of recognition as esteem (4.6).

4.2   Charles Taylor: The Politics of Difference

It will be recalled that Taylor's analysis of the politics of recognition is based on a fundamental distinction between what he refers to as the 'politics of universalism' and the 'politics of difference'. In section 3.2, I showed how the politics of universalism focuses on individuals' capacity for rational autonomy. It contends that respect is due to those individuals in light of this capacity, and that such respect is expressed in the form of individual rights (1995b: 233–5). This is a familiar sort of political theory, most readily associated today with what I have referred to as procedural liberalism. In this section, I shall argue that the politics of difference is Taylor's version of what I am calling the politics of esteem. This form of politics focuses on 'the potential for forming and defining one's identity, as an individual and also as a culture' (1995b: 236). It holds that it is in virtue of having this potential that one should receive recognition, and that such recognition is expressed in measures designed to protect such identities. As I argued in section 3.5, although Taylor does not use the word 'esteem' to refer specifically to this sort of recognition, I believe that his account makes most sense if the distinction between respect and esteem is correlated with the distinction between universalism and difference. Again, the sort of political theory that centres on such an idea of recognition is a familiar part of the contemporary political landscape. I would suggest that it can be associated, for instance, with contemporary forms of communitarianism which place the protection and care of communities at the heart of their political project.[6] In this section, I shall focus on Taylor's analysis of the politics of difference. I shall suggest that it deals with two very distinct issues. One concerns the proposition that all cultures should be judged to be of equal value. The other concerns the legitimacy of political measures designed to ensure the survival of a culture. Although both of these issues concern recognition as esteem, I shall argue that they have no necessary connection. I shall now consider each issue in turn.

With regard to the issue of cultural value, it is important to understand Taylor's account of what I am calling the context of esteem. He argues that all individuals are necessarily located in a 'horizon of meaning', 'frame' or 'framework' which they use to make sense of the world. As he says, 'the horizons within which we live our lives and which make sense of them have to include . . . strong qualitative discriminations' (1989: 27). They 'articulate' our 'sense of the good, the holy, and the admirable' (1995b: 256). The discriminations made within such horizons provide both the material from which individuals' identity formed and, at the same time, the ethical vocabulary by which they orientate themselves in the world. In light of this analysis of the context of esteem, why might an exponent of the politics of difference argue for the presumption that all cultures are of equal value? Taylor puts it like this:

> If withholding the presumption is tantamount to a denial of equality, and if important consequences flow for people's identity from the absence of recognition, then a case can be made for insisting on the universalization of the presumption as a logical extension of the politics of dignity. Just as all must have equal civil rights, and equal voting rights, regardless of race or culture, so all should enjoy the presumption that their traditional culture has value. (1995b: 253)

In his essay, Taylor illustrates this argument by reference to the so-called campus wars or culture wars that have intermittently broken out in American universities since the early 1990s. He suggests that, if the demand for the recognition of equal value were successful, it would have profound implications for the syllabi of universities' humanities courses. If the canon as it is presently constituted expresses a series of judgements about the superiority of the dominant culture, then the implication is that it must be radically revised in order to include works by all of the cultures presently excluded from it. As Taylor says, demands have been made 'to alter, enlarge, or scrap the canon' in order to shift its balance away from 'dead white males' and toward 'women and . . . people of non-European races and cultures' (1995b: 251). Such a revision is necessary, both to treat all citizens equally and to avoid the psychological harm that exclusion from the canon causes.[7]

Taylor admits that he can see the force of this demand for cultural equality. He accepts that 'there is something valid in this presumption' of equal value: 'the claim is that all human cultures that have animated whole societies over some considerable stretch of time have something important to say to all human beings' (1995b: 252). If they did not, why would they endure? Taylor is nevertheless determined to reject the presumption in this form. As he says, 'it can't make sense to demand as a matter of right that we come up with a final concluding judgment that their value is great, or equal to others' (1995b: 254). He offers at least three distinct reasons against it. First, it would be patronizing: 'the giving of a judgment on demand is an act of breathtaking condescension' (1995b: 254–5). Such a judgement would in fact betray the opposite attitude to esteem. It would say: 'We shall exercise our power to esteem you since you need esteem, regardless of whether or not you actually deserve it.' It would thus express the sense of superiority that the judge has to the object of their judgement. Second, the judgement would be ethnocentric. In attempting to esteem a culture without seriously studying it, we have only our own standards to rely on. Hence our judgement is ethnocentric, revealing an unjustified preference for our own standards. Third, the judgement would be homogenizing. Taylor puts it like this: 'The peremptory demand for favorable judgments of worth is paradoxically – perhaps tragically – homogenizing. For it implies that we already have the standards to make such judgments. The standards we have, however, are those of North Atlantic civilization. And so the judgments implicitly and unconsciously will cram the others into our categories' (1995b: 255). Since we apply our own ethnocentric standards, and do not take others' standards seriously into consideration, the effect is to misinterpret those other cultures by seeing them solely from our own point of view.[8] These criticisms notwithstanding, Taylor admits that 'it would take supreme arrogance to discount [the] possibility' that long-standing cultures 'are almost certain to have something that deserves our admiration and respect' (1995b: 256). For this reason, he concludes, it 'makes sense to insist as a matter of right that we approach the study of certain cultures with a presumption of their value' (1995b: 253–4).

The second issue that Taylor deals with under the rubric of the politics of difference is cultural survival. It is here that the difference between his position and that of supporters of the politics of universalism becomes clear. In contrast to the procedural liberalism described in section 3.2, Taylor defends what he refers to as a 'non-procedural' form of liberalism (1995b: 249). It is non-procedural since it does not claim to be neutral between different ways of life; in fact, it is 'grounded very much on judgments about what makes a good life – judgments in which the integrity of cultures has an important place' (1995b: 248). This does not mean that Taylor entirely abandons the politics of universalism for the politics of difference. He argues, rather, that a group may take measures to try to ensure the survival of its culture, but only if these measures are consistent with fundamental rights. While Taylor accepts that these rights must be defended in all circumstances, he believes that they should be distinguished 'from the broad range of immunities and presumptions of uniform treatment that have sprung up in modern cultures of judicial review'. The latter *may* sometimes be overridden, and thus the goal of uniform treatment abandoned, in the name of 'cultural survival' (1995b: 248). In this way, Taylor hopes, the claims of individual rights can be balanced against claims for cultural protection. To put this in terms of recognition, he hopes that claims for the recognition of individual autonomy can be balanced against claims for the recognition of the identity of distinct cultural groups.

In order to see what Taylor's non-procedural liberalism looks like in practice, let us consider the case of Quebec. As I showed in the previous chapter, Taylor rejects the version of the politics of universalism which he calls procedural liberalism. In particular, he rejects its assumption that a commitment to equality of concern entails a commitment to uniformity of treatment. Taylor believes that such a political theory lies behind the Canadian Charter of Rights and Freedoms which seeks to forge an identical relationship between every Canadian citizen and the state. By contrast, his non-procedural liberalism is committed to equality of concern, but not to uniformity of treatment. In the case now under consideration, Taylor argues that, within the framework of the Charter of Rights and freedoms, it is justifiable to recognize Quebec as a distinct society. In the words of the Charlottetown Accord of 1992, it should be acknowledged that Quebec 'constitutes within Canada a distinct society, which includes a French-speaking majority, a unique culture and a civil law tradition' (§1c). The official acknowledgement of Quebec's particular cultural identity would mean that certain measures could be taken to protect this identity. Thus the government of Quebec could legitimately enact policies to protect the French language so long as these measures did not violate citizens' fundamental rights (Taylor

1995b: 246–8). As Michael Walzer puts it, Quebec 'can require French signage; it cannot ban English newspapers' (1994: 100). In other words, compulsory French signage is justified in order to protect Quebec's cultural identity, but English newspapers are permitted so that citizens' basic rights are not violated.

4.3   Axel Honneth: The Principle of Achievement

In chapter 3, we saw Honneth argue that respect is due to all humans in light of their universal capacity for rational agency. By contrast, he contends that esteem, the final mode of recognition which he identifies, is due to individuals in light of those distinct characteristics that mark them out as different from one another. As Arto Laitinen puts it, esteem is given to someone '*qua* a certain kind of person' (2002: 463). To be specific, Honneth argues that individuals deserve esteem in virtue of their 'concrete characteristics' (1995: 121) or 'traits and abilities' (1995: 125, 129). They are not esteemed simply because they are associated with a particular culture or because they have a particular social identity, but rather because they possess specific features which distinguish them as unique individuals. It is not the case, however, that all unique traits are valuable. Whilst only some people are exactly six feet tall, being this height does not have any ethical significance. Honneth's argument is that individuals deserve esteem if they have traits and abilities which contribute to the achievement of 'societal goals' (1995: 122). Esteem is the reward for particular individuals who have helped their society to accomplish its objectives. As he puts it, 'the social standing of subjects is . . . measured in terms of what they can accomplish for society within the context of their particular forms of self-realization' (1995: 127). At one point, Honneth suggests that, in early capitalist societies, esteem was allocated according to a 'principle of achievement' (2003: 147). Although he uses this phrase to refer to a value system that he rejects, I see no reason why the idea of a principle of achievement cannot be broadened in order to describe the general logic behind the allocation of esteem.[9]

Honneth's thesis, then, is that esteem is the type of recognition which may be given in acknowledgement of those individual traits and abilities which help to advance 'societal goals'. In order fully to understand this thesis, it is necessary to consider the character of such goals. Here Honneth's position is very close to Taylor's. His assumption is that each society has certain goals or values that help to define its identity. As he puts it, each particular society has a set of 'ethical goals and values' that comprises its 'cultural self-understanding' (1995: 122). The collective identity of a society is defined not just in terms of a concrete set of institutions or a formal system of laws. It is also characterized by a distinctive set of values which are linked together to form a more or less coherent scheme. Honneth refers to this aspect of a particular society as its 'intersubjectively shared value-horizon' (1995: 121) or 'value-system' (1995: 124). For example, one society may value obedience to authority over free-thinking creativity, whilst another may value individuality over familial loyalty. One society may be more egalitarian than libertarian, whilst another may be more committed to tradition than to innovation. It follows that the qualities in virtue of which esteem is due may vary from time to time and from place to place. If particular individuals possess traits and abilities which help to further one or more of their society's collective aims, then they may enjoy esteem.

It is important to realize, however, that no contemporary society has a fixed system of values on which everyone agrees. With the collapse of 'traditional hierarchies of value', Honneth says, we have witnessed the emergence of a condition of 'value pluralism' (1995: 125) in which many values compete against each other for social precedence. I shall refer to these ongoing struggles over values as struggles for esteem.[10] As a result of such struggles, value systems are in a state of constant flux as the significance of some values waxes while that of others wanes. It is worth considering how this happens in more detail. Since societal goals are fairly abstract in character, there needs to be what Honneth calls a 'secondary interpretive practice' in which these goals are given 'supplemental cultural interpretations' (1995: 126). This means that there is a 'permanent struggle' to control 'the means of symbolic force' and to shape 'the climate of public attention' (1995: 127). To put this in more concrete terms, different groups attempt to raise the profile of the particular traits and abilities associated with their own members. If they succeed, and their particular characteristics become more highly valued, then they stand a greater chance of earning esteem. At the same time, if the characteristics associated with another group go into eclipse, then that group will have less chance of earning esteem. As a result of these struggles for esteem, contemporary societies are characterized, not by a fixed consensus, but rather by a series of temporarily stabilized agreements, on societal goals.

For Honneth, one important effect of such struggles for esteem is to unleash the developmental potential of this mode of recognition. He argues that, after the historical split of social honour into respect and esteem, two processes have helped an ever more complete realization of esteem to be achieved. He refers to the first of these processes as 'individualization'. In pre-modern societies, 'culturally typified status groups' enjoyed esteem in accordance with their particular place in the status hierarchy (1995: 123). In modern societies, by contrast, the subject enters 'the contested field of social esteem as an entity individuated in terms of particular life-history' (1995: 125). In other words, it is now unique individuals rather than social groups who are the potential objects of esteem. Honneth refers to the second process as 'equalization'. In pre-modern status orders, there was a hierarchy of esteem in which members of a higher status group automatically earned more esteem than members of a lower group. Honneth argues that, in modern societies, this has been replaced by a 'horizontal competition' between values, and that this has resulted in the 'pluralization' of such values (1995: 122). I would argue that 'equalization' is a confusing term by which to refer to the result of this process. As I shall show in a moment, Honneth does not mean that all individuals should receive equal esteem. Instead, he insists that esteem is 'symmetrical', where this means that each individual has an equal *chance* of being esteemed (1995: 130).

Honneth's principal thesis is that individuals have a chance to earn esteem if their particular traits and abilities are in tune with the values of their society. An unwanted implication of this idea could be that, if individuals lack the relevant traits and abilities, they will not have a chance to be esteemed. For Honneth, this would be highly unsatisfactory, to say the least. This is because he believes that without esteem individuals cannot develop self-esteem, and without self-esteem they will be unable to achieve self-realization. It is for this reason that he takes great pains to try to show that, in contemporary societies, everyone does have the chance to earn esteem. In order to make this case, he uses his argument that, in modern societies, the twin processes of individualization and equalization have led to the pluralization of values. As a result of such pluralization, there is more chance that particular individuals' characteristics will be regarded by their fellows as worthy of esteem. Honneth emphasizes that this esteem will be 'symmetrical'. It is important to realize that, in this context, 'symmetrical' does not mean 'to the same degree'. There is not, in other words, a crude equality of esteem (1995: 129). Rather, it means 'that every individual is free from being collectively denigrated, so that one is given the chance to experience oneself to be recognized, in light of one's own accomplishments and abilities, as valuable to society' (1995: 130). In other words, although Honneth does not think that all individuals have an automatic right to be granted esteem, he does believe that they should have an equal 'chance' to earn esteem. As I shall argue below, this means that one of Fraser's main criticisms of Honneth's theory is misplaced.

In order to see how Honneth's account of esteem as a mode of recognition might play out in practice, it will be useful to consider a concrete example. Women's struggles to have their distinctive contribution to the economic reproduction of society appropriately acknowledged and valued would be one instance of the politics of esteem in practice. According to Honneth's analysis, 'bourgeois-capitalist' or 'developing capitalist' society was characterized by an ideologically distorted principle of achievement, which stated that 'each was to enjoy social esteem according to his or her achievement as a "productive citizen"'. He argues that this 'one-sided, ideological valuing of certain achievements' meant that other achievements – such those associated with 'household work' – were systematically undervalued (2003: 141; and see 148). From this perspective, political struggles such as wages-for-housework campaigns since the 1970s can be seen as strategies that feminists have used to try to change the ideological valuation of domestic labour. These campaigns have had various aims. One is to justify a redistribution of resources, and another is to justify a change in relations of power. But a further aim is to change prevailing social values so that women's labour receives the acknowledgement to which it is due. To put this in Honneth's terms, this aim should be to create the conditions in which it is possible for individual women to earn esteem for the labour they do.

4.4   Nancy Fraser: The Revaluation of Values

I began my exposition of Fraser's account of respect in section 3.4 by considering the possibility that she aligns recognition with an idea of esteem, rather than respect. Thus she contends that recognition is cultural in character, is located in the status order, and can be identified with multiculturalism and the politics of identity. Since this strongly suggests that recognition is to be understood as the acknowledgement of distinctive cultural identities, this would mean, to put it in my terms, that it is a matter of esteem. In fact, I argued in the previous chapter that the idea of respect does have a significant role to play in Fraser's political theory. To be specific, in those cases where injustice takes the form of a denial of people's universal features, universalist recognition is the necessary remedy. Having said this, it remains true to say that Fraser more frequently associates recognition with the acknowledgement of particularity. She argues that, where injustice results from the depreciation of distinctive cultural characteristics, justice requires such depreciation to cease. Already we can see that, on Fraser's account, a variety of measures may be taken in the name of recognition. My aim in this section is to examine those measures which can be said to follow a logic of esteem.

To begin with, let us consider how Fraser proposes to justify this type of recognition. She contrasts her position sharply with that of Taylor and Honneth. On her account, they endorse what could be called an 'identity model' of recognition, according to which the recognition of identity is justified, since otherwise people would be psychologically damaged and/or unable to achieve self-realization (2003: 29–30). In chapter 2, I discussed Fraser's reasons for rejecting this model of recognition. In its place, she offers a 'status model' of recognition, founded on the principle of parity of participation. According to this principle, a just society is one in which individuals are able to participate 'on a par with one another in social life' (2003: 30). This principle requires two conditions to be met. The 'objective condition' concerns the distribution of resources, and I shall examine it in detail in the next chapter. The 'intersubjective condition' is the one that is of particular relevance here. This 'requires that institutionalized patterns of cultural value express equal respect for all participants and ensure equal opportunity for achieving social esteem'. Hence it 'precludes institutionalized norms that systematically depreciate some categories of people and the qualities associated with them', since such depreciation denies those people 'the status of full partners in interaction' (2003: 36). In other words, one obstacle that can stand in the way of people's ability to participate as peers is a pattern of value that undervalues or belittles them. In this case, justice requires the replacement of such a pattern of value with one that makes participatory parity possible. As we shall see, what this means is that attention to particularity is justified whenever it is necessary to meet the intersubjective condition of parity of participation.

Before examining the specific measures that may be required to achieve participatory parity, it is worth noting Fraser's emphasis on the 'institutionalized' character of norms or patterns of values. She argues that misrecognition is not simply a matter of 'deprecatory attitudes or free-standing discourses' (2003: 29). Rather, the cultural dimension of recognition is located in what she calls the 'status order' of society. Following Max Weber's analysis in his essay 'Class, Status, Party' (1958), she argues that a group of individuals forms a status group if it occupies a shared position in the status order. This means that it is ascribed distinctive traits, where possession of those traits means that the group enjoys levels of respect, esteem and prestige different from those enjoyed (or suffered) by others. Concentrating on the objective effects rather than on the subjective experience of differential status, Fraser argues that 'status represents an order of intersubjective subordination derived from institutionalized patterns of cultural value that constitute some members of society as less than full partners in interaction' (2003: 49). If a status order exists, then some citizens cannot participate on a par with their fellows: 'To say . . . that society has a status hierarchy is to say that it institutionalizes patterns of cultural value that pervasively deny some members the recognition they need in order to be full, participating members in social interaction' (2003: 49).[11]

For Fraser, then, meeting the intersubjective condition of parity of participation requires a status order which enables citizens to participate on a par with their fellows. Institutionalized patterns of value must therefore be reformed whenever they present an obstacle to such parity. She considers a range of measures that may be taken to change such value patterns. Two ways of overcoming misrecognition are clearly related to the idea of esteem. The first method is to *upwardly revalue currently devalued identities*. Fraser's argument here is that a status hierarchy may exist in which members of one or more particular groups are not able to participate as peers with members of other groups since current patterns of cultural value malign or devalue them. In these circumstances, she suggests, it is necessary to change current value patterns so that this obstacle to parity is removed. According to the everyday understanding of recognition, this requires 'upwardly revaluing disrespected identities and the cultural products of maligned groups' (2003: 13). A second method of overcoming misrecognition is to *recognize cultural diversity*. This appears to be a more general version of the previous method. Rather than revaluing the identities of specific groups, the aim here is to ensure that all differences are valued. In this case, the everyday understanding of this form of politics suggests that this will entail 'recognizing and positively valorizing cultural diversity' (2003: 13). I would suggest that, to the extent to which this approach is successful, the first method of revaluing specific maligned identities will be unnecessary. In a society in which all cultural identities are valued, none is maligned.[12]

The relationship of other ways of combating misrecognition to the idea of esteem is less clear. The third method holds that one way of achieving parity of participation is to *remove excessive distinctiveness*. It is possible for members of a group to be recognized as different, but in an inappropriate manner or to a disproportionate degree.

Fraser says that it is possible to suffer from 'excessive ascribed or constructed distinctiveness' (2003: 47). In this case, the appropriate solution is to 'unburden' the group of its distinctiveness. The fourth method focuses on the groups that are presently advantaged. In some status orders, a dominant group may be able to secure a considerable advantage by passing off its particular values as universal. In this case, says Fraser, justice requires us to *expose hidden distinctiveness.* In other words, it is necessary 'to shift the focus onto dominant or advantaged groups, outing the latter's distinctiveness, which has been falsely parading as universal' (2003: 47). The final form of recognition that Fraser suggests may be necessary to secure parity of participation is the most radical. She argues that in some circumstances the best thing to do is to *deconstruct existing systems of identity.* Rather than upwardly revaluing a devalued identity, or devaluing an overvalued identity, the proposal here is to pull apart the system of identity itself. As she puts it, the aim is 'to deconstruct the very terms in which attributed differences are currently elaborated' (2003: 47). This would have the effect of 'transforming wholesale societal patterns of representation, interpretation, and communication in ways that would change everyone's social identity' (2003: 13).

In order to see how these different means of recognition might operate in practice, I shall return to two familiar cases. In chapter 3, I showed that Fraser opposes the ban on the wearing of Muslim headscarves in French public schools. One reason for her opposition is that the ban expresses the values of the dominant majority. Hence it is necessary to apply the fourth method considered above. It is necessary, in other words, to expose the way in which the law as it presently stands privileges that majority. The argument for lifting the ban could be expressed in terms of respect: the acknowledgement of the capacity for rational autonomy must include the protection of the right to freedom of religion. But it could also be expressed in terms of esteem: in order to recognize Muslims' identity appropriately (or perhaps to recognize cultural diversity in general), Muslim schoolgirls must be allowed to wear the hijab as a public declaration of their religious identity. This is a version of the first method that Fraser considers. It is to upwardly revalue devalued identities, and in particular 'to have hitherto underacknowledged distinctiveness taken into account' (2003: 47). Same-sex marriage is another case to which Fraser gives considerable thought. Here her argument is that 'marriage laws that exclude same-sex partnerships as illegitimate and perverse' constitute 'an institutionalized pattern of cultural value that constitutes some categories of social actors as normative and others as deficient or inferior: straight is normal, gay is perverse' (2003: 29–30). Thus it is necessary 'to remedy the injustice by deinstitutionalizing the heteronormative value pattern and replacing it with an alternative that promotes parity'. As I mentioned in section 3.5, one way to do this would be 'to deinstitutionalize heterosexual marriage' (2003: 39). This looks like a version of the third method considered above. It works by removing excessive distinctiveness, and in particular by eliminating 'those privileges' which are 'now reserved for advantaged groups' (2003: 73). Another way 'would be to grant the same recognition to homosexual partnerships that heterosexual partnerships currently enjoy by legalizing same-sex marriage' (2003: 39). This could be regarded as another version of the first method, involving the upward revaluation of currently devalued identities.

4.5   A Critical Comparison

I have now considered the principal features of the three versions of the politics of esteem under investigation in this book. It is now time critically to compare these three politics. In order to do so, I shall focus on the four particular issues introduced in section 4.1: the distinctiveness, context, justification and practice of esteem.

Distinctiveness of Esteem

The first issue that I want to examine is the distinctiveness of esteem as a mode of recognition. In particular, I want to consider whether the three theorists under investigation make a sufficiently clear distinction between this mode of recognition and respect. I have argued that Honneth does make such a distinction. Indeed, in this and the two previous chapters, I have followed his categorization of recognition into the three primary modes of love, respect and esteem. The positions of the other two theorists are less clear. While Taylor distinguishes between the politics of universalism and the politics of difference, he does not explicitly align this with a distinction between two different modes of recognition. Fraser identifies a range of means of achieving participatory parity, some of which – so I have argued – follow a logic of esteem. Yet she does not fully incorporate the distinction between esteem and respect into her political theory. Since I am persuaded by Honneth's account of the distinction between respect and esteem, I shall say no more about his theory here. Instead, I shall focus on Taylor and Fraser, arguing that both of them would be well advised to make the distinction between these two modes of recognition a central part of their political theories.

In section 3.5, I pointed out that Taylor only very rarely uses the word 'esteem' in his analysis of the politics of recognition. Instead, he uses the words 'recognition' and 'respect' interchangeably to talk about all forms of recognition. I would argue that, on his account, there is a single concept of recognition with two competing traditions of interpretation. While the politics of universalism contends that recognition requires subjective rights in order to protect rational autonomy, the politics of difference contends that cultural protection is necessary in order to safeguard the capacity to form identity. As a result of this analysis, Taylor tends to understand struggles for recognition as conflicts between these two forms of politics. Thus defenders of Quebec's claim for recognition as a distinct society are regarded as exponents of the politics of difference, while those Canadians who oppose Quebec's claim are understood to subscribe to the politics of universalism. If the problem is regarded in this way, then no principled compromise between these two positions looks possible. At the level of theory, every call by a collectivity for its culture to be acknowledged will be regarded as a threat to individual recognition, whilst any defence of a system of purely individual recognition will be seen as an affront to groups seeking acknowledgement as groups. At the level of practice, the protection of individual rights will be guaranteed only by resisting demands to further collective goals; and if collective goals are promoted, it is individual rights that will suffer. I would argue that a precarious balance between these forms of politics is struck at the point at which Taylor distinguishes between fundamental and non-fundamental rights. If a right is regarded as fundamental, then no method of cultural protection should be allowed to override it. But if it is not regarded as fundamental, then those who wish to protect culture need not worry about respecting it. Thus, since it regards recognition as a single concept subject to rival interpretations, Taylor's political theory is located on an unstable fault line between a politics of individual rights and a politics of collective protection.[13]

I want to argue that things would look very different if Taylor were to acknowledge that there are two distinct and mutually irreducible modes of recognition, rather than two competing interpretations of the same concept. Individuals stand in need of two different things. First, in order to have self-respect, they need to have their rights protected so that they can exercise their autonomy. Second, in order to have self-esteem, they need to have their culture acknowledged in an appropriate manner – where this may involve *inter alia* having their cultural works placed in the canon, and being allowed to take measures to protect their culture.[14] Both these sorts of measures are required, and neither can be a substitute for the other. As Honneth would put it, self-respect and self-esteem are both necessary conditions of self-realization. I have already argued that a distinction between these two modes of recognition is in fact implicit in Taylor's analysis. The recognition of the capacity for rational action identified by the politics of universalism is very different from the recognition of the capacity for identity formation on which the politics of difference is based. I would suggest that, if Taylor were to acknowledge that the first sort of recognition is respect for autonomy, and the second is esteem for identity, then he might be able to avoid some of the difficulties that I have identified. If he were to make a clear distinction between respect for rights and esteem for culture, then he would be able to argue that a rights system and an appropriate value horizon must coexist as complementary aspects of a society that can show due recognition to all of its members.

It would be foolish to claim that an appreciation of the differentiated nature of recognition would make it possible to eliminate all tensions between individual rights and cultural protections. I believe nevertheless that such an appreciation would make it easier to find a principled compromise between rights and protections. In order to see how this might work in practice, consider James Tully's interpretation of the legal battle over the language of public signs in Quebec (1995: 169–72). In 1976, the provincial government passed a law which was designed to protect the region's French *visage linquistique* by prohibiting the use of English on public signs. When a group of anglophone shopkeepers complained that the law violated their right to freedom of expression, the Quebec and federal courts ruled in their favour. Drawing on Avigail Eisenberg's (1994) analysis of this case, Tully suggests that the court began by fully recognizing the importance of freedom of expression in a language of one's choice, including on public signage. It then went on to argue, however, that this freedom could legitimately be curtailed in order to preserve and enhance the French language in Quebec. Finally, it considered whether there was a *via media* between these two competing but equally legitimate claims. Its answer was that if French was 'always' but not 'only' the language of public signs, then both sides could be accommodated. Making French compulsory on all public signs protected Quebec's *visage linquistique*, but not making it exclusive allowed individuals to display other languages alongside the French text.

Echoing my interpretation of Taylor's theory, Tully suggests that this legal battle has generally been interpreted as a conflict between individual rights and group rights, and therefore between the individual and the community. He contends that in fact it is better understood in terms of rival claims for the recognition of what Eisenberg calls 'identity-related differences'. It is clear that the English and French languages are important markers of identity for the anglophone and francophone communities in Quebec. In this case, the objective is to see how these two rival claims for the recognition of identity can be accommodated. I would argue that, although this interpretation is revealing, it does not go quite far enough. To put it in my terms, Tully suggests that at issue in this political battle are two competing sets of claims for esteem. I think, however, that there are in fact two different modes of recognition at work here. Certainly, the claim that all public signage must be in French in order to protect Quebec's cultural character can be seen as a claim for esteem. But the claim that individuals should be able to express themselves in a language of their choice is better interpreted as a claim for respect. Seen in this light, Tully's analysis of this conflict reveals something rather different from what he intended. Rather than demonstrate that rival claims for the recognition of identity-related differences can sometimes be accommodated, the 'always' but not 'only' solution shows that it is possible in some circumstances simultaneously to meet the demands to respect rights and to esteem cultural difference. Although I must admit that my analysis here has merely scratched the surface of a very complex issue, I hope that I have done enough to show how a clear distinction between respect and esteem may be of use in determining what justice requires in particular circumstances.

Turning now to Fraser, I have explained why she believes that two conditions must be met in order for parity of participation to be achieved. The objective condition, concerning the distribution of economic resources, suggests that all individuals must have a certain level of independence. They should not experience a degree of inequality that would make them reliant on others. Since this condition does not bear directly on the issues of respect and esteem, I shall defer further discussion of it until the next chapter. The intersubjective condition, concerning institutionalized patterns of cultural value, states that individuals should not experience cultural disparagement. This is the condition of particular concern to me here. In this and the previous chapter, I have shown that Fraser identifies a range of means of overcoming misrecognition, from universalist through particularist to deconstructive recognition. I have argued that some of these means follow a logic of respect, and others a logic of esteem. Thus universalist recognition, which may be required if people's universal features are denied, is a way of showing them respect. By contrast, particularist recognition, which is justified when distinctiveness needs to be taken into account, is a way of esteeming people. In spite of the distinction that I am drawing here, it is important to understand that for Fraser these two forms of recognition operate in exactly the same way. On her account, meeting the intersubjective condition of participatory parity always involves making modifications to the status order of society.

I want to argue that, while this account may make sense of those means of securing parity which follow the logic of esteem, it does not make sense of those means which follow the logic of respect. It seems reasonable to suggest that, in order to remove excessive distinctiveness, expose hidden distinctiveness, or deconstruct existing systems of identity, it will be necessary to change the pattern of cultural values. However, it sounds very odd to say that it is also possible to modify cultural values in order to recognize 'our common humanity' (2003: 45) by, for example, guaranteeing 'the full rights and equal protections of citizenship' (2003: 18). The problem is that instantiating a right is not just a matter of modifying cultural values; nor is it the purpose of such a right to end cultural disparagement. Rather, to instantiate a right is to create a legal guarantee backed by the force of the state, and its purpose is to provide a power or protection for the holder of that right (see Barry 2001: 275). What this suggests is that, even in circumstances in which the objective and intersubjective conditions have been met, all individuals may not be able to enjoy participatory parity. Even if there were a sufficiently equal distribution of resources, and a status order in which no individuals or groups were significantly disparaged, some individuals might still not be able to participate on a par with their fellows if their basic civil and political rights were not protected. For this reason, I think that it is necessary, at the very least, to modify Fraser's account. I would argue that, whilst the objective condition of parity requires a distribution of economic resources which guarantees independence, and the intersubjective condition requires a status order in which no one is disesteemed, an additional legal or political condition – which requires a system of rights capable of protecting individuals' autonomy – must also be taken into account. I return to this issue in section 5.4 below.

Context of Esteem

The second issue on which I wish to concentrate concerns what I have referred to as the context of esteem. With this idea I mean to highlight the background conditions that are necessary in order for the practice of esteem to be possible. For Honneth and Taylor, an intersubjectively shared value horizon provides the setting for assessments of individual contribution and cultural value. Fraser, by contrast, believes that patterns of value, which are anchored in the status order, may need to be manipulated in order to overcome misrecognition. I want to focus here on two particular aspects of these accounts. The first concerns the degree of abstractness of the context of esteem. Here my discussion will revolve around the charge that Taylor's account of esteem artificially separates value horizons from other more concrete aspects of the social order. The second issue concerns the degree of homogeneity of the context of esteem. Here I shall concentrate on a particular criticism that Fraser makes of Honneth. She argues that he mistakenly assumes that modern societies have a single coherent set of cultural values. Instead, she maintains, contemporary status orders are highly complex and differentiated, and this has significant consequences for the practice of esteem. Can Taylor and Honneth successfully answer these criticisms?

A number of Taylor's critics have focused on his contention that the worth of cultures must be tested within a shared horizon of values. According to these critics, this account is too abstract. Conceiving of value horizons and cultures in terms of ideas, goods and values, Taylor detaches them from the economic, social and political institutions in which they are inevitably located. Nicholas Smith points out that Taylor's hermeneutical approach has been criticized for 'linguistic idealism', since it abstracts 'linguistically constituted traditions from the systems of organized force which provide their material context' (1994: 21; and see 22, 25–6). On this point, Brian Barry suggests that, since Taylor is a follower of Herder, it is no surprise to find that he 'focuses on language' (Barry 2001: 66; cf. Markell 2003: ch. 2). The mildest criticism that can be made of such linguistic idealism is that, by overlooking the role played by concrete practices, it fails to provide a complete account of the practice of esteem. A more serious criticism is that such an account fails to appreciate that particular descriptions of cultures, drawing on particular value horizons, may serve particular political ends. As Amelie Rorty contends, since he is not aware that 'cultural descriptions are politically and ideologically laden', Taylor is not sensitive to the possibility that particular descriptions may serve the interests of some groups against others (1994: 158–9). The failure to acknowledge the vital role that power plays in shaping culture, and hence the failure to recognize that accounts of cultural identity can serve as means to political ends, means that such power is able to go on serving such ends undisturbed. To put this in terms of recognition, by focusing exclusively on culture, and by abstracting this from the systems of power in which culture is embedded, Taylor endorses a politics of esteem which may contribute to the oppression of those individuals marginalized by the existing distribution of power.

An examination of Taylor's use of the idea of 'culture' reinforces this criticism of idealism. Even if our attention is restricted to his essay 'The Politics of Recognition', here are just some of the examples that we can find. At the most general level, Taylor talks about 'modern culture' (1995b: 228, 232) and 'democratic culture' (1995b: 227). In a more geographically specific sense, he suggests that, when judging other 'cultures and civilizations', our standards 'are those of North Atlantic civilization' (1995b: 255). Finally, at the most concrete level, Taylor also offers examples of cultures in which the referent is a nation or a national minority. He talks, for instance, about the cultural distinctness of 'French Canadians, particularly Quebeckers' (1995b: 242) and of 'French culture in Quebec' (1995b: 246). Here the conception of culture being deployed refers to particular national groups, and it is probably this that he is assuming when he speaks of 'all human cultures' (1995b: 252). I would argue that Taylor is able to use the idea of culture to refer to such a wide range of different objects because he conceives of it in highly abstract terms. Only by thinking of a culture as a set of more or less coherent ideas and values, is it possible to regard both 'modern culture' and 'French culture in Quebec' as objects of the same kind.[15] For the purposes of a politics of recognition, however, a much more precise account of the object of recognition is required. Whilst it may make sense to argue that the distinctive culture of a national group could be an appropriate object of esteem, it is difficult to see how 'modern culture' could be. For this reason, I agree with Rorty that Taylor 'owes us an account of cultural differentiation' which provides 'criteria for distinguishing them that are narrower than the demarcation of natural languages and more precise than the differentiation of "ways of life"'. Such criteria should specify, for example, how cohesive a culture's identity must be, and how strong its degree of continuity through time, in order for it to be recognized as a distinct culture (1994: 156–7). Without such an account, it is impossible to decide whether Taylor's account of esteem is defensible or not.

Having said all this, I do believe that there are resources in Taylor's theory which he could deploy in order to answer the charge of idealism. When he is discussing issues of cultural value, it is not surprising to find that the idea of an intersubjectively shared horizon of value figures prominently in his analysis. This does not mean, however, that he is oblivious to the fact that there is an important connection between value horizons and the social and political institutions which lie behind them. Let me mention two instances where he explicitly acknowledges this sort of connection. In *Sources of the Self*, Taylor suggests that modern identity 'arose because changes in the self-understandings connected with a wide range of practices – religious, political, economic, familial, intellectual, artistic – converged and reinforced each other to produce it' (1989: 206). Here a connection is made between a way of thinking about the self and a set of concrete practices. Moreover, Taylor asserts that it was the practices that *produced* the self-understanding. The second example focuses more closely on values rather than ideas. In his well-known essay 'What's Wrong with Negative Liberty?', Taylor focuses on the relationship between the value of negative freedom and the institutions of liberal democracy. He argues that it would be illogical for anyone committed to this value not to support the institutions – including a free press, an independent legal system, and so on – which are necessary to sustain it (1985: 211–29). In this example, Taylor makes a connection between values and institutions. He argues, furthermore, that the institutions provide the indispensable context of the values. I conclude that he is aware of the relationship between particular ideas and values and their institutional context. Whilst he argues that the assessment of cultural value must occur within the context of a horizon of value, he does not think that such a horizon is a free-floating set of ideas and values without any material counterpart. Instead, he appreciates that each horizon has a specific material context, a set of social practices and institutions without which that horizon could not be sustained. I conclude that Taylor can and should use his account of the relationship between particular ideas and values and their institutional context in order to answer the criticism of idealism.

Turning now to the second issue concerning the context of esteem, I want to consider Fraser's charge that Honneth exaggerates the degree of homogeneity to be found in contemporary status orders. On her reading, Honneth follows Emile Durkheim's assumption that there is 'a single, overarching pattern of cultural value' (2003: 59; and see 103 n.58). Fraser argues that this assumption is patently false. As she says, would-be Critical Theorists today 'cannot conceive society as a culturally homogenous bounded whole, in which political claims can be adjudicated ethically, by appeal to a single shared value-horizon' (2003: 198). There are a number of dimensions to the complexity of modern status orders. First, they are 'hybridized' in the sense that cultural influences flow across all social boundaries (2003: 55). Second, they are 'institutionally differentiated': there are a variety of social sites – including *inter alia* the institutions of the family, law, education and religion (2003: 55–6) – which possess their own relatively autonomous patterns of cultural value. Third, status orders today are 'ethically pluralistic' in the sense that there is a wide variety of communities of value in existence (2003: 56). Fourth, they are 'intensely contested': since there is a great diversity of value communities, sets of values always exist in terms of which criticisms of dominant values can be made. Finally, in contemporary societies, 'status hierarchy' is regarded as 'illegitimate' (2003: 56). In short, Fraser argues that in modern capitalist societies 'the cultural order is hybridised, differentiated, pluralistic, and contested, while status hierarchy is considered illegitimate' (2003: 69). It follows from this analysis that the practice of esteem will be more complicated than it would be if there were a single unified pattern of cultural value. In order to achieve status equality, it may be necessary to make changes in many different subsystems of cultural value. Yet the very complexity of the status order may render this task highly problematic. A change in one part of this order may have unintended effects in other parts. There may even be what Fraser calls 'perverse effects' in which the outcome of intervention is the exact opposite to that intended (2003: 86).

Is Honneth guilty as charged? Does he offer an over-simple account of the context of esteem? Is Fraser right to argue that this context is in fact highly pluralized and indeed fragmented? To begin with, it must be conceded that, according to the hermeneutic tradition within which both Honneth and Taylor are working, an authentic judgement about the value of a culture or the social contribution of members of a particular group must be made in terms of values shared by both parties. The only alternatives are relativism or ethnocentrism. According to the first option, each set of values is appropriate in its own context, but inappropriate in any other. According to the second, one set of values can be used to evaluate another set although the latter not recognize or perhaps even understand the former. Yet, as Taylor acknowledges, the need for shared values with which to make an authentic judgement does not mean that such values already exist. The obvious fact of value pluralism tells against such a possibility. For Taylor, then, the identification of a set of shared values must be the result of a joint effort in which all parties strive to establish a common understanding. Seen in this light, this criticism of Honneth could be rewritten in the following way: since he assumes that the practice of esteem takes place in the context of a unified and homogenous culture, he fails to appreciate the need for a joint effort to find common values.

Certainly, it is true to say that Honneth talks of a society's value horizon or its cultural self-understanding in the singular. At these points, it must be conceded, he does not place sufficient emphasis on the heterogeneity of the context of esteem. At the same time, as I showed in section 4.3, Honneth gives considerable prominence to the process of the pluralization of values in contemporary societies. He notes that, in modern societies, a condition of 'value pluralism' has emerged in which many incompatible values vie for public attention (1995: 125). Indeed, he places considerable emphasis on the ongoing debates and disagreements within a particular value community about the relative importance of different values. I would suggest that this picture is difficult to reconcile with Fraser's claim that Honneth assumes a 'single, overarching pattern of cultural value' or pictures 'society as a culturally homogenous bounded whole'. It is true to say that, for Honneth, if such disagreements over value are to be meaningful, they must be conducted in terms of other – perhaps more abstract – values on which all parties do agree. But it would be misleading to infer from this that he believes that society is united by a shared agreement on a single set of cultural values. In fact, he is adamant that the converse is the case.

I conclude that Honneth's position is much closer to Fraser's than she might care to admit. Since both accept and indeed emphasize the inevitability of disagreement about values in contemporary societies, their positions are characterized by differences of focus rather than of substance. While Fraser concentrates on the 'pluralized, fractured, and cross-cutting' character of contemporary status orders (2003: 198), Honneth concentrates on the background agreement on values which makes this foreground disagreement possible and meaningful. Even in a hybridized, differentiated, pluralistic, contested and anti-hierarchical status order, there can be a relatively stable but not completely fixed horizon of values. Indeed, if such a horizon did not exist, then it would be difficult to know in virtue of what there would be *a* status order at all.

Justification of Esteem

The third issue that I wish to consider concerns the justification of esteem. Do the theorists under investigation in this book offer plausible accounts of the reasons why someone (or something) should be esteemed? As we have seen, Taylor argues that the works of a particular culture may be included in a society's canon if the value of those works can be demonstrated in a hermeneutic encounter with that culture. Honneth, in marked contrast, suggests that esteem depends on the degree of an individual's achievement. For Fraser, it is not that the object has some property in virtue of which it deserves esteem. Rather, esteem is a property of structures of prestige which are able to facilitate parity of participation. Regarding the justification of esteem, I want to focus on two particular questions. First, is Taylor right to think that the case for the recognition of a culture depends on proof of its value? Second, is Honneth right to claim that esteem can be earned only by an individual who makes a contribution to societal goals?

With regard to the issue of cultural value, I think it is important quickly to dismiss a couple of common criticisms of Taylor's position. According to Barry, Taylor 'tries to whistle a tune about the equal value of cultures while at the same time continuing to sing the old song about incommensurability' (2001: 265). The first thing to note about this claim is that the two theses it identifies – let us call them *equal value* and *incommensurability* – are logically incompatible. If cultures really were incommensurable, then it would be impossible to compare them, and hence impossible to know that they were of equal value. Putting this aside, it is important to realize that even Barry himself has to concede that Taylor does not endorse the first thesis. While suggesting that Taylor has 'considerable sympathy for the notion that cultures can be said to be of equal value', Barry admits that he in fact accepts only a 'presumption' of value (2001: 265–6). With regard to the thesis of incommensurability, Barry has to develop a tortuous argument in order to attribute it to Taylor. Lighting on Taylor's claim that 'this is the way we do things around here' does not make sense in multicultural societies, Barry infers that Taylor would endorse the counterfactual thesis that, in a world of monocultural societies, this claim would make sense (2001: 279–80). That is to say, in societies with homogeneous and bounded cultures, it would be legitimate to invoke facts about that culture in a normative argument. It is important to note, however, that even if Taylor did endorse the counterfactual claim – which I doubt – even this would not get him to the thesis of incommensurability. Saying that 'this is the way we do things around here' does not imply that our way of doing things cannot be meaningfully or legitimately compared to your way of doing things over there.

As we have seen, Taylor's argument is that esteem is justified if and only if the culture in question can be shown to be of value in an actual hermeneutic encounter. Some critics have argued that this rests on a fundamental misconception about the grounds for esteem. To appreciate what is at issue here, let us consider the case to which Taylor refers when analysing the claim that all cultures should be judged of equal value. He argues that the case for including the works of a particular culture in the curricula of university humanities courses must rest on a demonstration that these works are at least as good as (if not better than) works already in the canon. According to the critics, this argument misunderstands the reasons why people want their culture to be esteemed. The case for inclusion does not rest on claims about equal (or greater) value. It rests, rather, on the claim that the works of all the major cultural groups in society should be included in the canon because that canon should reflect all of their identities. Thus Lawrence Blum argues that equality 'is misplaced in the realm of culture' (1998: 51). His argument is as follows:

> recognition need involve no evaluative judgment at all, nor is it particularly appropriate, or even natural, to engage in assessing the culture of the student or the cultural group, when all that is at stake is recognizing that forms of cultural expression, and historical experiences, of the cultural group in question are important to that student, and that in the context of a school, they warrant a public, institutional acknowledgment. (1998: 56)

To take up Blum's own example, American public schools should offer education in Spanish in order properly to acknowledge the Hispanic-American children present in those schools. To put the argument at its briefest, a culture deserves esteem because the group associated with it is part of the society from which esteem is demanded.[16]

According to Blum, then, the case for esteeming a culture does not depend on a claim about its putative value. It depends, rather, on the claim that such esteem is a way of showing appropriate acknowledgement to the people – individuals or groups – who associate themselves with that culture. I want to argue that Blum's critique, as it stands, depends on the elision of two different arguments, one concerning the canon *per se* and the other concerning the provision of facilities for particular groups. While his critique does have something important to say about the latter issue, it is irrelevant to the former. With regard to the first issue, I agree with Taylor that, since the canon is necessarily defined as the best which has been thought and said, it is necessary for society to engage in hermeneutic deliberation about what that best is. In this case, to say that the cultural works of a particular community should be included in the canon simply because that community is part of society is to make a fundamental category mistake. Esteem must involve what Blum calls 'evaluative judgment'. Hence I agree with Taylor that one should approach the study of cultures presuming that they have some value, and if they are shown to have value, that they may deserve a place in the canon. Having said this, there is another problem concerning unfair exclusion from the canon which does need to be taken seriously. There may be particular cases in which the debate about what should be included is unfair since it is based on criteria that suit the advocates of some works and not others. These selective criteria typically favour those works already included in the canon. However, the solution to this problem is not to demand that the excluded works be included as of right, but rather to ensure that the criteria for inclusion are fair, and the best way to do this is to make sure that these criteria are themselves part of society's hermeneutic deliberations.

With regard to the second issue, I agree with Blum that in certain circumstances special facilities should be provided for particular groups in order to show them appropriate recognition. To take the particular case on which he concentrates, it could be argued that Hispanic-American children should have the choice of an English- or a Spanish-language education so that they are not systematically disadvantaged by an educational system in which they are taught only in their second language. I think, however, that the reason for providing lessons in Spanish is not to acknowledge cultural value, but rather to show equal concern for all individuals.[17] As Peter Jones puts it, 'if we seek to deal fairly with cultural diversity, it is not cultures that will be the ultimate objects of our concern but the people who bear them' (1998: 36). To put this in terms of recognition, the provision of lessons in Spanish is not an act of esteem for Hispanic culture. Rather, it is a way of showing equal concern for those citizens whose first language is Spanish.[18] To generalize this point, I would argue that two issues need to be kept separate. It is one thing to say: in order to show all individuals equal concern, some of them must be provided with special facilities. But it is quite another thing to say: in order to recognize all cultural groups, works by all such groups should have a place in their society's canon. While the former requires only the appropriate acknowledgement of the *existence* of a particular culture (and its importance to those individuals who are associated with it), the latter would require an assumption of the *value* of that culture. This, I have suggested, is a bridge too far.

As I showed in section 4.3, Honneth argues that esteem may be due to individuals in virtue of their contribution to societal goals. He hopes that, in light of the pluralized value horizons of contemporary societies, everyone will have a chance to earn such esteem. It could be argued that this is an excessively restricted view of this mode of recognition. Honneth limits the grounds for esteem to what he refers to at one point as 'individual accomplishments and abilities' (1995: 126). His argument is that esteem is deserved for those distinctive features of individuals which enable them to make a contribution to the common good. There are two distinct restrictions at work here. First, Honneth rules out esteem for any sort of collective entity. He agrees with Laitinen that 'only persons can be recognizees' (2002: 466). Thus Honneth would disagree with Taylor's claim that it is possible to show esteem for a culture by including its works in the canon. Second, it is an individual's 'accomplishments and abilities', rather than their identity *per se*, which are the grounds for esteem. Individuals should not be esteemed just for being Muslim, speaking Spanish, or being Ulster-Scots. In order to have a chance of being esteemed, they need to show that their particular traits and abilities have made a contribution to societal goals. I would suggest that, given this restricted view of the third mode of recognition, Honneth is not able to account for many of the varied forms that the politics of esteem can take in practice. Here it is often the case that recognition is demanded for distinctive cultures. But Honneth's account of esteem would rule these demands illegitimate. A couple of examples will help to illustrate this point. First, to return to Blum's example, it would be impossible to argue on the grounds of esteem for the provision of public education in Spanish. Since speaking Spanish cannot be regarded as an accomplishment or ability which contributes to societal goals, it does not deserve to be publicly acknowledged. Second, on Honneth's account, it is difficult to see how a case could be made for lifting the French government's ban on the wearing of conspicuous religious symbols in public schools. Once again, wearing such symbols cannot be seen as an accomplishment or trait that makes a contribution to the common good.

I would argue that it is because Honneth offers such a narrow interpretation of esteem as individual contribution to societal goals that he is forced to contemplate the possibility of a fourth mode of recognition for cultural identity *per se*. It is clear that, in order to meet the 'demand that a minority communal culture be socially esteemed for its own sake' (2003: 167), it would be necessary to breach the two restrictions that Honneth places on recognition as esteem. This demand is for a collective identity rather than an individual (or set of individuals) to be esteemed, and for identity itself, rather than achievement, to be the grounds of such esteem. Although it is probably true to say that the introduction of this fourth mode of recognition would bring Honneth's account more closely into line with the current debate about cultural recognition, it seems to me that it would also bring with it a whole new set of problems. In particular, Honneth's fourth mode of recognition would suffer from the same problems as the presumption of cultural equality. That is to say, it would be vulnerable to Taylor's criticism that this presumption is patronizing, ethnocentric and homogenizing. As we have seen, Taylor's conclusion is that, in order to attribute value to a culture, it is necessary seriously to evaluate it. Honneth's proposal violates this injunction, appearing as it does to offer esteem on demand. Furthermore, as we shall see in the next subsection, this fourth mode of recognition would also run into all the problems encountered by the proposal that there should be a right to cultural survival.

If I am right to suggest that Honneth is tempted to introduce a fourth mode of recognition because he interprets the third too narrowly, then this implies that the way to avoid this temptation is to widen his interpretation of the third. Such a reinterpretation would retain the idea of contribution, while dropping the claim that this must be understood narrowly in terms of individual accomplishments and abilities. My proposal would be that the grounds for esteem should be broadened to include not just individual traits and abilities, but also aspects of cultural identity. But esteem would not be granted just because a particular identity is distinctive (or because, without it, people would suffer psychological harm), but because it is an important part of the cultural character of society as a whole. A couple of examples should help to make the nature of my proposal clear. First, it could be argued that French Muslims contribute a distinctive Islamic element to French public culture. To give one small example, the idea of *zakat* can be used to add an important dimension to public debates about charity and welfare.[19] Second, it could be argued in a similar vein that Ulster-Scots language, history and heritage deserve esteem since they are a vital ingredient of the cultural mix in Northern Ireland and beyond. On my account, in short, esteem may be due in light of the contribution which a distinctive culture makes to the culture of society as a whole.

Practice of Esteem

I refer to the fourth and final issue which I wish to investigate further as the practice of esteem. With this phrase, I mean to focus on the sorts of concrete measures that esteem may entail in practice. Many commentators think that, according to Taylor, a group may be allowed to take practical measures to ensure the survival of its culture. On Fraser's reading, Honneth contends that all individuals have an automatic right to be esteemed. Fraser herself suggests that a variety of modifications – including the deconstruction of existing identity-systems – may be made to the existing pattern of cultural value in order to ensure that it does not present an obstacle to parity of participation. Since I have already shown toward the end of section 4.3 why I think that Fraser's criticism of Honneth is mistaken, the discussion that follows will focus on Taylor and Fraser. First, I shall ask if Taylor really believes that the survival of cultures should be guaranteed. Second, I shall ask whether Fraser is right to argue that deconstruction can be considered one of the forms that recognition may take in practice.

In section 4.2, I argued that, when reading Taylor's essay 'The Politics of Recognition', the issue of cultural equality must be kept separate from the issue of cultural survival. With regard to the latter issue, many of Taylor's critics have read in his essay a commitment to guarantee cultural survival, and they have almost universally condemned that commitment. Stephen Rockefeller argues as follows: 'There is an uneasy tension . . . between Taylor's defence of the political principle of cultural survival and his espousal of open-minded cross-cultural exchange' (1994: 92–3). That is to say, defending a rigid principle of cultural survival may undermine the possibility of each culture learning from others in such a way that all may be transformed. In a similar vein, Anthony Appiah contends that Taylor defends a form of politics which seeks to guarantee 'the survival of certain "societies"'. However, if the survival of that 'society' is understood as its continued existence for descendants of the current population, then for Appiah it is 'not at all clear that this aim is one we can acknowledge while respecting the autonomy of future individuals' (1994: 157). In other words, we may only be able to guarantee the survival of a society by limiting the autonomy of its future generations to act as they wish. It may, for instance, only be possible to defend the practice of arranged marriage by limiting the right of individuals to marry outside of that group.[20] For Barry, while the 'aspiration that a collective identity should never be lost' is legitimate, the creation of collective right to guarantee its survival is not (2001: 66; cf. 67–8). As a result of similar reflections, Walzer argues that, whilst a guarantee of cultural survival may be appropriate in societies with a long-established majority culture such as Norway and Quebec, it is simply not appropriate in 'immigrant societies' such as the USA and federal Canada. Since immigrants knew the risks they were taking in moving to these societies – societies which they knew were based on a strong ideal of individual rights – there should be no guarantee that immigrant cultures will survive (1994: 102–3).

Although I agree with Walzer's conclusion, I nevertheless want to offer at least a partial defence of Taylor's position. I shall do so by reasserting the difference between the issues of cultural value and cultural survival. This will enable me to argue that it is possible to interpret Taylor's account in such a way that he makes no commitment to guarantee cultural survival. To begin with, it must be emphasized that Taylor makes a clear distinction between these two issues. As he says, there are two distinct sorts of demand that can be made regarding culture. The first 'is that we all recognize the equal value of different cultures', and the second 'is that we let cultures defend themselves, within reasonable bounds' (1995b: 250). Certainly, it is possible to connect these two issues. It could be argued, for instance, that all cultures should be able to defend themselves precisely because they are all of equal value. However, it is also perfectly possible to separate these issues. On the one hand, it could be argued that all cultures should be able to take reasonable actions to defend themselves, while rejecting the claim that they are of equal value. On the other hand, it could also be argued that all cultures are of equal value, whilst rejecting the claim that they should be allowed to try to ensure their survival.

Given that these two issues are distinct, I shall now focus specifically on cultural survival itself. It is worth repeating the exact words that Taylor uses to describe the demand that he is analysing. This is 'that we let cultures defend themselves, within reasonable bounds'.[21] There are two elements to this formulation. First, groups are allowed to defend their cultures. Second, they must do so within reasonable bounds. Note what the first element does not say. It does not say that the state has a duty to defend the cultures of groups living within its jurisdiction. It says, rather, that the group associated with a particular culture may be permitted to take action to defend it. Turning to the second element of Taylor's formulation, it suggests that there are limits to what a group may do in order to defend its culture. By implication, some actions that it might want to take are illegitimate. This prompts the question: what reasonable actions may a group take in order to protect its culture? As we have seen, the critics contend that Taylor believes that groups can legitimately demand guarantees of cultural survival. But I believe that an alternative reading of his position is possible. According to this alternative account, he holds that a group may make claims and propose policies and laws which are designed to increase the chances of the survival of its culture, so long as such demands and proposals are part of the normal day-to-day business of democratic politics. If a particular group is able to advance its claims successfully, and thus to influence the formulation of policy and to ensure the passage of particular laws, then it may be able to advance its culture's cause. But this does not imply that the state has committed itself to guarantee the survival of that particular culture. Rather than proposing a guarantee of cultural survival, Taylor simply suggests that groups should have a fair opportunity to pursue the goal of cultural survival. If the critics' reading is right, that he holds out a promise of cultural survival, then I agree with them that his position is indefensible. But if my reading is right, then I believe that Taylor's position can be saved.

Finally, it is worth asking whether permitting a community to take measures to protect its culture could be regarded as an act of esteem. There are, I think, two possible interpretations of Taylor's position. On the one hand, it could be argued that it has no relevance for esteem. The argument simply says that a political order may establish certain laws, enact certain policies and so on, which aim to protect a particular culture. But this does not mean that by so doing it esteems that culture (beyond perhaps the minimal acknowledgement involved in recognizing the protection of that culture as a legitimate political goal). If the Northern Ireland Assembly gives financial support to initiatives to preserve the Ulster-Scots language, it is simply carrying out the wishes of the current political majority. It need not commit itself to the claim that Ulster-Scots culture is of value. On the other hand, it could be argued that such political measures are closely bound up with esteem. Measures taken to protect the Ulster-Scots language may have important consequences for the self-esteem of those who associate themselves with that language. They may be able to hold their heads high in Northern Ireland, the United Kingdom and on the international stage. According to this interpretation, then, taking measures to protect cultures has everything to do with esteem. According to the usual reading of Taylor's position, he thinks that states are obliged to support (or even guarantee) the survival of cultures. In this case, it could be said that, by so doing, they esteem such cultures. I have offered an alternative reading which places his analysis of the issue of cultural survival firmly in the context of the quotidian business of democratic politics. On this account, cultural survival is simply regarded as a legitimate democratic goal for groups. In this case, it is difficult to see in what sense accepting the legitimacy of such a goal could constitute an act of esteem.

Turning now to Fraser, I want to consider whether her method of deconstruction can be considered one of the forms that esteem may take in practice. In section 4.4, I showed why she thinks that in some circumstances it is necessary, not to upwardly revalue a devalued identity or to devalue a currently overvalued identity, but to radically transform the existing system of values so that no one's identity remains untouched. As she says, this method will involve 'deconstructing the symbolic oppositions that underlie currently institutionalized patterns of cultural value' (2003: 75). I want to argue that the idea of deconstructive recognition is in fact a contradiction in terms. No application of the method of deconstruction can appropriately be considered an instance of recognition, and no form of recognition can involve the method of deconstruction.

In order to make this case, I would suggest that there are two ways in which Fraser's account of deconstructive recognition might be read. On the first reading, Fraser believes that this method can be used to remove a particular status inequality, such as that between sexual identities. At present, men are valued above women. This differential valuation operates in part through a series of cultural associations, such as the contrasts between strength and weakness, reason and emotion, and so on. In order to correct this differential valuation, it is therefore necessary to break this chain of association. In other words, there must be a process of revaluation in which the distinction between men and women is separated from these other distinctions. I would argue that, while the effect of such a process of revaluation is to remove particular oppositions which underlie existing differences, this way of modifying an existing status order is not deconstructive in any substantive sense of that term. The distinction between men and women itself is not radically challenged. In fact, it is best understood as an instance of Fraser's first method, involving the upward revaluation of a currently devalued identity. In this particular case, such a revaluation is achieved by changing or removing some of an identity's existing associations. In Fraser's own words, its effect would be 'to redress disrespect by revaluing unjustly devalued group identities, while leaving intact both the content of those identities and the group differentiations that underlie them' (1995: 82). On this reading, then, such a practice is a form of recognition, but it is not deconstructive.

The second way of reading Fraser's account of deconstructive recognition suggests that it involves not merely the revaluing but the dissolution of all existing identities. Rather than disentangling one particular difference from its associated contrasts, the aim here is to destabilize the distinction at its very root. In the case of sexuality, the aim would be 'to sustain a sexual field of multiple, debinarized, fluid, ever-shifting differences' (1995: 83; and see 2003: 76). I would argue that, while this method of changing cultural values can certainly be considered a form of deconstruction, it cannot be regarded as a form of recognition. In all ordinary uses, recognition is understood as a practical act of positive evaluation. At the beginning of the current chapter, I argued that esteem, as a particular form of recognition, involves the public attribution of positive value to an object in light of some distinctive characteristic of that object. In this case, I would argue that deconstruction, in the radical sense suggested by this second reading, cannot be considered a form of recognition in any accepted sense. This type of deconstruction does not acknowledge, but rather destroys, existing identities. On this reading, then, such a method is deconstructive, but it is not a form of recognition.

In light of this analysis, I suggest that it is best completely to abandon the idea of 'deconstructive recognition'. On the one hand, if the practice which Fraser describes is a form of recognition, then it is deconstructive only in a very attenuated sense of this word. In this case, I would suggest that the adjective 'critical' might capture Fraser's meaning more successfully than 'deconstructive'. On the other hand, if the practice which she describes can appropriately be described as one of deconstruction, then it cannot be considered a form of recognition.[22] Having said this, it is important to emphasize that it does not follow from this decoupling of deconstruction and recognition that deconstruction cannot be a way of achieving participatory parity. It may be that, in some circumstances, parity can be achieved only by destroying an existing identity system. What does follow is that not all ways of achieving parity can appropriately be considered forms of recognition. Some means of achieving participatory parity are forms of recognition, including the revaluing of devalued identities and the devaluing of overvalued identities. But others are not, including in particular the creation of shifting fields of multiple differences. In short, Fraser's political theory outlines a range of cultural methods by which it may be possible to achieve participatory parity, but only some of these methods may be considered forms of recognition. Deconstruction is not one of them.

4.6   Conclusions

My aim in this chapter has been to conduct a critical comparison of the accounts of esteem found in the three theories of recognition of especial interest in this book. Let me sum up the results of my investigations into the four issues on which I chose to focus. First, I argued that it is vital to establish a clear distinction between respect and esteem, in order to appreciate that the protection of rights and the protection of cultures are two distinct – and by no means necessarily incompatible – goals. My argument that Fraser should introduce a third condition of participatory parity which concerns the protection of individual rights will be developed in detail in the next chapter. Second, I suggested that Taylor should make the link between horizons of value and their material contexts more explicit, in order to avoid accusations that his account is too abstract and idealist. This would bring him closer to Fraser in her emphasis on the institutional basis of status orders. I also argued that it was possible to synthesis Fraser's account of such orders and Honneth's account of value horizons. While the former focuses on the fact of reasonable disagreement, the latter pays attention to the background agreement which makes such reasonable disagreement possible. I should stress that to assume that there must be such an agreement is not to commit oneself to the claim that it is constant, fixed and entirely without ambiguities or lacunae. Third, I argued that, while the case for inclusion in the canon must involve the assessment of value, the case for the provision of special facilities for specific groups need not do so. This means that it is possible to defend a number of political measures associated with the politics of recognition on the grounds of equal treatment rather than cultural recognition. I also argued that, if Honneth were to widen his conception of the principle of achievement so that it can encompass cultural as well as individual contributions to societal goals, he could then avoid the temptation to introduce a fourth mode of recognition for cultural identity *per se*. Fourth, by distinguishing between cultural protection and cultural survival, I argued that a group may legitimately propose measures in defence of its culture so long as such measures are compatible with fundamental rights. I also argued that, whilst in some circumstances deconstruction may be a means of securing participatory parity, it is not appropriately considered a form of recognition.

I have now completed my overview of the three primary modes of recognition that Honneth identifies. The next three chapters focus on three further features of the political theory of recognition. As I shall show, however, aspects of these three modes will also feature in my investigations of the links between recognition and redistribution, recognition and democracy, and recognition and the idea of struggle. In chapter 5, for instance, I return to the argument that Fraser needs to include a third dimension in her analysis of recognition in order to deal with issues concerning respect. To give another example, in my analysis of struggles for recognition in chapter 7, I shall discuss examples of struggles which are motivated by the felt absence of esteem.

5

Recognition and Redistribution

5.1   Introduction

In 1972 Selma James founded the International Wages for Housework campaign. Its principal demand was that women receive fair wages for all of the unwaged work that they do (Malos 1995). This campaign has been one significant strand in feminist politics for more than three decades now. It can be regarded as the progenitor of later campaigns such as those for Pay Equity and Comparable Worth (Treiman and Hartmann 1981). A vigorous debate on the issue of wages for housework continues up to this day. In 2004, for example, James engaged in a debate with Melissa Benn in the *Guardian* newspaper. Expressing considerable concern about the very idea of wages for housework, Benn feared that its effect would be to reinforce gender stereotypes according to which women should remain in the domestic sphere looking after their husbands and children, while men remain in the public sphere of paid labour. In reply, James reasserted the case for paying wages for women's currently unwaged labour, arguing that 'validating caring work . . . is the first step to radically changing the whole division of labour and the economy'. In this campaign for wages for housework, it is possible to see two distinct, albeit closely related demands at work. The first, most obvious demand is to reform the economic structure of society in the name of distributive justice. This is not simply a matter of moving resources from men to women, but also a matter of changing structures such as the division of labour which perpetuate maldistribution. The second, rather less obvious demand is that women's work needs to be revalued as an integral part of the effort to secure justice. Hence James says that caring work must be 'recognized: measured, valued and paid for'.[1] Here 'valued' sits alongside but separate from 'paid for'. The implication is that, at least with regard to this issue, economic and cultural justice must go hand in hand.

Campaigns such as that for wages for housework should be welcomed by those commentators who are unhappy about what they see as the displacement of legitimate concerns about injustices rooted in the economic structure of society by what they regard as relatively ephemeral concerns about identity and difference. Brian Barry can be seen as a fairly typical representative of this view. In response to the charge that egalitarian liberals are 'blind' to 'difference', he contends that 'it is multiculturalists who are blind to the ever-widening differences that are such a deplorable feature of most contemporary societies (2001: 64). However, it is not cultural differences that Barry has in mind, but rather differences in income and wealth, and disparities in 'the quality of education and healthcare available to people with different incomes' (2001: 63–4). Richard Rorty is also concerned about the displacement of concerns about money and power by concerns about identity and difference. He also thinks that, in leftist academia, culture has been allowed to push economics aside (2000: 13), and he points out what he sees as the 'dangerous consequences of developing a left that neglects class and money by focusing on the elimination of prejudice and sexism' (2000: 18). While he accepts that recognition – in the limited sense of the elimination of residual stigma – is important, he argues that anyone concerned with social justice should give much more attention to redistribution. Hence he recommends that leftist students 'spend more time thinking about what will happen if American wages continue to sink toward the level of the global wage market' (2000: 19). Anne Phillips captures the spirit of these arguments well: 'Difference . . . seems to have displaced inequality as the central concern of political and social theory. We ask ourselves how we can achieve equality while still recognizing difference, rather than how we can eliminate inequality' (1997: 143).

Although she identifies herself as a political theorist of recognition, Nancy Fraser also shares these concerns that the rise of the politics of recognition has been at the expense of what she calls the politics of redistribution. She believes that recent years have witnessed the emergence of a 'new constellation' in which recognition has come into the ascendancy while redistribution has gone into decline. In a striking shift of emphasis, she argues, concerns about class and social equality have been largely eclipsed by concerns about identity and difference (2003: 7, 88–9). It is in light of this concern that Fraser argues that it is necessary for political theorists to resist this wholesale shift from redistribution to recognition. Instead, she contends, a theory of social justice must be formulated in which redistribution and recognition play equal parts. In response to Fraser's thesis, a number of other theorists of recognition have entered this debate. Axel Honneth, in particular, engages in a lengthy exchange with Fraser in their jointly authored book *Redistribution or Recognition?*, published in 2003. Unlike Fraser, Honneth does not regret the recent shift of attention from distribution to recognition. Indeed, since he contends that recognition is 'the fundamental, overarching moral category' (2003: 2–3), he has reason to welcome its rise to prominence. To be specific, Honneth contends that a suitably differentiated account of recognition can provide the basis for a theory of justice on its own. In sharp contrast to Fraser, Honneth believes that the conception of recognition can underpin an account of justice which can deal with all matters of economic distribution.

Is Fraser right to argue that redistribution and recognition must be placed beside one another as the two halves of a dualistic theory of justice? Or is Honneth right to argue that all matters of redistribution can be considered matters of recognition?

In this chapter, I shall give detailed consideration to these questions, in order to determine what the right relationship between accounts of recognition and accounts of redistribution should be. To this end, I begin by presenting a sketch of Fraser's dualistic theory, in which redistribution and recognition are regarded as two analytically distinct, although practically intertwined, aspects of justice (5.2). I then consider Honneth's alternative monistic theory, according to which injustices of distribution can be understood as injustices of recognition (5.3). In the analysis that follows, I concentrate on several areas of contention between Fraser and Honneth. In particular, I focus on their accounts of the nature of capitalism, the social theories that they think are needed in light of these accounts, and the moral philosophies that can be associated with these social theories (5.4). By working through these various issues, I hope to come to a considered judgement about the proper relationship between recognition and redistribution (5.5).

5.2 Nancy Fraser: Redistribution, Recognition and Participation

As I have just said, Fraser believes that what she refers as the 'politics of difference' or 'identity politics' has displaced the 'politics of equality' or 'class politics' (2003: 8). She contends that this displacement is deeply misguided. Any account of social justice that focuses on cultural recognition to the neglect of economic redistribution will inevitably fail properly to understand the nature of injustice. She argues that, since culture and economy are closely entwined, any acceptable theory of justice must be able to integrate the politics of recognition and the politics of redistribution. In order to make this case, Fraser begins by examining what she calls the 'folk paradigms' of recognition and redistribution (2003: 11). These paradigms are intended to encapsulate the essential features of the two very distinct ways of thinking about justice that inform our contemporary political life. She focuses in particular on the sorts of collectivities with which these two forms of politics are concerned. Theories of redistribution concentrate on collectivities defined primarily by their location in the economy. Fraser offers the example of class as an ideal-typical collectivity which suffers purely economic injustices (2003: 13, 16–17). To remedy these injustices, it is necessary to reform the economic structure of society. Theories of recognition, by contrast, focus on groups defined primarily by their cultural identity. Fraser offers the example of groups of individuals defined by their sexuality as an ideal-typical case of those who suffer purely cultural injustices (2003: 13, 17–18). As we saw in section 4.4, the remedies for such injustices must change the status order of society.

In contrast to this everyday account, Fraser wants to argue that 'virtually all' collectivities are in fact two-dimensional in character. They are defined by both economic and cultural characteristics, where neither set of characteristics is reducible to the other. She offers gender and 'race' as examples of such bivalent collectivities. These groups are characterized by their position both in the class structure and in the status order, and hence the injustices from which they suffer are both economic and cultural in character (2003: 19–23). Fraser goes on to argue that even class and sexuality are bivalent collectivities. The only difference is that, in these collectivities, the injustices experienced are 'rooted' in economy and culture, respectively. In the case of class, for instance, 'the ultimate cause of class injustice is the economic structure of capitalist society', so that the status component of this injustice is 'less weighty' than the economic (2003: 10–11). On the basis of this analysis of two-dimensional collectivities, Fraser reaches several important conclusions about the character of modern societies. First, in such societies, class and status – and economy and culture – are differentiated or empirically divergent (2003: 48, 64, 66). There is, as she says, a 'partial decoupling of the economic mechanisms of distribution from the structures of prestige' (2003: 53). It is because they are differentiated that some faulty social theories assume that they are disconnected. Second, economy and culture are in reality entwined and interpenetrating social spheres (2003: 48, 64, 66). There is no zone of society which is purely economic or purely cultural: '*every* practice' is 'simultaneously economic and cultural, albeit not necessarily in equal proportions' (2003: 63). This means that an adequate social theory must enable us to understand how closely connected they are. Third, Fraser believes that it is because ordinary folk (and some social theorists) are dazzled by the surface appearance of two separate spheres that they fail to see their deeper interconnection (2003: 62). She argues that it is this faulty account of economy and culture that underpins the two folk paradigms which assume that redistribution and recognition can be dealt with as two separate aspects of justice.

If Fraser's analysis is correct, it follows that any theory of justice which focuses exclusively on either economy or culture is bound to be inadequate. On the one hand, she condemns ways of thinking about justice that underrate the importance of culture and corresponding injustices of misrecognition. Thus she rejects all forms of 'economism' which contend that, since all injustices are rooted in the economy, they will disappear once maldistribution is remedied. Economistic understandings of justice neglect the inevitable cultural component of all injustices. Here Fraser gives the example of the 'African-American Wall Street banker who cannot get a taxi to pick him up' as a simple demonstration that not all injustice is rooted in the economic structure (2003: 34). On the other hand, Fraser also condemns various ways of thinking about justice that underrate the importance of the economy and injustices of maldistribution. Thus she rejects all forms of 'culturalism' which contend that, since all injustices are rooted in the cultural order, they will disappear once misrecognition is remedied (2003: 53–4). She argues that Honneth has such a 'reductive culturalist view of distribution' (2003: 34; cf. 102 n. 51). In other words, he attempts to explain all matters concerned with distribution in ultimately cultural terms.

Given her rejection of both economism and culturalism, Fraser needs to find a form of social analysis adequate to the conditions to be found in contemporary capitalist societies. Such a form of analysis must be able to appreciate that, in these societies, culture and economy are differentiated yet interpenetrating, and that recognition and redistribution are analytically distinct yet inevitably co-present aspects of all matters of justice. In this case, Fraser believes, what is needed is a form of analysis that she calls 'perspectival dualism'. Only this approach, she argues, can adequately theorize 'the complex connections between two

orders of subordination, grasping at once their conceptual irreducibility, empirical divergence, and practical entwinement' (2003: 64). The
key feature of perspectival dualism is that it regards recognition and
redistribution as 'two analytical perspectives that can be assumed with
respect to any domain' (2003: 63). Each can be applied to either aspect
of the social order, no matter how cultural or economic it may initially
appear.[2] It is possible to take the standpoint of recognition when
examining the economy. For example, the aspect of income-support
programmes that causes unintended cultural stigma can be scruti-
nized.[3] It is also possible to apply a redistributive perspective to culture.
For example, an analysis can be conducted of the transaction costs
involved in not coming out as gay in public life (2003: 63). Thus each
perspective may have illuminating things to say about either aspect of
the social order. Fraser concludes that perspectival dualism
is a suitable method of social analysis for modern times. It can distinguish between recognition and redistribution, whilst understanding
their 'mutual imbrication', and without reducing either of them to the
other (2003: 64).

It follows from this analysis that in any theory of justice adequate
to contemporary conditions, redistribution and recognition must play
equal parts. More strongly, it is necessary to bring redistribution and
recognition together into a 'single normative framework' (2003: 33).
To this end, Fraser places a normative principle of 'parity of participation' at the heart of her political theory, according to which 'social
arrangements' must 'permit all (adult) members of society to interact
with one another as peers' (2003: 36). She then seeks to identify the
obstacles that stand in the way of such participation. Fraser argues
that, since both misrecognition and maldistribution can prevent
citizens from participating as peers, both will need to be remedied if
parity of participation is to be achieved. Misrecognition can take a
variety of forms, including 'cultural domination' (in which one group
is subjected to another's alien values), 'nonrecognition' (in which a
group is 'rendered invisible' by dominant patterns of cultural value)
and 'disrespect' (in which a group is belittled by stereotypical images
found in those value patterns) (2003: 13). Since misrecognition takes
many forms, so can its remedies. Recognition may involve *inter alia*
the upward revaluation of 'disrespected identities', the positive valuation of diversity in general, or the wholesale deconstruction of the
value patterns on which misrecognition is based (2003: 13, 44, 73).[4]
In all cases, the objective is the same: to remove the cultural barriers
which prevent some from being others' peers, and so to fulfil what
Fraser calls the 'intersubjective condition' of parity of participation
(2003: 36). Maldistribution can also take on a variety of forms,

including 'exploitation' (in which what is rightfully the worker's is taken by someone else), 'economic marginalization' (in which one is restricted to low-wage work or denied work altogether) and 'deprivation' (in which one does not enjoy an adequate standard of living). The ways of overcoming these different forms of maldistribution also vary, although all will involve altering the economic structure of society. They could include the redistribution of income and wealth *per se*, democratizing investment decisions or radically transforming the economic structure of society (2003: 13, 73). In all cases, the objective is the same: to remove the economic barriers which prevent some from being others' peers, thus fulfilling the 'objective condition' of parity of participation (2003: 36). In this way, Fraser's principle of parity of participation brings recognition and redistribution together as two mutually irreducible moments of justice.

5.3   Axel Honneth: Redistribution as Recognition

Honneth agrees with Fraser that any account of social justice must make space for both redistribution and recognition. However, since he regards recognition as the most fundamental normative category, he is not concerned about its eclipse of redistribution. In order to make his case for the importance of recognition, Honneth believes that his point of departure must be different to Fraser's. He claims that she begins with an analysis of the political objectives of new social movements. He has two reasons for rejecting such a starting point. First, since the demands of such movements have been filtered through the 'bourgeois public sphere' (2003: 116), so that certain demands have been allowed through and others suppressed, they do not give an accurate picture of everyday experiences of injustice. Second, Fraser's analysis risks 'idealization', since it focuses on appealing social movements such as feminism, and overlooks unappealing movements such as neo-Nazism (2003: 116, 121–2). Against this account, Honneth contends that it is necessary to examine the 'institutionally caused suffering and misery' that exist 'prior to and independently of political articulation by social movements' (2003: 117). What is required, in other words, is to go behind the already articulated political demands found in the public sphere in order to examine 'the everyday dimension of moral feelings of injustice'. By doing so, Honneth hopes to produce 'a "phenomenology" of social experiences of injustice' (2003: 114). That is to say, he intends to provide a nuanced description of what it is actually like to experience specific injustices.[5]

As a result of this phenomenological investigation, Honneth claims that, no matter how varied experiences of suffering may be, they nevertheless have a common 'normative core' (2003: 131): all such experiences result from the violation of expectations about recognition. As he says, 'the experience of the withdrawal of social recognition – of degradation and disrespect – must be at the center of a meaningful concept of socially caused suffering and injustice' (2003: 132). However, although misrecognition is at the core of all suffering and injustice, it is not a unitary substance. In fact, it takes three distinct and mutually irreducible forms. The first is maltreatment. As we saw in section 2.3, Honneth argues that physical injuries such as 'torture and rape' damage subjects' integrity, and so undermine their bodily self-confidence. The second form of misrecognition is disrespect.[6] In chapter 3, it was argued that people are disrespected if they are not treated as rationally autonomous beings. The third form of misrecognition is denigration. It was argued in chapter 4 that if distinctive identities are not valued, or if contributions to society are not ack-nowledged, then subjects' self-esteem may be put at risk. From this taxonomy of forms of misrecognition, it is possible to deduce a corresponding taxonomy of recognition. Although in each case it involves the public attribution of positive value by one party to another, re-cognition operates in three different modes. Love, the first form of recognition, involves the powerful emotional attachment of an individual to their significant others. As Honneth says, it is expressed in 'loving care for the other's well-being in light of his or her individual needs' (2003: 139). The second form of recognition is respect. Hon-neth argues that all individuals should enjoy equal respect for possessing features which all other human beings possess. Finally, with regard to the third form of recognition, Honneth suggests that, in the 'prestige order' of bourgeois capitalism, each person enjoys 'social esteem according to his or her achievement as a "productive citizen"' (2003: 141).[7]

For Honneth, these three modes of recognition do not just describe relationships between subjects; they also make possible particular relationships of subjects to themselves. In other words, the experience of each of these forms of recognition leads subjects to regard themselves in a particular way. As Honneth says, 'only social relations that require an attitude of mutual recognition contribute to the development of a positive self-relation'. Corresponding to the three forms of recognition and misrecognition just described, then, there are three types of self-relation. First, 'in intimate relations', subjects have the opportunity to 'understand themselves as individuals with their own needs' (2003: 142). Honneth argues that, if people are shown loving concern, then they are able to develop self-confidence. Second, 'in legal relations', they can 'understand themselves as legal persons owed the same autonomy as all other members of society' (2003: 142). Being respected thus makes self-respect possible. Third, 'in loose-knit social relations', people have the chance to 'understand themselves as individuals with their own needs' (2003: 142). Being esteemed then leads to self-esteem. Honneth argues that, if people experience these three types of self-relation, then they can achieve what he calls 'individual self-realization' (2003: 174). In light of this analysis, it is possible to specify the conditions necessary for such self-realization to be possible. First, without 'care and love', Honneth contends, 'children's personalities cannot develop at all' (2003: 138). Thus the circumstances must be in place for such care and love to be possible. Second, the realization of respect requires the maintenance of a system of civil, political and social rights. In such a system, one can be 'respected as a legal person with the same rights as all other members of society' (2003: 140). Third, the idea of achievement must be generalized so that everyone's contribution to the society has a fair chance of being appreciated. There must be, in other words, a horizon of value which gives all individuals an equal opportunity to earn esteem. If these three conditions of recognition are in place, then individuals will be able to achieve self-realization (2003: 174).

In sharp contrast to Fraser, then, Honneth contends that recognition should be the principal normative category of a theory of social justice. He believes, furthermore, that 'the conception of recognition, when properly understood, can accommodate, indeed even entails, a modified version of the Marxian paradigm of economic distribution' (2003: 3). In other words, all normative issues concerned with the distribution of economic power and resources can be understood as matters of recognition. In order to understand why, it is necessary to examine Honneth's account of the nature of capitalist societies, and in particular his account of the relationship between culture and economy in such societies. A brief analysis of three propositions will suffice to indicate the main contours of this account. First, Honneth argues that 'material distribution takes place according to certainly contested but nevertheless always temporarily established value-patterns' (2003: 142). In other words, how goods and resources are shared out depends on the values prevalent at a particular time in the society in question. Second, he suggests that 'the cultural values involved in the institutional constitution of the economic sphere . . . give it a particular shape in the form of a division of labor and a distribution of status' (2003: 155–6). The form that the economy takes, and in particular who gets which jobs and what social standing is attached to those jobs, is influenced by the prevailing cultural values. Third, Honneth contends that, even in 'distribution struggles', in which participants see themselves 'aiming at a redistribution of material resources . . . cultural interpretations play a constitutive role' (2003: 157–8). That is to say, when a group of people is fighting for a wage rise or for the abolition of inheritance tax, their struggle is profoundly influenced by a particular account of culture. Taking these three claims together, it is clear that, on Honneth's account, culture has a pivotal role to play in the economy.

This account of the nature of capitalism is closely entwined with Honneth's advocacy of a particular form of social theory. To understand this connection, consider his assertion that it is impossible to identify aspects of capitalist society which are purely economic in character. As he says, 'it is not advisable to theoretically isolate purely economic or systemic factors from cultural elements with regard to the capitalist economic order' (2003: 156). It is possible to read this statement in two different ways. On a weak reading, since culture permeates all aspects of the social order, any explanation of that order must have a hermeneutic element. On a much stronger reading, since 'cultural elements' have a key role in explaining the 'capitalist economic order', an explanation of that order must begin with and centre on the interpretation of cultural values. Given my understanding of Honneth's account of capitalism, I think that he would endorse this latter reading. In contrast to Fraser's dualism, then, Honneth's social theory gives priority to the hermeneutic interpretation of cultural values. In general, the task of such a theory is to determine whether the prevailing set of cultural values encourages the achievement of individual self–realization by facilitating the creation and maintenance of adequate relationships of recognition. In the specific circumstances of contemporary capitalist society, the task is to understand how the principle of achievement established in bourgeois capitalism and, more recently, the principle of equality which has informed the development of welfare capitalism play a key role in determining the possibility of self-realization. This account of Honneth's social theory also helps to explain why he believes that issues of economic justice can be understood in terms of recognition. Since the economy is regulated by normative principles, struggles for redistribution are in fact struggles to be recognized according to these principles. Hence struggles for redistribution are a subspecies of struggles for recognition.

5.4   A Critical Comparison

Thus far this chapter has presented a comparison and contrast between two very complex theories of social justice. Fraser is what might be called an 'integrated dualist': she argues that redistribution and recognition need to be placed side by side, as two conjoined yet distinguishable elements of a theory of social justice. Honneth, by contrast, is what might be called a 'differentiated monist': he regards recognition as the fundamental normative category, although he emphasizes that three distinct principles of justice can be derived from it. From their different perspectives, these two theorists reach different conclusions on a whole range of issues. I would argue that three areas of contention are of particular importance. First, while Fraser argues that culture and economy are mutually irreducible and equally important aspects of the social order, Honneth contends that culture plays a leading role in shaping the economy. Second, in contrast to Fraser's 'perspectival dualism', Honneth gives a foundational role to the hermeneutic analysis of cultural values. Third, while Fraser defends an account of moral philosophy in which redistribution and recognition are the two necessary conditions of parity of participation, Honneth argues that a combination of love, respect and esteem is necessary to secure the conditions of self-realization. These three areas of contention will now be investigated in greater detail.[8]

The Social Order

In the second round of the debate between Fraser and Honneth, each of them directly addresses the other's claims about the nature of capitalism. Against Honneth, Fraser argues that, while the 'market order is culturally embedded . . . it is not directly governed by cultural schema of evaluation' (2003: 214). She concludes that he 'vastly exaggerates the role of recognition in capitalist society . . . he takes valid insights about the ubiquity and irreducibility of culture and inflates them beyond all recognition' (2003: 216). It is hard to disagree with Fraser's judgement. Indeed, Honneth's claims about the importance of cultural factors come close to a commitment to cultural determinism. In his defence, Honneth seeks to distance himself from any such commitment: Fraser's accusation that he analyses 'market processes in terms of "cultural" recognition alone' is, he says, 'fundamentally wrong' (2003: 248). He claims that his goal was 'much more modest':

rather than aiming to produce an 'explanatory' account of modern capitalist societies, he 'sought only to reveal the moral "constraints" underlying social interaction on different levels in this form of society' (2003: 249). It could be argued that Honneth's rejoinder is analogous to Engels's claim in his 1890 letter to Bloch: 'According to the materialist conception of history, the *ultimately* determining element in history is the production and reproduction of real life' (in Tucker 1972: 760). For Honneth, of course, it is culture, not the economy, which plays the role of ultimate determinant.

Honneth's defence of his position is highly disingenuous. Certainly, it does not square with many of the claims that he made in his first statement of his position, including, for instance, his contention that economic distribution 'takes place according to' certain value patterns (2003: 142). Indeed, even in his reply to Fraser's critique, he cannot quite let go of his strong thesis about the role of culture in economic processes: 'I continue to assume that even structural transformations in the economic sphere' depend 'at least' on the 'tacit consent' of 'those affected' (2003: 250). Thus Honneth wavers between a strong and a weak thesis about the role of cultural values in economic relations. The problem is that both of these theses present him with serious problems. On the one hand, if he endorses the strong thesis that the cultural determines the economic, then he could provide a complete explanatory account of capitalism. However, Fraser is right to argue that this thesis is implausible. On the other hand, if Honneth endorses the weak thesis that the cultural merely has a role in shaping the economic, then he would have abandoned the ambition of providing a full explanation of capitalism. That is to say, if he were to acknowledge that there are some non-cultural constraints on economic behaviour, then he would have to accept that some struggles for economic resources would not be instances of struggles for recognition. Thus Honneth's principal claim about the relationship between recognition and redistribution would fall.[9]

Fraser's dualistic account of capitalist society, for its part, has attracted a number of criticisms. Iris Marion Young argues that political economy and culture cannot be separated. As she declares: 'Political economy is cultural, and culture is economic' (1997: 154).[10] Judith Butler agrees with Young. She argues that when Fraser characterizes queer struggles as 'merely cultural', her implication is that real oppression is rooted in political economy (1998: 38). *Pace* Fraser, Butler argues that the cultural and economic aspects of the social order cannot be neatly separated from each other. She makes this argument by showing how the social regulation of sexuality is 'central to the functioning of political economy' (1998: 39). To be specific, she contends that the social order produces two sexualities: heterosexuality, which is considered normal, and homosexuality, which is considered deviant. As a consequence, pressure is placed on individuals to be heterosexual and to form heterosexual families (1998: 40). In this way, the system for the reproduction of sexuality helps to underpin the gender division between men and women which is vital to the functioning of the economic system (1998: 40–1). Butler's conclusion is that, since the cultural and the economic are inseparable (1998: 43), Fraser's dualistic account must be rejected. In her reply, Fraser reasserts her claim that there are very real differences between the two dimensions of the contemporary social order. Butler's anti-dualism, she contends, obscures 'actually existing divergences of status from class' (2003: 30). Addressing Butler's own example, she argues that the sphere of sexuality is relatively disconnected from the sphere of political economy. The eradication of homophobia, for instance, is unlikely significantly to affect the operation of the economic system. Or, to refer once more to one of Fraser's own examples, the case of an African-American broker on Wall Street who cannot get a taxi to stop for him vividly illustrates the relative independence of cultural and economic injustice (2003: 16). Fraser concludes that, since a change in one dimension of the social order need not be accompanied by a change in the other, her dualism makes more sense than Butler's monism.

In order to assess the relative strengths of Fraser's and Butler's positions, it is vital to distinguish two levels of analysis that they both conflate. For the purposes of the current argument, let us call these the analytical and the empirical levels. Fraser's thesis is that the cultural and the economic are analytically distinct but empirically intertwined. Butler's rival thesis is that, since the cultural and the economic are always co-present at the empirical level, the analytical distinction does not make sense. Hence, she declares, 'the very practices of sexual exchange confound the distinction' between the cultural and the economic (1998: 43). So far as the first level of analysis is concerned, Butler fundamentally misunderstands the nature of an analytical distinction. By its very nature, such a distinction is justified if it enhances the explanatory power of the theory in which it figures, even if the objects that it distinguishes are always intertwined in practice (cf. Markell, 2006). For this reason, Fraser's defence of her analytical distinction between the cultural and the economic need make no reference to the empirical relationship between these two dimensions of the social order. With regard to the empirical level of analysis, Butler argues that Fraser falsely assumes that collectivities based on sexuality are purely cultural. Fraser is adamant, however, that this is an ideal-typical characterization of such collectivities.

As she says, 'the ideal type I sketched earlier for heuristic purposes may be inadequate to the real-world complexities'. 'In general', she concludes, 'even such an apparently one-dimensional status category as sexuality has a distributive component' (2003: 24–5). Hence, at this level of analysis as well, Butler's criticism of Fraser's dualism is misplaced.

However, although Fraser's account of culture and economy as two dimensions of the social order is not threatened by Butler's critique, it is more difficult for her to dismiss the charge that her dualistic account is not exhaustive. Here critics have argued that, in addition to the economic and the cultural, there is a further dimension to the social order. As Young says, there is a 'third, political, aspect to social reality, concerning institutions and practices of law, citizenship, administration, and political participation' (1997: 151). Similarly, Brian Barry argues that the problem with Fraser's 'crude dichotomy' is that it 'squeezes out . . . the possibility that the injustice suffered by homosexuals is the lack of equal legal rights' (2001: 275). I would suggest that the best way to make the argument that politics is a third aspect of the social order is to offer an analysis of collectivities involved in political struggles that parallels Fraser's own analysis. As we saw in section 5.2, her argument that collectivities based on ideas of class, sexuality, gender and 'race' are 'bivalent' supports her thesis that culture and economy are the two mutually irreducible dimensions of the social order. If it could be shown that collectivities also have a third, political aspect which cannot be reduced without remainder to the other two, then this would demonstrate that politics must be regarded as the third dimension of the social order. To make this argument, I shall focus on two specific examples.

First, consider Leonard Feldman's account of the politics of the homeless which he uses to argue that Fraser is wrong to overlook what he calls the 'specifically political dynamics of injustice' (2002: 419). Acknowledging that the homeless suffer from cultural stigmatization, and that they are disadvantaged by the prevailing distribution of resources, he argues that they also suffer from distinctively political injustices, which are the responsibility of the state (2002: 422–3). As an example of such injustice, Feldman analyses policies which have been put into place in a number of American states. While these are designed to solve the problem of homelessness, in practice they add to the problem. Here he talks about 'punitive state policies' – such as legislation which bans outdoor sleeping – which are presented in the guise of 'a compassionate politics of state-sponsored and funded redistribution' (2002: 425–6). The effect of these policies 'is to turn the homeless into outlaws – into noncitizens whose everyday coping strategies place them outside the law' (2002: 426). Feldman contends that the homeless also seek distinctively political solutions to the injustices that they face. Certainly, they want the stigma from which they suffer to be removed, and they want more resources to be directed their way, but they also demand to be included as full citizens in the life of their polity (2002: 428–31).

Second, consider the case of national minorities. Members of such groups claim that, within the existing state, the minority status of their nation means that they are in all sorts of ways marginalized: their representatives in the state legislature are outnumbered, resources flowing into their territory are disproportionately low, the minority status of their language puts them at a disadvantage compared to speakers of the majority language, and so on.[11] It is important to emphasize that these are distinctively political obstacles. While they may have cultural or economic aspects, they cannot be entirely reduced to either of these categories. The disadvantages caused by the minority status of a language, for instance, are the product not solely either of particular patterns of cultural value or of a particular distribution of resources. They are caused, rather, by the structural position of the minority language community within the state. In reaction to these disadvantages, many national minorities demand to be accommodated fairly within the existing political system. Once again, it should be emphasized that this is a distinctively political remedy to the obstacles that national minorities face. The demand for the national minority to be granted special status is neither simply a demand for a change in patterns of cultural value nor a demand for a redistribution of resources. It is, rather, a demand that the constitutional framework of the state be altered in order appropriately to accommodate the special position of this national minority.[12]

This analysis of the homeless and of national minorities could be extended to many other collectivities. In each case, it could be shown that such groups are defined by their political as well as cultural and economic characteristics. They occupy a specific place in the political structure, as well as the status order and economic structure of society. It follows that such groups suffer from political as well as cultural and economic injustices, and they seek distinctively political as well as cultural and economic remedies for these injustices. The implication of this analysis, then, is that politics must be regarded as a third dimension of the social order, one that cannot be reduced without remainder to a combination of culture and economy. As we shall see shortly, it follows that this further dimension of the social order must be fully incorporated into any adequate analysis of that order.[13]

Having conducted this examination of Fraser's and Honneth's analyses of the capitalist social order, it may be worth saying in conclusion that neither of these theorists really try to theorize capitalist society as a totality. In the introduction to their jointly authored book, they refer to the way in which 'economic inequalities are growing, as neo-liberal forces promote corporate globalization' (2003: 2). However, their sketchy remarks on the nature of capitalist societies fall a long way short of an adequate explanatory account of the current state of global capitalism; and nor do they engage with the rapidly growing literature on this subject.[14] Fraser offers a solitary reference to David Held et al.'s *Global Transformations,* published in 1999. The closest that Honneth comes is a reference to Frank Parkin's 1971 book *Class Inequality and Political Order.* Nor do they engage with the contemporary literature on the role of culture in economic processes.[15] Indeed, Fraser's key source here seems to be Max Weber's classic essay on 'Class, Status, Party' (1958). To make this criticism is not to imply that Fraser and Honneth should, or possibly could, be equally expert in all of the areas of research of relevance to their goals. However, since one of Fraser's and Honneth's key claims is that they intend to overcome the division of labour between different sorts of expert in order to theorize capitalism as a totality, then some engagement with the relevant literatures might reasonably be expected. Without such engagement, their debate remains at an unsatisfactory level of abstraction. More than this, it means that the empirical accounts of the social order on which their theories of justice are meant to depend are inadequate.

Social Theory

Since both Fraser and Honneth believe that there is an intimate link between an account of how the world is and an account of how that world should be explained, these critical remarks about their descriptions of the social order also bear on their social theories. Turning first to Fraser, Honneth suggests that there is 'something arbitrary' about her advocacy of perspectival dualism. Why, he asks, should we employ the two analytical perspectives of "economy" and "culture" rather than, say, "morality" or "law" (2003: 156)? In one sense, there is nothing arbitrary about Fraser's choice of these two perspectives. This is because it follows directly from her account of capitalist society. If economy and culture are the two key sub-systems in such a society, then Fraser's perspectival dualism is justified. In another sense, however, Honneth is quite right to question her choice of redistribution and recognition as the only relevant analytical perspectives. In the previous subsection, I agreed with those critics who argue that there is a third, political dimension to the social order. It would follow from the logic of Fraser's argument that there must also be a third aspect to a social theory which is capable of explaining that order. In principle, Fraser is open to the suggestion that further 'modes of social ordering' and 'types of subordination' could be added to her analysis (2003: 67–8). In practice, however, she strongly resists proposals to add a third category to her social theory. Responding to Honneth's suggestion that there is 'a conflict dynamic . . . over the appropriate interpretation of the principle of legal equality' (2003: 151–2), she contends that perspectival dualism 'conceives law as pertaining to both dimensions of justice, distribution and recognition' (2003: 220). She believes, in other words, that the explanation of any dispute about the law can be divided without remainder into a combination of cultural and economic elements.

Is Fraser right to argue that all legal and political conflicts can be satisfactorily explained by use of a social theory which combines only two distinct analytical perspectives? Or are her critics right to argue that, since there is a distinctive third element to the social order, this must be included in any social theory which hopes to comprehend that order? As Barry argues, '[a]utocracy, repression and persecution are not reducible to economic inequality, but no more are they perspicuously classified as "cultural misrecognition"' (2001: 275). One way in which to decide between these two positions is to consider the role of the state in matters of justice. By demonstrating that the state may be both a source of injustice and a means of overcoming such justice, I shall now show that Fraser's social theory needs to be able to conceptualize the state – and that it cannot do so by combining cultural and economic perspectives alone. To begin with, recall the argument in the previous subsection that all collectivities have a political dimension. Feldman argues that the homeless suffer from distinctively political injustices for which the state is responsible. He contends that its punitive policies trigger the struggles of the homeless for political inclusion. Many commentators contend that national minorities also experience a range of distinctively political injustices, including those arising simply from their status as minorities in a state dominated by a majority. In these circumstances, national minorities struggle to be fairly accommodated (and/or to secure some degree of autonomy) within the existing state. In both of these examples, it is the institutions and policies of the state that are responsible for these distinctively political injustices. It is the policies of the state that govern the homeless, and it is the structure of the state that determines the condition of national minorities. Furthermore, since misrecognition is institutionalized in the structures of the state, the remedy for such misrecognition must involve the reform of that state. The state is the organization capable of modifying the existing status order, intervening in the existing economic structure, and changing its own rules and procedures, in order to eliminate obstacles to justice.

Looking at Fraser's own account of the causes of and remedies for injustice, it might be thought that she would agree with this analysis. For one thing, she emphasizes the fact that cultural values are rooted in institutions. As she says, 'institutionalized patterns of cultural value' include 'marriage laws . . . social-welfare policies . . . and policing practices'. Such laws, policies and practices are of course products of the state. For another thing, she acknowledges that cultural injustices can take legal and/or political forms. Thus she remarks that 'misrecognition is juridified, expressly codified in formal law' and 'institutionalized via government policies' (2000: 114). Hence she appears to accept that at least some injustices of misrecognition can be associated with the state. Yet, in spite of this implicit acknowledgement of the role of the state, it is curiously absent from her theory of justice. As Feldman suggests, although the state is vital to Fraser's political project as the agency capable of realizing justice, she offers no account of that state. She does not specify, for instance, what it is comprised of, how its actions are determined, and what the limits to its power are. As he says, Fraser assumes that the state is a 'neutral delivery service' (2002: 418; and see 434; cf. Markell 2003: 26–7). That is to say, it is a mechanism that can be used to carry out the actions needed to secure justice without its own dynamics interfering with the execution of such actions. Nor does she follow through on the possibility that the state is itself a potential source of political 'oppression and hardship' (2002: 411; and see 418–19). In short, the state is a conceptual blindspot in Fraser's argument (2002: 411). It is an invisible but omnipresent agency which may be responsible for some injustices, and which is at the same time charged with overcoming such injustices.

If Fraser does refer to the state, she assumes that its actions are either cultural or economic. As Feldman argues, she views the state 'bifocally' – as an agent of either cultural or economic justice (2002: 416–17). Thus she maintains that legal and political injustices can be regarded as the result of a combination of a particular set of cultural values and a particular distribution of economic resources. Legal rules or political policies merely juridify or institutionalize such misrecognition and maldistribution. This, however, forces her to take up some very awkward positions. At one point, for instance, she refers to 'redistribution as the remedy for male domination' (2003: 8). Here Fraser tries to argue that the restructuring of power relations can be considered a form of redistribution. The problem is that it is the power structure which determines, or at least delimits, the distribution of resources within that structure. In general, Fraser's dualism elides important distinctions between formal legal rules and cultural value patterns, on the one hand, and between political power and economic imperatives, on the other. With regard to the first of these distinctions, there is a significant difference between the status order and the legal order. At best, the latter could be regarded as a sub-system of the former, marked out by the formality of its rules and by the fact that they are backed up by the force of the state. So far as the second of these distinctions is concerned, there is a significant difference between political power and economic imperatives. Only the crudest sort of 'economism' would support the proposition that the former can be entirely explained by reference to the latter. As we have seen, Fraser argues that Honneth's social theory is reductionist. Yet I would maintain that Fraser's perspectival dualism is reductionist too. The only difference is that it seeks to explain all social phenomena in terms of a combination of cultural and economic factors, rather than in terms of cultural factors alone.[16]

So far as Honneth is concerned, Fraser brings two closely interrelated charges against his social theory. First, if he accuses her of arbitrariness, she accuses him of foundationalism. She argues that, on his account, 'moral psychology settles everything in advance'. He gives moral psychology a 'foundationalist' role which undermines the 'relative autonomy' of other modes of inquiry (2003: 206). Second, if Honneth condemns Fraser for being no more than a dualist, she condemns him for being a monist. She argues that 'Honneth's social theory, like his moral psychology, is monist'. It views 'all social processes through the single lens of interpersonal psychology' and so views capitalism 'exclusively from the perspective of recognition' (2003: 213). Bringing these two charges together, Fraser argues that, since Honneth's social theory gives a foundationalist role to moral psychology, and neglects the independently significant role of both cultural and economic analysis, it is unable to understand contemporary capitalist society. In his reply to these charges, Honneth argues that 'Fraser overdramatizes both the importance of moral psychology to my proposal and the significance of its ethical point of departure'. He then explains that he invokes 'moral-psychological conside-rations . . . only insofar as they are to support the social-theoretical thesis that social integration works through forms of mutual recognition', and it is this thesis that 'represents the key to determining the purpose of social justice' (2003: 258).[17]

I believe that the success of Fraser's critique depends on the character of Honneth's conception of self-realization. In order to see what I mean, consider two possible interpretations of this conception. On one interpretation, Honneth's conception of self-realization is purely psychological. That is to say, self-realization is to be understood as a condition that humans may achieve if certain psychological conditions are in place. On this interpretation, a normative theory which declares that a just society is one that enables self-realization is indeed a form of psychological foundationalism. This is because it allows the requirements of justice to be fully determined by a subjective psychology. Such a theory contends that it is because humans have a particular psychological make-up that justice must take the form it does. This interpretation of Honneth's idea of self-realization seems to be borne out by an examination of his reply to Fraser's critique. Although the purpose of Honneth's reply is to refute the suggestion that his theory of justice depends on a form of psychological foundationalism, the argument that he offers undermines that purpose. In particular, it is difficult to see why he uses the word 'only' as he does here, since his argument gives 'moral-psychological considerations' an absolutely central role in his 'social-theoretical thesis' about social integration. It is this thesis which then determines what form justice should take. On this interpretation, then, psychology does indeed play a foundational role in Honneth's account of justice. To put it rather crudely, a psychology of recognition determines a sociology of recognition, which determines an ethics of recognition.

On an alternative interpretation, however, Honneth's conception of self-realization is understood more broadly. According to this reading, self-realization requires the establishment not just of psychological, but also of specific cultural and political, conditions. Such an interpretation can draw support from Honneth's account of the tripartite nature of justice, in which recognition does not just take the form of love and care for one's significant others. In addition, recognition as respect requires the creation of a system of subjective rights, and recognition as esteem requires the maintenance of a horizon of values in which all citizens have a chance to gain esteem. On this account, then, the conditions of self-realization are not just psychological, but also cultural and political in character. It would follow that, since Honneth's normative theory does not derive the conditions of justice from a purely psychological account of self-realization, it cannot be considered a form of psychological foundationalism. However, I would argue that this way of answering Fraser's charge is somewhat disingenuous. In section 2.3, I suggested that although Honneth does indeed regard self-confidence, self-respect and self-esteem as the three necessary conditions of self-realization, he gives the first of these a key role to play. To be specific, self-confidence is the necessary precondition for both self-respect and self-esteem, and hence for self-realization itself. As Honneth himself says, love is the 'basic requisite' for all further modes of recognition (1995: 176). It must be concluded that he cannot escape the charge of foundationalism in this way.

This discussion connects back to my analysis in section 2.5 of Fraser's charge that Honneth – and also Taylor – allow their normative theories to be dangerously dependent on empirically disputable psychologies of recognition. Against Fraser, I argued that, since all normative theories inevitably depend on the validity of certain empirical propositions, it is not sufficient simply to point out such dependence. In the present context, then, it could be argued that it is not enough to show that Honneth's theory is a form of foundationalism. He could simply accept this characterization, arguing that the indisputable strength of his social psychology lends decisive support to his normative theory. In this case, it would also be necessary to show that this foundationalism is not true. Without this demonstration, Honneth would see no reason to abandon his theory. In fact, Fraser does not take Honneth on at this level. Her argument is that, since this psychology *might* not be true, he should not rely on it. She does not try to show that, since his social psychology *is* empirically flawed, he should not rely on it. In this case, however, my earlier conclusion stands: since all normative theories must depend on empirical support, simply pointing out such dependence does not mean that the normative conclusions must be abandoned. This is true even if the empirical support in question can be characterized as a form of foundationalism.

Moral Philosophy

Just as there is an intimate link between Fraser's and Honneth's accounts of capitalist society and their social theories, so there is also an intimate link between these theories and their moral philosophies. They conceive of the purpose of a theory of justice in very similar ways. To be specific, both believe that such a theory must meet two conditions. First, it must be able to provide good reasons to support the principles of justice which it articulates. Second, these principles must be able to guide practical judgements about justice. Fraser, for her part, claims that her theory is able to articulate 'substantive requirements of justice' whilst 'eschewing ethical foundations' (2003: 230; and see 232–3). In other words, it can tell us what justice requires in practice, and it can do so without reference to any particular conception of the good life.[18] Honneth questions the claims that Fraser makes for her theory. He argues that, since her idea of 'social participation' must be 'filled in' by 'recourse to ethical considerations', her goal of formulating what he characterizes as a 'teleological liberalism' is quite impossible (2003: 178–9; and see 259, 262). He concludes that, since Fraser must provide a detailed account of what she means by participation which will inevitably draw on a particular conception of the good, it cannot be normatively binding all citizens. In her defence, Fraser argues that she rejects 'both teleological sectarianism and proceduralist formalism' in favour of what 'could be called *thick deontological liberalism*' (2003: 230). In this way, she reasserts her claim that her theory can provide practical guidance in matters of justice, whilst at the same time being normatively binding on all reasonable citizens. Does Fraser or Honneth get the best of this exchange?

In order to answer this question, it will be useful to focus on the principle of parity of participation which lies at the centre of Fraser's theory of justice. To begin with, let us consider her claim that this principle is 'nonsectarian' in the sense that it 'can justify claims for recognition as normatively binding on all who agree to abide by fair terms of interaction under conditions of value pluralism' (2003: 14). In order to prove that the principle of parity can meet this demanding condition, she attempts to show that it can be deduced directly from the idea of equal moral worth (2003: 231). If such a deduction worked, it would show that, since no one could reasonably reject this conception of equality, no one could reasonably reject the principle of parity either. In this case, such a principle could provide authoritative guidance in matters of justice in societies marked by value pluralism. The problem with this argument, however, is that a wide variety of normative principles can, and have been, deduced from an idea of equal moral worth. Indeed, Ronald Dworkin argues that virtually all modern political philosophies are committed to such an idea (e.g. 1986: 297–301). In this case, it is difficult to see what is special about the principle of participatory parity. This principle could reasonably be rejected by the many different sorts of egalitarian who endorse the idea of equal moral worth but dispute the particular deduction that Fraser makes from this idea. It would follow that, since the principle of parity is not normatively binding for all reasonable citizens, it fails to meet one of the two conditions that Fraser sets for it.

With regard to the second condition, Fraser claims that the principle of participatory parity is capable of providing practical guidance in matters of justice. It could be argued, however, that, since her theory fails to provide a detailed account of the nature of participation, the principle of parity cannot serve as a practical guide in matters of justice. She offers very few details about what participation means in this context, except to refer to participation 'in social life' (2003: 29; cf. 2000: 113; 2001: 24, 25, 40 n. 11). Without an account of 'social life', the means needed to participate in it, and the purpose of such participation, Fraser's theory cannot guide practical judgements about justice. Here Kevin Olson provides a useful development of Fraser's own theory. He argues that, in this context, active participation in co-operative endeavours must be regarded as the 'privileged' form of participation (2003). The meaning of this sense of participation is captured in what Olson calls the 'participatory ideal', according to which citizens should have 'maximal opportunities to participate in politics and culture' (2003: 6). In practice, he contends, an 'enabling' state will be necessary to secure participatory parity (2003: 7). Such a state will provide a 'guarantee of enablement' which ensures that citizens are able effectively to participate in political debate (2003: 11). Although I must emphasize that this is Olson's rather than Fraser's view, I nevertheless think that it is a logical and defensible extension of her theory. However, there is a serious problem with this extension of Fraser's account. If, as I have just argued, the principle of participatory parity fails to meet the condition of non-sectarianism, then how much more clearly does the idea of the enabling state fail to meet the same condition. In Honneth's words, it is without a doubt 'filled in' by 'recourse to ethical considerations'. It must be concluded that Fraser is caught on the horns of a dilemma: the more she tries to make sure that her theory of justice is non–sectarian, the less practical guidance it can provide; but the more she attempts to ensure that it meets the condition of practicality, the less persuasive is the claim that it is non-sectarian. Fraser fails to demonstrate that she can escape this dilemma.

Turning now to Honneth, we have seen that his moral philosophy is grounded on a conception of recognition. He believes that, if a complete set of relationships of mutual recognition were in place, all individuals would be able to achieve self-realization. Fraser's critique of Honneth's approach exactly mirrors his critique of hers. She argues that he is caught between 'the requirements of nonsectarianism and determinacy'. On the one hand, he can avoid sectarianism only by denying 'that his conception of human flourishing has any substantive content'. On the other hand, without substantive content, his theory of justice 'could not be able fairly to mediate conflicts across different value horizons' (2003: 225; and see 228).[19] In reply, Honneth denies that he faces the choice between procedure and substance which Fraser describes. However, while Fraser seeks to evade her dilemma by claiming to derive the principle of parity from an uncontroversial norm of equality, Honneth seeks to ground his normative conclusions in certain empirical facts about human relationships. To be specific, he argues that the correct theory of justice is the one that enables us to establish and maintain the necessary conditions of individual self-realization. Is Honneth able to refute the criticisms that Fraser makes of his account?

Honneth's strategy is very different from Fraser's. He seeks to infer the 'ought' of normative recognition from the 'is' of social integration. Thus Christopher Zurn suggests that 'the desired end-state – namely, that each individual be able fully to realize her or his self in non-coercive relations of recognition – is ineradicably drawn from the existential conditions of identity development' (2000: 119). Critics have argued that, in doing so, he has violated the fact–value distinction. The problem with this is that it is logically incoherent to try to derive a normative judgement – that justice should take a particular form – directly from an empirical fact – namely, that social relations are mediated by relations of recognition. One way in which Honneth could close this gap between the 'is' and the 'ought' would be explicitly to endorse a normative principle which states that a just society is one that provides the conditions for people's self-realization. As long as he did not try to claim that this principle could be derived directly from an empirical account of social integration, then the structure of his argument would be logically coherent and defensible. But I suspect that Honneth would seek to deal with this problem rather differently. As a Critical Theorist, he believes that his approach to social analysis and criticism is distinguished from its rivals by its claims to be able to locate an 'intramundane element of transcendence' in existing reality (1994: 259). According to Critical Theory, in other words, there is something about how things are in the world which points beyond this existing world to a better future. The task of this theory is thus to show that reality is already governed by normative criteria that can be used as the basis for the critique of this reality. This would suggest that the very project of Critical Theory, at least as Honneth conceives it, is built right over the fault line between 'is' and 'ought'. Unfortunately, a proper evaluation of this ambitious claim would take me beyond the confines of this chapter.

5.5 Conclusions

This chapter has focused on three issues central to the debate about the proper relationship between recognition and redistribution in a theory of social justice. Beginning with accounts of the social order, it went on to consider social theory, and ended by examining moral philosophy. In my concluding remarks, I want to return briefly to each of these areas in turn. With regard to the analysis of the social order, I argued that Honneth must abandon the implausibly strong thesis of cultural determination in favour of the weaker thesis of cultural influence. This would mean admitting that some parts of the social world are not governed by cultural values and, therefore, that not all struggles for redistribution can be understood as a subset of struggles for recognition. While Fraser's account of the nature of the social order is more successful, I argued that, by focusing entirely on the cultural and the economic, her perspectival dualism fails to take account of the political dimension of the social world. So far as social theory is concerned, I have suggested that, if Honneth does not endorse a purely psychological conception of self-realization, then he can evade Fraser's critique.[20] Following my argument about Fraser's account of the social order, I recommended that she incorporate a third, political dimension into her social theory. Since the state has a key role in helping and hindering parity of participation, it must be included in any comprehensive social analysis. The final theme discussed in this chapter was moral philosophy. Regarding Fraser's attempt to derive her principle of parity of participation from an idea of equal moral worth, I contended that, since many other principles could be derived from such an idea, her demonstration does not prove that it would be unreasonable to reject her particular principle. Honneth seeks a different solution to the same problem, appearing to justify his normative principles of recognition by reference to an empirical thesis about the nature of social integration. In this way, he defends a form of Critical Theory in which an account of how the world should be is based on an account of how the world is.

What all of this suggests is that the best way forward may be to try to synthesize Honneth's and Fraser's theories. On the one hand, Fraser's analysis of the economic dimension of justice can make good a lack in Honneth's theory. Given the failure of his cultural determinism, it follows that a complete theory of justice must include a further dimension in which the analysis of economic processes plays a central part. On the other hand, Honneth's analysis of the political dimension of justice can make good a lack in Fraser's theory. Given the inadequacy of her two-dimensional conception of justice, it follows that a complete theory of justice must be able to comprehend its specifically political aspects. In addition, in light of Fraser's critique of psychological foundationalism, I would argue that if a political theory of recognition chooses to include a psychological dimension, this must remain independent of cultural, economic and political dimensions. Finally, both Fraser and Honneth should accept that, while it may make sense to regard non-sectarianism as a regulative ideal, it is not wise to imagine that it will ever be possible to realize this ideal in practice. Only if a political theory of recognition were to take all of these points on board could it provide a comprehensive account of the necessary conditions of participation, and hence provide practical guidance in matters of justice.

6

Recognition and Democracy

6.1 Introduction

Since 1867, a number of seats in the New Zealand Parliament have been reserved for Maori representatives. For more than 120 years, there were four Maori seats; this number went up to five in 1993, six in 1999, and seven in 2002. Individuals who identify themselves as Maori can choose to be put on either the Maori or the general electoral roll. This means that some Maori legislators are elected by Maoris alone. Before 1993, this system of reserved seats operated alongside a first-past-the-post electoral system. But after extensive research, consultation and deliberation, New Zealand moved to a mixed member proportional system. This gave each citizen two votes – one for a local representative and one for a party list. With this system in operation, the number of seats held by each party is proportionate to its number of votes. These two elements of the New Zealand political system in conjunction – reserved Maori seats and the MMP electoral system – mean that today the proportion of Maori Members of Parliament roughly matches their proportion in the population at large.[1] This political set-up has a high level of support. Many regard it as the best way of ensuring fair political representation for all of New Zealand's citizens. Iris Young sees it as part of an exemplary case of 'differentiated solidarity', by which she means an ideal of integration which 'aims to balance values of generalized inclusion and respect with more particularist and local self-affirmation and expression' (2000: 221; cf. n. 38).[2] However, this political system is not without its critics.

For instance, Dr Don Brash, leader of New Zealand's National Party, spoke in 2004 about Maoris getting 'greater civil, political or democratic rights' than other New Zealanders, and about the 'divisive race-based features' of the political system.[3]

This brief sketch of some elements of New Zealand's political system gives us an important insight into the intimate relationship between recognition and democracy. One thing that individuals want recognition for is their identity as political actors. They do not just want to be respected as rationally autonomous agents, and to be esteemed for their distinctive identity or social contribution. They also want to enjoy the rights and powers of citizenship. Perhaps this particular form of recognition could be called 'representation'. Seen in this light, it is possible to understand why representation is always a key political battleground in a democratic political system. Who is to count as a citizen is perhaps the fundamental political question. Individuals and groups are continually striving to gain representation or to protect the representation they currently enjoy. Furthermore, since it is those currently inside the system who decide who should be represented, and how they should be represented, we could say that democracy determines recognition. At the same time, no democracy would exist if it did not provide at least a minimal level of representation for those over whom it claims authority. In this sense, we could say that recognition is a necessary condition of democracy itself. Putting the two sides of this analysis together, a conundrum appears. On the one hand, recognition is a necessary condition of democracy; without suitable recognition, democracy is impossible. On the other hand, it is democratic deliberation that determines the content of recognition; without democracy, recognition is unspecifiable. In short, democracy determines justice, but justice is a necessary condition of democracy. Following Nancy Fraser, I shall refer to this conundrum as the circularity of democratic justice. Since it is at the heart of the relationship between recognition and democracy, the exploration of this conundrum will be the central theme of this chapter.

All three political theorists of principal concern to me in this book are committed democrats. Fraser, Honneth and Taylor believe that a just society must be, amongst other things, a democratic society. All three of them endorse a version of the principle of democracy. They all believe that, since the laws of a polity significantly affect the sort of lives which citizens can lead, it is only right that they should have a say in the formulation of these laws. As James Tully puts it, *quod omnes tangit* – 'what touches all must be agreed to by all' – is a basic political principle in all constitutional democracies (2001: 24; cf. Habermas 1994: 112; Young 2000: 23). In addition, all three of them endorse the principal elements of the currently hegemonic model of democracy as a political system in which citizens vote periodically for representatives whose job is to help carry out their parties' manifestos. Fraser, Honneth and Taylor also agree that a democratic polity must have certain features, including individual freedoms such as those of speech and assembly, regular elections at various levels of government, a choice of parties and representatives in those elections, and an independent judiciary enforcing the rule of law (e.g. Young 2000: 18). However, the details of their preferred model of democracy, and the nature of the justification which they offer for that model, vary considerably. Each of them endorses his or her own particular conception of democracy as the context in which a politics of recognition can be located and claims for recognition adjudicated. Taylor draws on the republican political tradition in order to defend an account of democracy as 'participatory self-rule'. Fraser is committed to a strongly deliberative account of democracy, in which the content of justice can be determined only in democratic debate. For Honneth, democracy should be understood as a system of reflexive co-operation in which citizens consciously engage with their fellows in order to solve collective problems and achieve important human goods together.

Three features of these models of democracy are of particular importance if our aim is to understand their accounts of the relationship between democracy and recognition. The first concerns the relationship of democracy to society. Can a democratic political system be regarded as separate from the rest of society, or must it be seen to be rooted in some way in that society? Both Taylor and Honneth endorse the latter option, but Fraser provides some reasons for thinking that they should not do so. I want to know who is right. The second theme concerns the nature of political representation. It might be thought likely that as political theorists of recognition these three thinkers would be tempted to defend a system of group representation – at least as a supplement to a system of individual representation. As we shall see, however, none of them succumbs to this temptation, defending instead a model of democracy in which the individual citizen forms the basic unit of the political system. I want to find out why this is so. A third theme concerns what I shall call the status of the values of democracy. All three of these theorists seek to show that the realization of their models of democracy would not require a particular conception of the good to be imposed on all citizens, irrespective of their own particular ethical values. I want to determine whether any of them successfully makes their case. Having considered each of these three themes, I shall be in a position to examine the character of the relationship between democracy and recognition to be found in these models of democracy. As I have said, Fraser explicitly acknowledges that her conception of 'democratic justice' is circular: democracy determines justice, but justice is a necessary condition of democracy. I want to ask if this way of thinking about the relationship between democracy and recognition is coherent and defensible.

In this chapter, then, I want to understand how these three theorists' commitment to a particular account of recognition leads them to a particular model of democracy, and I want to assess the cogency of the case that each of them makes for the connection between this account and this model. The chapter is divided into the following sections. First, I sketch Taylor's ideal of democracy as participatory self-rule (6.2). Then I outline Honneth's social and political ideal of democracy as a system of reflexive co-operation (6.3). Following this, I show how Fraser articulates a version of deliberative democracy based on the normative standard of parity of participation (6.4). Having set out the essential features of these models, I shall discuss the three themes which I have just enumerated, considering their accounts of the nature of the political community, individual versus group representation, and the status of the values of democracy (6.5). At the end of the chapter, I shall reach a number of conclusions about the character and cogency of the links made between democracy and recognition in each model (6.6).

6.2   Charles Taylor: Participatory Self-rule

Taylor's ideal of democracy is a system of 'participatory self-government', or 'participatory self-rule' (1995b: 192, 199). In such a democracy, citizens take an active part in determining their common destiny together. If such an ideal is to be realized in practice, Taylor believes that it is necessary to modify the standard model of liberal democracy in certain specific ways. In her insightful account, Ruth Abbey suggests that he seeks to recover the deliberative aspects of the liberal tradition, and also to draw on the civic humanist account of politics, in order to give a much more significant role to 'debate, discussion and compromise' in political life (2000: 131). I shall suggest that Taylor identifies two conditions in particular which must be met if his ideal of participatory democracy is to be realized in practice. According to the first condition, the vigorous democratic participation of all citizens requires the inculcation of a sense of the common good and a sense of patriotic attachment to that good. A second necessary condition is that the unity necessary for such deliberation should not come at the price of unjust exclusion of some individuals from citizenship. By examining these two conditions in detail, it will be possible to understand why Taylor believes that genuine democratic decisions can be made only in circumstances in which all citizens are appropriately recognized.

With regard to the first of these conditions, Taylor argues that citizens must have a sense of themselves as a political community 'that shares some common purposes and recognizes its members as sharing in these purposes' (1995b: 276). All citizens must regard themselves as parts of a community, and they must recognize their fellows as other parts of that same community. In particular, this recognition takes the form of an acknowledgement that citizens have a number of goals in common. It is only by so doing that citizens can form a cohesive unit capable of engaging in meaningful deliberation together. As Taylor asks: 'If they are not mutually acquainted, or if they cannot really understand one another, how can they truly engage in joint deliberation?' (1998: 144). There is a further element to this first condition. In addition to seeing themselves as parts of a community of common purpose, citizens must also have a sense of patriotic identification with their polity. Such patriotism – defined as 'strong citizen identification around a sense of the common good' (1995b: 194) – provides citizens with reason to take part in democratic debate. As Taylor says, in a free regime, citizens' patriotism is the motivation for their public participation (1995b: 192–3). In short, he believes that, in the circumstances he describes, citizens have both the capacity and the motivation to engage in democratic deliberation together.

However, while Taylor maintains that a sense of collective identity is vital for a flourishing democracy, he is aware that this same argument can be used to justify the exclusion of some people from citizenship. There is, he says, 'something in the dynamic of democracy that pushes toward exclusion' (1998: 143). Taylor's thesis is that, although formally speaking, democracy is government of all the people by all the people, there is in practice a tendency for some citizens to be excluded from this process. This tendency arises from, and is justified by reference to, the idea that the body politic must have 'a strong collective identity' (1998: 144). If it is assumed that such an identity is a necessary condition of meaningful democratic dialogue, then the danger of exclusion arises from the belief that some groups, regarded as different in some way from the norm, threaten that necessary unity. Taylor highlights two principal modes of exclusion. First, a group may be denied formal citizenship since it is seen to be of a different ethnicity from the dominant group. Hence it is prevented from entering the democratic conversation, or it is expelled from it. The position of Turkish guest-workers in Germany would be a case in point here (1998: 143). For reasons that will become clear in a moment, this can be called a case of 'outer exclusion'. Second, a group that enjoys formal citizenship is nevertheless not able to take part in democratic deliberation. Here Taylor refers to the Jacobin tradition in France, which demands that all new citizens assimilate to existing cultural norms. He gives the example of 'the French overreaction to Muslim adolescents' wearing the veil in school' (1998: 147). This is a case of what Taylor himself calls 'inner exclusion' (1998: 148). Although those who suffer from this form of exclusion are formally a part of the citizen body, they are in practice unable to play a part in it.

Given this analysis of the 'dynamics of democratic exclusion', Taylor seeks to defend a model of democracy in which the sense of common identity necessary for participation does not unfairly exclude some people from citizenship. This means that the relevant conception of political community must be compatible with a wide diversity of identities. In order to achieve this goal, Taylor believes that it is necessary to rethink the relationship between identity and difference. He suggests that we try to see difference in complementary rather than competitive terms, so that we regard those who are different from ourselves as contributing something to the common good which we ourselves cannot provide. Thus differences should be regarded as reasons to join together rather than as things which should keep us apart; we should come together *because of,* not *in spite of,* our differences. Only in this way, Taylor contends, will a people be able to 'bond together in difference without abstracting from their differences' (1998: 153). Another way in which he describes the same idea is to say that it is a matter of 'sharing identity space' (1999: 281). To share such space is to find a new way of political belonging in which democracy can thrive without exclusion.

With these considerations in mind, it is possible to understand how Taylor's model of democracy and theory of recognition are related. In chapters 3 and 4, I sought to show that Taylor relies on a distinction, which he does not make wholly explicit or consistently clear, between two forms of recognition. I argued that this distinction between respect for autonomy and esteem for identity is necessary in order to make sense of his argument that, in certain circumstances, a polity can advance a conception of the good so long as it does not undermine individuals' fundamental liberties. Quebec, for instance, can take measures to defend its francophone culture without threatening its citizens' basic freedoms. To put this in terms of recognition, this province can find ways of esteeming its culture whilst still respecting individual citizens.[4] I want to suggest that, in the context of his model of democracy, we see Taylor once again trying to find a *via media* between these two forms of recognition.

I shall begin by considering recognition as esteem. I would suggest that there are two distinct forms of esteem to be found in Taylor's democratic model. The first is the one already familiar from my earlier discussion in chapter 4. This comes to the fore when Taylor takes pains to emphasize that, although all must be included in the political community, the price of entry should not be assimilation. Individuals and groups should not be compelled to conform to a narrowly defined conception of identity in order to gain citizenship. On this account, people are to be acknowledged for their distinctive identities, for what makes them different from others. As Taylor puts it, citizens must have a 'sense of being heard', which is only possible when 'they know themselves to be valued in a certain way' (1995b: 277). Explicitly using the language of recognition, he argues that a 'given point of view' should not be 'screened out and discounted in advance through prejudice or the nonrecognition of its protagonists' (1995b: 276). The second form of esteem has not been previously discussed in this book. This can be seen at work in Taylor's argument that a sense of political community is a necessary condition of an effectively functioning democracy. The implication of this argument is that each citizen must recognize all others as fellow members of their political community if they are to be able to engage in democratic deliberation together. It should be emphasized that, in this case, individuals and groups are not esteemed as distinctive individuals with their own identities. Rather, they are esteemed by virtue of the identity which they share with other members of their polity. In short, while the first form of esteem acknowledges what is unique about people, the second form acknowledges what they have in common.

Turning now to respect, I want to argue that there are also two distinct forms of this type of recognition to be found in Taylor's democratic model. The first of these is familiar from my analysis of his theory in chapter 3. There I showed why Taylor believes that respect should be shown to individuals in light of their capacity for autonomy. Individual rights are thus to be understood as means of protecting this autonomy. In the context of his model of democracy, he reaffirms the importance of this form of respect. Individual rights and freedoms are the necessary basis for a fully functioning participatory democracy (1995b: 199, 257–8). I would suggest, rather more tentatively, that it is possible to find a second form of respect in Taylor's account of democracy. Here the idea of autonomy familiar from the first form is shifted from the individual to the collective level. Just as individuals should be able to run their own lives, so whole bodies of citizens should be able collectively to determine their common fate. This idea can be seen in Taylor's characterization of 'democracy as a system of collective self-government' (1995b: 272). Perhaps we could say that, whilst an individual should be treated as a singular self-governor, a people should be treated as a collective self-governor. In both cases, it is assumed that individuals and peoples are treated with respect when they are able to determine the conditions under which they live. Thus Taylor's version of the principle of democracy can be understood as a collective version of recognition as respect. To argue for democracy is to argue that peoples – as well as individuals – should be respected. To bring this discussion to a close, we can see that Taylor regards recognition as a necessary precondition of democracy. Without the right sort of esteem and respect in place, democracy is impossible.

6.3   Axel Honneth: Reflexive Co-operation

Honneth's views on democracy are developed most fully in an article entitled 'Democracy as Reflexive Cooperation' (1998), which takes the form of a critical commentary on the American pragmatist John Dewey's account of democracy. Honneth emphasizes two aspects of democracy: first, it is a mode of political organization that can contribute to the rational solution of collective problems; and second, it is not only a mode of political organization, but is also rooted in society. In order to understand his perspective on democracy, it will be useful to begin by examining two other perspectives that Honneth rejects. In the first place, he dismisses a type of republicanism which he associates in particular with Hannah Arendt. He argues that, since such a model of democracy regards participation in political life as the highest human good, it is incompatible with the plurality of values to be found in contemporary societies (1998: 777). In other words, since many citizens do not consider political participation to be the most important aspect of their lives, a republican polity would be intolerant of their particular ways of living.[5] Furthermore, Honneth argues, Arendt's model does not provide criteria by which to judge therelative merits of different models of democracy (1998: 778). Here his point seems to be that republicanism declares every self-governing political community to be a democracy, without being able to judge whether any one of them is better than any other (Owen, forthcoming: MS9).

Honneth also rejects what he calls 'proceduralism', a model which contends that democracy is constituted by fair and just procedures that enable citizens to solve their problems in a rational and legitimate manner. According to Honneth, although this theory – which he associates with Jürgen Habermas – marks a considerable advance over republicanism, it still has significant problems. To begin with, he argues that Habermas's model is guilty of a 'one-sided restriction of democracy to the political sphere', since it assumes a 'politically constituted public sphere' in which citizens are able to exercise their autonomy (1998: 778–9). In making this assumption, he overlooks 'the prepolitical relations of socioeconomic equality' which must be present in order for citizens to be able to exercise that autonomy effectively. In other words, only if certain social and economic conditions are in place will citizens be able to take part in democratic deliberation. Furthermore, this model cannot explain why citizens might have a commitment to political participation. According to Honneth, Habermas must assume that they 'share so much common ground with all others that at least an interest can emerge in involving oneself actively in political affairs'. Habermas is forced to assume such an interest since he fears that, if he tried to explain why citizens have a commitment to democracy, he would be endorsing what Honneth calls an 'ethical understanding of politics' (1998: 779).

The reasons that Honneth gives for rejecting these two models of democracy impose certain requirements on his own model. In light of his critique of republicanism, his model (1) must be compatible with the value pluralism to be found in contemporary societies, and (2) must provide criteria for assessing the relative merits of different democratic models. Given his rejection of proceduralism, it follows that his alternative (3) must not be restricted to the political sphere, and (4) must explain why citizens would want to engage in democratic deliberation. These two pairs of requirements provide the rationale for the two principal aspects of Honneth's model of democracy. I now consider each of these aspects in turn.

As Honneth observes, Dewey's case for democracy is based on two interrelated but distinct arguments. One of these is what he calls an 'epistemological argument' (1998: 773). This begins with a particular understanding of the character of scientific endeavour. Dewey believes that scientific progress will be more certain, the greater the number of researchers concerned with a particular problem, and the more freely they are able to make a contribution to the analysis of that problem. He similarly regards democracy as a method by which a public can solve its collective problems. By analogy, the more citizens included in public debate about these problems, and the more freely they can make contributions to that debate, the more rational the solutions that will emerge from it. Here Honneth finds an argument for making as many individuals as possible citizens, and an argument for ensuring that the status of citizenship comes with guaranteed civil, political and social rights, so that citizens can make an effective contribution to democratic deliberation. The greater the extent to which these two conditions are met, the more rational the democracy.[6]

In addition to the epistemological argument, Dewey also emphasizes the role that the experience of communal co-operation must play in a democracy. Honneth endorses this idea, arguing that a healthy democracy is one in which citizens have the everyday experience of making their own contribution to the common good.[7] More specifically, a democratic political system is one in which citizens consciously co-ordinate their actions in a way beneficial to all members of society. Thus democracy is a system of 'reflexive co-operation'. For Dewey, communal co-operation takes the form of a just division of labour. On his account, so Honneth argues, 'democratic ethical life' is 'the outcome of the experience that all members of society could have if they related to each other cooperatively through a just organizing of the division of labour' (1998: 780). In other words, if the economy is arranged so that each individual is able to make his or her own unique and valuable contribution to the social good, and each recognizes that their fellow citizens make their own particular contributions likewise, then they would each be able to regard their fellows as part of the same co-operative community. Whilst Honneth endorses the spirit of this idea, he argues that today this cannot be achieved simply through 'a normatively inspired restructuring of the capitalist labor market' (1998: 780). It is not possible for everyone to make a contribution to society simply through the paid labour that they do. Instead, society must be arranged in such a way that all members of the democratic polity can have the opportunity to make a contribution to the common good.[8]

Bringing these two aspects of Honneth's model together, we can see that democracy as a 'reflexive form of community cooperation' (1998: 765) combines elements found in the alternatives to political liberalism that Honneth rejects. As in proceduralism, there is an emphasis on the rationality of deliberation; and, as in republicanism, there is an emphasis on the importance of political community. We can also see how Honneth's model of democracy meets the four requirements he sets. First, since this model avoids imposing a single set of values on all citizens, it is compatible with value pluralism. Although there is, and must be, a conception of the common good, each individual relates to this conception as a 'higher-order value'. Thus a regime endorsing this common good is tolerant of all citizens' specific sets of values. Second, the epistemological argument for democracy provides a way of judging the relative merits of different democratic models. As we have seen, Honneth believes that the more citizens are included in deliberation, and the more effectively they are included, the more rational the solutions they can achieve to their collective problems. Third, Honneth's model meets the requirement to locate democracy in society as well as in the public sphere. As he says, on his account, democracy is a social ideal as well as a political ideal (1998: 780). In other words, it is rooted firmly in a particular account of social relations as well as describing a particular set of political arrangements. Fourth, this model of democracy is also able to explain citizens' motivation. Honneth argues that the experience of co-operative endeavour gives citizens reason to participate in the democratic life of their polity.

In light of these reflections, it is possible to understand how Honneth's model of democracy and his theory of recognition are connected. To begin with, recall that two of the necessary conditions of his ideal of self-realization have 'development potential'. Different social and political arrangements can make it more or less likely that individuals will enjoy self-respect and self-esteem. We can now identify the elements of Honneth's democratic model which correspond to these two aspects of self-realization. Here David Owen's analysis provides a useful way forward: 'what form of polity', he asks, 'would secure the intersubjective conditions of each [aspect] taken by itself'? (Forthcoming: MS 16.)[9] First, imagine a democratic ideal that focuses exclusively on respect. For Owen, this would point to 'a *proceduralist* conception of the democratic polity in which individuals are regarded as equal persons in a sovereign association' (forthcoming: MS 17). In such a polity, more respect can be shown, and more self-respect can be achieved, to the extent that individual rights are generalized (so that more individuals are included as citizens) and de-formalized (so that those citizens enjoy substantial basic rights). Now imagine a democratic ideal that was concerned only with esteem. This would suggest 'a (classical) *republican* conception of the democratic polity in which individuals are regarded as equal members of a self-governing political community' (forthcoming: MS 17). In this sort of polity, more esteem can be shown, and more self-esteem can be achieved, to the extent that the conditions of esteem are individualized (so that individuals, rather than collectives, are the objects of esteem) and equalized (so that social esteem is a matter of pluralism rather than hierarchy).[10]

As we know, Honneth's 'formal conception of ethical life' seeks to make space for *both* of these aspects of recognition, arguing that neither on its own would be sufficient to ensure that individuals could achieve full self-realization. It is for this reason that Honneth endorses what Owen describes as 'a political ideal of radical democracy which combines a commitment to securing democratic procedures of rational deliberation' with 'a commitment to democratic political community' (forthcoming: MS 17). It is clear, then, that recognition as respect and recognition as esteem play key roles in Honneth's model of democracy. Whilst the one-sided proceduralist conception of the democratic polity would provide what Owen calls 'the maximal conditions of the experience of respect-recognition', and the one-sided republican conception would provide 'the maximal conditions of the experience of esteem-recognition', only Honneth's synthesized ideal would create the conditions in which both respect and esteem could be maximized. It is only if all citizens are fully included, and all are properly valued, that they will be able to achieve full self-realization. Hence there is a very close connection between Honneth's formal conception of ethical life and his model of democracy. For Owen, indeed, Honneth's account of democracy as reflexive cooperation 'is simply the expression of this formal conception of ethical life as a social and political ideal' (forthcoming: MS 18; cf. Markell 2003: 3).

6.4   Nancy Fraser: Radical Democracy

In previous chapters, we saw that Fraser defends a theory of social justice in which the principle of 'parity of participation' plays a central part. She believes that, in order for such parity to be achieved, two conditions must be met. The objective condition requires a particular distribution of resources, and the intersubjective condition requires a particular pattern of cultural values. Together these conditions ensure that all individuals are able to participate in society on an equal footing with others. This is as far as my presentation of Fraser's theory has gone hitherto. As a result, it has left a number of important questions unasked, prominent amongst which are the following. First, who is to decide how best to meet these two conditions? Second, how is this decision to be reached? It is in answer to these questions that Fraser gives a vital role to democracy. To be specific, she adopts what she calls 'a modified version of the standpoint of democratic justice', according to which justice can be determined only in democratic debate (2003: 72; cf. Shapiro 1999). From this standpoint, there is no yardstick independent of democratic procedures which can be used to measure justice. Only by following the correct deliberative procedures can we determine what justice requires. The rationale underlying this conception of democratic justice is the same as that underlying ideas of democratic legitimacy. Thus, Fraser argues, if a principle of justice is to obligate those people to whom it is intended to apply, then they must have a say in determining that principle (2003: 44). As we shall see in a moment, they have such a say in democratic processes of public deliberation.

Fraser is aware that this account of democratic justice must confront an important problem of circularity. On the one hand, two vital preconditions of inclusive deliberation are fair redistribution and recognition. That is to say, only if all citizens have sufficient economic resources and adequate social standing can they play a full part in democratic deliberation. Absent such resources and standing, their voices will not be heard, and their perspectives will be overlooked. On the other hand, in order to determine what just redistribution and recognition are, there must be inclusive deliberation. *Ex hypothesi*, only if all citizens play a full part in democratic deliberation can we know what economic and cultural justice require (2003: 42–3). To bring these two sides of the circle together, it is necessary for all citizens to participate in democratic debate in order to determine how the norm of parity of participation should be applied; but the very reason for applying the norm is to remove the obstacles to full participation. In short, inclusive deliberation requires just redistribution and recognition; but just redistribution and recognition require inclusive deliberation. Fraser does not believe that this circularity constitutes a fatal weakness in her argument. Rather, she suggests, it simply gives expression to the 'reflexive character of justice as understood from the democratic perspective' (2003: 44). In other words, circularity is exactly what one would expect of a conception of democratic justice. Fraser shows how this circularity manifests itself in practice by pointing to situations in which second-order claims are raised 'about the conditions in which first-order claims are adjudicated'. In such circumstances, citizens seeking to determine the appropriate policy in particular circumstances may end up asking whether all those who need to be included in this debate are in fact able to take part. In this way, the prevailing criteria for citizenship and the rules of inclusion in the sphere of democracy are called into question. Thus, Fraser claims, 'one expresses the reflexivity of democratic justice in the process of struggling to realize it practically' (2003: 44).

In light of this conception of justice, Fraser is able to specify the role of democracy in her theory of recognition. She argues that the purpose of democratic deliberation is to apply the norm of participatory parity to particular cases. Indeed, she insists that this norm 'must be applied dialogically and discursively, through democratic processes of public debate' (2003: 43; cf. 2001: 41 n. 19). Without such debate, there would be no way of knowing what justice requires. In practice, applying the standard of participatory parity dialogically will involve a number of closely interrelated tasks. The first of these is to test the validity of claims for recognition (and redistribution) in order to decide which claims are just. As Fraser says, 'the status model submits claims for recognition to democratic processes of public justification' (2000: 119). For example, a particular social group may demand the public recognition of its religion since it claims that without such recognition its members cannot participate on a par with other citizens. It is then the task of the democratic public to decide whether this claim is just. In order to do so, citizens will also have to engage in a second task. As Fraser puts it, they must deliberate 'about how best to implement the requirements of justice' (2003: 70). That is to say, citizens will have to decide which practical measures are necessary to secure parity of participation. This will involve *inter alia* determining the effects of specific policies in practice. An example that Fraser uses here is *l'affaire foulard* which has been mentioned in earlier chapters. One purpose of democratic debate in this particular case would be to determine the effects of wearing the foulard on the status of Muslim girls (2003: 42; cf. 2001: 41 n. 18). If it presents an obstacle to their ability to participate as peers, then it is incompatible with justice. However, if it is simply an expression of their religious and/or cultural identity, no different from wearing a cross or a yarmulka, then it is compatible with justice. Bringing these various tasks together, we can say that, for Fraser, the role of democratic deliberation is to determine the content of justice.

From what I have said so far, it may appear as if the citizens of a democracy have licence to make whatever decisions they wish. Things are not quite as straightforward as this, however. It is important to emphasize that, for Fraser, democratic deliberation must work within one particular, strictly defined constraint. This is the standard of parity of participation itself. The range of 'policies and programs' (2003: 72) from which citizens make their choices must be compatible with this standard. It is not open to them to make decisions which would make it harder for some people to participate on an equal footing with others. Fraser is most explicit about this constraint on democracy when recommending a division of labour between those she calls 'philosophers', on the one hand, and democratic citizens, on the other (2003: 72). She argues that the role of philosophers is to engage in the conceptual analysis of parity of participation, and in particular to determine the range of laws, policies and institutions which are compatible with that standard. Thus they may judge that both the institutionalization of gay marriage and the de-institutionalization of straight marriage, both allowing the wearing of the foulard and banning the display of all religious symbols in state-funded schools, are all compatible with participatory parity. It is only when the range of options compatible with participatory parity has been determined that citizens take over. It is then their task to engage in democratic debate in order to make a choice within this set of options. As Fraser says, while the task of philosophers is to delimit the set of political options which are 'compatible with the requirements of justice', it must be left to citizens themselves to decide collectively between these options (2003: 72).[11] In making this distinction between the work of philosophers and that of citizens, Fraser contends that she has limited the role of philosophy in order to maximize the role of democratic citizens.

Given this constrained role for citizens, what does democratic deliberation actually look like? Fraser argues that, in such deliberation, parity of participation becomes the *'principal idiom of public reason'*, the 'preferred language for conducting democratic political argumentation' (2003: 43). When citizens meet to discuss their collective problems, they use the terminology of participatory parity in order to guide their discussions. Furthermore, in these deliberations, citizens are guided by 'some heuristics' (2003: 72) which are derived from this normative standard. To be specific, deliberators must accept that recognition and redistribution are both fundamental. They must also take what Fraser calls the 'problem of the frame' into account: they must ask who the subjects of justice are, and decide which issues are best dealt with at regional, national and global levels (2003: 87–8). The standard of parity thus sets the terms on which democratic deliberation takes place, and it is the principal source of guidance on judgements about the justice of particular policies and actions. It specifies the range of options compatible with justice, and also guides choice within that range. Operating within these constraints, democratic deliberation is a matter of 'hermeneutical reflection on matters that are context-specific, including what citizens value in addition to justice, given their histories, traditions, and collective identities' (2003: 72). In other words, so long as they work with the language of participatory parity in the manner just specified, citizens can introduce arguments drawing on their own values in order to argue for particular laws, policies and institutional arrangements.

Fraser uses this account of democracy as part of the justification for her theory of recognition. In earlier chapters, I considered why she believes that such a theory should be based on the principle of parity of participation. It is worth recalling that much of the justification for this standard depends on the claim that it is 'deontological' (2001: 31).[12] Since citizens endorse different and often conflicting sets of values, it is essential that they establish a common standard which they can use to order their lives together. It is now possible to see how this social co-ordination is to be achieved in practice. Procedures of democratic deliberation, guided by the standard of participatory parity, provide the method by which citizens are able to order their lives together in a way consistent with the requirements of justice. That is to say, through suitably constrained democratic deliberation, citizens can determine the conditions of their collective existence. With this in mind, let us return finally to Fraser's account of the relationship between democracy and recognition. We can now see what she means by emphasizing the circularity of her conception of democratic justice. Beginning at one point on the circle, it appears that democracy determines justice. In democratic deliberation, citizens decide who should get what sort of recognition. Beginning on the opposite side of the circle, however, it seems that justice constrains democracy. Citizens cannot choose to treat people in ways that violate the norm of parity of participation. They cannot, for instance, pass a law which lowers some people's social standing below an acceptable minimal level. In a phrase, democracy determines justice, but justice constrains democracy.

6.5 A Critical Comparison

Up to this point, I have presented the essential elements of three models of democracy. In this section, I present a critical analysis of these models which revolves around three closely intertwined but distinguishable themes. First, I analyse their rival interpretations of the nature of the political community. Then I compare their different reasons for favouring individual rather than group representation. Finally, I consider their competing understandings of the status of the values of democracy.

The Nature of Political Community

As I have explained, both Taylor and Honneth believe that the sphere of democratic deliberation must stand in a particular kind of relationship to society as a whole. In order for democracy to flourish, the character of social relations outside the political system must take a particular form. Whilst Taylor thinks that citizens must have at least some goods in common in order to bind them together into a political community, Honneth believes that it is vital for the health of democracy for people in their daily lives to understand that they are making a contribution to societal goals. In slightly different ways, then, both of these theorists think that the health of democracy depends on individual citizens playing their own particular part in their polity. Taylor argues that individuals should come together to form a political community precisely because they are different. Honneth contends that individuals deserve esteem in virtue of traits and abilities which enable them to make a distinctive contribution to societal goals. A shared assumption of both of these accounts appears to be that the relevant differences and contributions will be both compatible and complementary. In other words, no difference or contribution will conflict with any other, and all of them will fit together to form an integrated whole. This could be called a 'symphonic' idea of political community: just as a symphony orchestra needs brass, woodwind, string and percussion players to form a harmonious whole, so a thriving democracy needs citizens who each have a complementary role to play in their political community.

Two criticisms of these closely related accounts are particularly pertinent in the context of a discussion of the politics of recognition.[13] First, it may be argued that they present an over-optimistic picture of the relationships between citizens in modern democratic polities, in which the possibility of harmonious co-operation is greatly exaggerated. In complex modern polities, the fact of pluralism means that what Taylor refers to as 'common purposes' (1995b: 276), and what Honneth refers to as 'societal goals' (1995: 122), do not exist. Against the idea that all individuals have complementary contributions to make, it may be argued that there is an important range of cases in which such contributions conflict with one another. Whilst one group may be in favour of the legalization of same-sex marriage, another group may be bitterly opposed to such a change. Whilst one group may support the ban on the wearing of religious symbols in schools, another group may struggle vigorously against such a ban. Furthermore, the assumption that there is a common good to which all citizens can contribute brings its own dangers. Here Joseph Schumpeter's critique of what he calls the 'classical doctrine of democracy' comes to mind. He suggests that, according to this doctrine, 'there exists a Common Good, the obvious beacon light of policy, which is always simple to define and which every normal person can be made to see by means of rational argument' (1942: 250). Schumpeter argues that this idea of a common good overlooks the fact that the many different values to be found in modern societies cannot be rationally reconciled. In this case, he concludes, this idea is a dangerous illusion which can serve to legitimate the self-interested actions of rulers who can suggest that their actions are undertaken in the name of people as a whole. To put this in terms of the current argument, the idea that there are 'common purposes', or 'societal goals', can legitimate the non-recognition of those individuals and groups whose conceptions of the good are incompatible with those purposes or goals.[14]

The first part of this criticism can be put aside fairly quickly. It is wrong to suggest that any political disagreement must undermine a sense of common purpose. In extreme circumstances, of course, a society can be torn apart by political disagreement. But in all circumstances short of such extremes, political disagreement is simply a part of the normal business of democracy. It could even be argued, extending Honneth's argument slightly, that each particular political perspective makes a distinctive contribution to the whole. The second part of this criticism cannot be dismissed so easily. Here it is worth distinguishing between two different claims that could be attributed to Taylor and Honneth. First, a healthy democracy must have a strong sense of common purpose. Second, each citizen must think of him or herself as making a distinctive contribution to that purpose. I would accept the first claim. To reject it, one would have to argue that a polity can survive without any sense of common purpose. It is the assumption that such a sense is needed which underlies a range of popular political practices, including civic education, citizenship ceremonies and pledges of allegiance. By contrast, I would reject the second claim. I think that, while a sense of common purpose is required, this need not be understood in terms of distinctive and complementary contributions. In this case, it might be useful to recast the language of commonality. Talk of 'common purposes' and 'shared goals' sounds highly teleological, suggesting the idea of a polity in which citizens come together in order to achieve their common aims. Michael Oakeshott's idea of a civil association can be used to show that no such aim is required. According to Ian Tregenza, 'civil association can be understood as association governed by noninstrumental rules, or association devoid of an extrinsic purpose' (2004: 6). In a civil association, individuals join together without believing that any common purpose gives them reason to do so. Indeed, as Tregenza continues, Oakeshott believes that 'the freedom of *cives* "is not tied to a choice to be and to remain associated in terms of a common purpose: it is neither more nor less than the absence of such a purpose or choice"' (2004: 9, citing Oakeshott 1975: 158). If we think of the modern democratic polity as a civil association, it might be possible to imagine citizens coming together to deliberate in order to determine their common fate, without thinking that they share any common purpose beyond this. Hence, I would suggest, it is possible to defend Taylor's and Honneth's thesis about the necessity of shared purposes by giving such purposes a less teleological reading.

The second criticism of Taylor's and Honneth's account of political community suggests, not that some citizens will have contributions to make which are in direct conflict with those of others, but that some of them will not have a contribution to make at all. If the lack of something to contribute means that citizens do not have an incentive to participate in deliberation, then a problem of motivation arises. In order to appreciate the import of this criticism, recall Honneth's contention that there is no automatic entitlement to esteem. Rather, he argues, citizens should have equal opportunities to earn esteem.[15] Earlier in this chapter, however, I considered his argument that the experience of esteem is necessary in order to give individuals reason to participate in politics. Putting these two points together, it follows that, if some individuals do not successfully win esteem, they will lack a motive to participate in politics. Since they are not valued, they will have no reason to engage in democratic debate. The worst consequence of this could be a vicious downward spiral of increasing marginalization and decreasing self-esteem. It may be that disaffected young people and ethnic minorities find themselves in this category (Young 2000: 144). As we have seen, Honneth's hope is that, since esteem is individualized and equalized in modern societies, there is every chance for individuals to earn esteem. He knows, however, that such esteem cannot be guaranteed. Hence, if his thesis about the motivating power of esteem is true, then it is very likely that at least some citizens will be culturally unvalued and will therefore feel politically marginalized.[16]

If it is accepted that the problem of motivation is real and serious, and if it is accepted that such motivation is weakened if citizens are not esteemed, then one possible way out might be to defend an automatic entitlement to esteem. As I argued in chapter 4, however, such a notion is absurd. In this case, absent such an entitlement, there is a very real chance that some citizens will not be esteemed. Another possible way out might be to show that esteem and motivation are not linked in the way that Honneth imagines. To be specific, in order to show that a lack of esteem does not undermine motivation, it is necessary to show that other sources of motivation exist. At this point, several possibilities present themselves. It could be argued that the citizens of modern democracies are motivated – and, in a limited sense, united – by enlightened self-interest. According to this thesis, each individual thinks that it is better to follow certain procedures of dispute resolution rather than abandon these procedures for bloody anarchy. From this perspective, democracy can be understood as a set of minimal procedures designed to co-ordinate action and resolve disputes, rather than a means of determining an illusory common good. However, the problem with such an account of motivation is well known. For it to be persuasive, it is essential that co-operation remains in every individual's self-interest. If it ceases to be so, then individuals who have nothing to gain thereby will have no reason to continue to participate in the affairs of – or even to stay loyal to – their polity. A second possibility could again draw inspiration from Oakeshott's idea of a civil association. From this perspective, the motivation to participate could be explained as a duty to help secure the continued existence of the association, rather than a desire to contribute to the common good. The problem here is to explain where this duty comes from, and to show why people have good reason to comply with it. A third possibility would be to turn to an account of motivation which relies on the idea of recognition, but not the specific conception of esteem that has been assumed up to this point. Here it seems to me that there are two options. The first would be to broaden the conception of contribution, just as I sought to do in section 4.5, so that esteem may be due in light of the contribution which a distinctive culture makes to the culture of society as a whole. By so doing, it would become more likely that most citizens would experience esteem. The second option would be to rely on an idea of respect, rather than esteem. In this case, the idea would be that in a polity in which all citizens were shown due respect, they would, as a result of experiencing such respect, have sufficient motivation to participate in democratic deliberation. A detailed exploration of these various possibilities would take me beyond the bounds of this book.

Individual versus Group Representation

One implication of the case-study with which this chapter began is that there may be circumstances in which it is appropriate to single out particular groups of citizens for special treatment regarding the way they are represented in the political system. In the case in question, the rationale for the system of reserved seats for the Maori in the New Zealand Parliament is that it is necessary in order to ensure that all citizens enjoy fair representation. It could be argued, however, that this justification for special treatment goes against the principle of political equality which lies at the heart of democracy, according to which all individual citizens are to count for one, and no one for more than one. Seen in this light, special representation stands in need of special justification. There are a number of contemporary political theorists who do claim to offer such justification. Prominent among them are Will Kymlicka, who argues for what he calls 'special representation rights' (1995: 31–2), and Iris Young, who defends 'the special representation of groups' (2000: 122). It is interesting to note, however, that none of the three theorists on whom I have chosen to focus engage with this idea of group representation. Instead, their accounts of democracy focus on the individual citizen as the basic unit of that system. In this subsection, I want to determine whether Kymlicka's and Young's justifications for group representation should persuade Taylor, Honneth and Fraser to adopt such political practices themselves.

To begin with Kymlicka, he contends that there are two possible grounds for special representation rights. First, they may be necessary in order to ensure that a 'national minority' is able to be self-governing (1995: 142). Second, they may be necessary in order to overcome 'some systemic disadvantage or barrier in the political process which makes it impossible for the group's views and interests to be effectively represented' (1995: 141). For the purposes of the current argument, I shall put the first rationale aside, since it opens up whole new cans of worms. Regarding the second rationale, Kymlicka discusses several complications which must be faced. With regard to reserved seats in particular, he asks which groups should be so represented, how many seats they should have, and how representatives can be accountable to those who elect them (1995: 144–7). In the light of these complications, he concludes that a case for special representation – including reserved seats – can be made, but that this is best seen as 'a temporary measure on the way to a society where the need for special representation no longer exists' (1995: 141).

Young's defence of the special representation of groups can be seen as part of her argument for '*differentiated* citizenship', by which she means a form of political membership in which some people are incorporated not just as individuals but also as members of particular groups (1989: 251). Famously in *Justice and the Politics of Difference*, she proposes that 'a democratic public should provide mechanisms for the effective recognition and representation of the distinct voices and perspectives of those of its constituent groups that are oppressed or disadvantaged'. To be specific, there should be public funding for 'self-organization of group members', 'group analysis and group representation of policy proposals in institutionalized contexts', and 'group veto regarding specific policies that affect a group directly' (1990: 184). A decade later, in her *Inclusion and Democracy*, Fraser says that young has 'bracketed' the third of these proposals, since it has proved 'particularly controversial' (2000: 144 n. 27); but she still defends modified versions of the first two. Responding to the 'frequently heard complaint' that existing 'norms of representation' do not fairly represent all groups in the political system (2000: 121), she defends a system of 'group representation' which she characterizes as 'differentiated group practices as an important enactment of political inclusion'. To be specific, her argument is that group representation is able to facilitate the inclusion of 'otherwise excluded or marginalized social perspectives' in public discussion (2000: 123). She discusses a range of means of achieving such representation, including not only reserved seats, but also quotas in party lists, redistricting, multi-member constituencies and proportional representation (2000: 148–53). Her conclusion is that in particular circumstances each of these means may be an appropriate way of ensuring fair representation.

As I have suggested, none of the three theorists of particular interest to me in this book entertains the possibility that demands for recognition may entail a need for group representation. Certainly, all of them are concerned about the ways in which individuals may suffer political marginalization and exclusion; and all of them have specific proposals to make about how such problems may be overcome. Taylor emphasizes the need for a sense of political community which does not exclude particular citizens. Honneth argues that all citizens must be formally included in democratic deliberation, and must enjoy the capacities they need to take an active part in such deliberation. Fraser now accepts that there is a third, political dimension of justice, according to which citizens should not be excluded by, for instance, 'single-member distinct winner-takes-all electoral rules that deny voice to quasi-permanent minorities' (2003: 68). But this acknowledgement does not lead her to the conclusion that such 'quasi-permanent minorities' should enjoy special representation. Indeed, I have argued that all three theorists' gazes generally remain fixed on the individual citizen. Taylor defends fundamental individual rights, arguing that measures to protect cultures can only override other 'privileges and immunities' (3.5). While he can be read as endorsing the idea that cultural survival is a legitimate political goal, I have suggested that he is better interpreted as allowing people to defend their cultures by ordinary democratic means (4.5). Honneth is adamant that only individuals can enjoy respect by bearing rights (3.3), and he insists that the shift from a collective to an individualized system of esteem is a matter of moral progress (4.3). While he is tempted to introduce a fourth mode of recognition for cultural identity, he never makes this an integral part of his theory (4.5). Fraser explicitly rejects group rights (3.5), and emphasizes that it is individuals who are to enjoy parity of participation.

Are these three thinkers right to ignore calls for group representation? Are their reasons for focusing on individual citizens also reasons to rule out special provision for groups? Even Kymlicka and Young, although they both defend group representation, raise concerns about its consequences. 'Reserving seats for particular groups', Young worries, 'can tend to freeze both the identity of that group and its relations with other groups in the polity' (2000: 149). She is also concerned that such measures will have the perverse consequence of perpetuating the marginalization of the group, and will make it difficult to ensure that holders of the reserved seats are accountable to their electors (2000: 150). Kymlicka points out the difficulties of correctly identifying marginalized groups, suggesting that, on Young's scheme, 80 per cent of the US population would have to be included (1995: 145). He also raises concerns about the lines of accountability between groups and their special representatives (1995: 147–8). To this list we can add Fraser's concern that the instantiation of group rights entrenches 'status distinctions in forms that are difficult to change' (2003: 82).

Might these drawbacks outweigh the advantages of group representation? I would suggest that it depends on the exact nature of the scheme being proposed. To explain, consider a number of features of the Maori system. First, the number of reserved seats is not fixed. It increased from four in 1867 to seven today. There is no reason why this number cannot be changed again. This answers part of the worry about the freezing effect of such schemes on relations between this particular group and others in the polity. Second, it would be possible in principle for a non-Maori to be elected to a Maori reserved seat. There is no crude assumption that individuals can be represented only by someone with the same identity. This answers part of the worry about the freezing effect of such schemes on group identities. Third, to be on the Maori electoral roll, one only has to be self-identified as Maori. There is no suggestion that there could be a return to the system prior to 1975 in which people were classified as Maori if at least one parent was 'full-blood'. This feature also undermines the concern that the scheme would have the effect of 'essentializing' identities. Fourth, given the two distinct electoral rolls, it is possible for some Maori representatives to be elected by Maoris alone. Kymlicka suggests that this may answer the concern about accountability, since it will be clear that these representatives are accountable to the Maori (1995: 147–8). Fifth, the whole system of reserved seats could be abolished. Indeed, if in the future the effect of the MMP electoral system introduced in 1993 was to further increase the number of Maori legislators elected through the main electoral system, then the rationale for reserved seats would gradually wither away. Once more, this answers the charge that such a scheme locks the group into unchanging relations with others in the polity. From these reflections, I conclude that in particular circumstances group representation may be a necessary and legitimate supplement to individual representation. It may be justified in order to guarantee that all interests and perspectives within a given polity enjoy equal voice. In this sense, group representation can be seen as recognition transposed to the sphere of democracy.

The Status of Democratic Values

All three theorists on whom I have focused in this book seek to show that the advocacy of their particular model of democracy is compatible with the diversity of ethical values to be found in modern pluralistic societies. All of them believe that there are high stakes involved here. If it is not possible to provide what Fraser would call a 'nonsectarian' justification for a model of democracy, then some citizens will experience a conflict between their own values and the values of democracy. In this case, the model in question will not be able to provide a set of procedures that can be used to co-ordinate citizens' actions in a way that is consistent with the requirements of justice. For this reason, Taylor, Fraser and Honneth all attempt to show that a non-sectarian justification for their particular model of democracy can be provided. It is my purpose in this subsection to determine whether any of them is successful.

To begin with Honneth, I showed in section 6.3 why he believes that his model of democracy can explain why citizens will wish to participate in democratic deliberation by reference to their experience of communal co-operation. In that section, I referred to his remark that Habermas is forced to assume citizens' interest in political participation since he is concerned that any attempt to explain such an interest – or perhaps to give reasons for having such an interest – would involve endorsing an 'ethical understanding of politics' (1998: 779). In light of this remark, it is necessary to ask if Honneth avoids the problem that concerns Habermas. If the sense of community embodied in the experience of reflexive co-operation is compatible with value pluralism, then there would be no problem for Honneth to deal with. This, however, does not seem likely. Fraser's criticism – considered in section 5.4 – that Honneth fails to steer a course successfully between 'the requirements of nonsectarianism and determinacy' (2003: 225) suggests that he fails to avoid this problem. In this case, if the sense of community he invokes does embody a particular ethical vision which at least some citizens will not be able to endorse, then they will find that their particular values clash with those values associated with the political community itself.

Honneth, like Taylor, is concerned about this charge of sectarianism. He explicitly rejects the republican model of democracy which makes 'political participation itself . . . a central part of the lives of all society's members'. 'Such a strong ethicization of politics', he argues, is 'scarcely compatible with the actual value pluralism of modern societies' (1998: 777). Hence, in order to avoid such an 'ethicization of politics', an acceptable model of democracy must be compatible with the pluralism of values to be found in contemporary societies. Talking about Dewey's theory, Honneth suggests that the American pragmatist faces the same problem, wanting to reconcile 'the factual pluralism of value orientations' with the need for 'an individual orientation toward a jointly shared good'. The solution which he believes Dewey favours is to understand the latter 'as that end to which each individual must be able to relate in the sense of a higher-order value' (1998: 778). Honneth's hope is that he can use the same solution himself. In this way, he believes, a suitably modified version of Dewey's theory of democracy 'opens a third avenue' between 'an overethicized republicanism and an empty proceduralism' (1998: 780). It does so by regarding 'democratic ethical life' as the outcome of the experience of co-operative participation in social life.

It seems to me that there are two distinct ideas at play here. The first is the claim that the higher-order value of democracy trumps all lower-order values to be found in particular ethical outlooks. The second is the claim that the experience of reflexive co-operation provides citizens with non-sectarian reasons for accepting the legitimacy of their particular democratic system. With regard to the first claim, let me consider a specific example. If I am both a Catholic and a democrat, then at those points at which my religious and political commitments clash, I will accept that the latter should override the former. I may, for instance, accept the legality of divorce despite my own moral convictions, since the law governing divorce was passed in accordance with democratic procedures that I endorse. In a sense, I am both against and in favour of divorce.[17] If this 'trumping' argument worked, then Honneth would be able to demonstrate that his model of democracy is compatible with value pluralism. Either citizens' particular preferences and democratic outcomes would cohere; or, if they did not, citizens would allow the democratic outcome to trump their own preferences. However, against Honneth, I would contend that this argument is more an expression of hope than a presentation of reasons for thinking that citizens will accept the priority of justice. Of course, many citizens in modern pluralist societies do frequently rank their commitment to democracy above their own particular commitments. But all the interesting and problematic cases occur when they do not. Simply to state that citizens will relate to the common good as a higher-order value is not to give a substantive reason for thinking that they will.

This leads us to the second claim. Here Honneth may provide a reason by arguing that citizens' awareness that they are co-operating by making their own contributions to societal goals gives them good cause to accept the priority of the democratic system that embodies those societal goals. Unfortunately, my argument in the first subsection of 6.5 tells against this possibility. There I suggested that Honneth – and Taylor – greatly exaggerate the possibility of harmonious co-operation between the citizens of modern democratic polities. Either each citizen's particular contributions to societal goals conflicts with the contributions of others; or, more strongly, such goals do not exist. Hence there is little possibility of an experience of reflexive co-operation which could lead citizens to accept the legitimacy of their democratic community. I sought to preserve the essence of Honneth's – and Taylor's – argument by reinterpreting their idea of an awareness of societal goals as an awareness of sharing a common fate. However, since the latter notion is deliberately less substantive than the former, it does not seem likely that the awareness of a common fate would provide a good enough reason for citizens to allow democratic values to trump their own.

It will come as no surprise to find that Fraser is also concerned about the potential clash between democratic values and other values that citizens reasonably hold. After all, it is her term 'non-sectarian' that I have used to frame this discussion. Fraser's own solution to this problem is to restrict the range of options between which citizens can choose. As we saw in section 6.4, citizens deliberate together in order to determine whether particular claims for recognition (and redistribution) are justified. However, it must be emphasized that they only have the power to decide between a range of options, all of which are compatible with the principle of parity of participation. They cannot choose options which lie outside this range, and they cannot choose the principle itself. Indeed, Fraser's account of a division of labour between philosophers and citizens suggests that philosophers could rule certain claims and proposals out of court before they ever came to democratic debate. Consider, for example, proposals to abolish a law against the incitement to racial hatred, or to introduce a new tax which would disproportionately increase the financial burden on the poor. The philosophical experts might decide that these proposals violated the intersubjective and objective conditions of participatory parity, respectively. Both proposals could create new barriers to parity, the first by making it possible legally to incite violence against a particular group, and the second by creating a situation in which some people lack the necessary resources to be able to participate effectively in democratic deliberation. According to the logic of Fraser's argument, it would seem to follow that philosophers could declare these proposals illegitimate before they ever reached the deliberative forum. If my reading of Fraser's position is right, then I would suggest that at this point the circle of democratic justice has broken apart: it has become a straight line in which the philosophical specification of the general limits of justice precedes citizens' democratic deliberations about specific claims of justice.

It can be argued that this is a highly undemocratic position, since it takes away from ordinary citizens the right to determine the most fundamental principles of their association. I want to argue that it is also incoherent, since it is impossible to distinguish the respective roles of philosophers and citizens in the way that Fraser suggests. To see what I mean, recall her proposal that philosophers engage in 'conceptual analysis' in order to determine the limits of participatory parity, while citizens engage in 'hermeneutic reflection' in order to choose options within those limits (2003: 72). To be specific, the role of citizens is to deliberate 'about how best to implement the requirements of justice' (2003: 70) by drawing on goods that they value 'in addition to justice' (2003: 72). Fraser's hope is that, if philosophy precedes democracy, then justice will precede ethics. In other words, while specific arguments on how to implement the principle of parity will be sectarian, the principle of parity itself will not. I would argue, however, that this is a completely implausible account of the relationship between philosophy and democracy. In order for it to make sense, Fraser must assume that conceptual analysis involves no element of hermeneutic reflection. In other words, it must be possible to specify the limits to the principle of parity without any need for the interpretation of that principle. But this is impossible. Recall my argument in section 5.4 that participatory parity is not the only principle that can be deduced from the premiss of moral equality. Political theorists have identified many other egalitarian principles which they claim to have deduced from the same premiss. Whether or not my argument is successful, the very fact that I have made it shows that things are not as Fraser hopes. The very fact that I have called into question her justification of the principle of parity is a practical demonstration that hermeneutic interpretation is an inevitable part of the practice of articulating normative principles. It follows that no clear distinction between conceptual analysis and hermeneutic reflection can be made, since the former activity is as interpretive in character as the latter. In this case, it also follows that no clear distinction can be made between the non-sectarian justification of the principle of parity and sectarian deliberation on the application of that principle. It may also follow that there is a role for citizens in shaping – rather than just applying – the principle of parity itself.

Finally, I want to consider Taylor's response to this dilemma. I have shown that he draws considerable inspiration from the republican tradition of political thought. From this perspective, he contends that modern Western societies should be understood as 'citizen republics' in which people 'decide their own fate through common deliberation' (1985: 245). There are two distinct but interrelated elements here: the first is a commitment to the principle of 'participatory self-rule'; the second is a belief that democratic deliberation is the essential medium for the exercise of such rule. It could be argued that this commitment to republicanism makes Taylor's justification of his model of democracy sectarian. If he believes that political participation in the collective life of one's community is an important – perhaps even the highest – human good, so that without such participation humans will inevitably lead severely diminished lives, then his model of democracy will come into conflict with the immense variety of goods endorsed by the citizens of modern polities. In this way, Honneth's reasons for rejecting Arendt's republicanism – summarized in section 6.3 – would also apply to Taylor's model of democracy.

Taylor is aware of the criticism of sectarianism levelled against republicanism. As he says, 'to treat' self-rule 'as the republican tradition does . . . would take us beyond the bounds of procedural liberalism'. He acknowledges that 'liberalism cannot incorporate' Arendt's 'political ideal' (1995b: 199). This suggests that one must endorse either republicanism or liberalism. At some points, it appears that Taylor would take the first, republican option. For example, discussing liberalism in his essay 'The Politics of Recognition', he argues that 'it can't and shouldn't claim complete neutrality'; indeed, it is 'also a fighting creed' (1995b: 249). A parallel response to the current criticism would be to confess that it is necessary to offer a strongly ethical justification for democracy, one that cannot and should not pretend to be compatible with all of the values held by citizens in modern societies. However, there are also points at which it appears that Taylor takes the second, liberal option, arguing that his model of democracy can be justified in non-sectarian terms. The evidence for this interpretation can be seen at those points at which he suggests that his model of democracy uses republican ideas merely to modify existing liberal democracy. To be specific, this model does not assert that political participation is the highest human good. Nor does it claim that fundamental individual rights may be sacrificed for the sake of the political community. As I showed in sections 3.2 and 4.2, Taylor is committed to the defence of fundamental individual rights, and would allow particular 'immunities and presumptions of uniform treatment' to be overridden only in the name of 'cultural survival' (1995b: 248). In this way, Taylor could argue that the justification for his participatory model of democracy is not vulnerable to the charge of sectarianism. These two distinct ways in which Taylor might respond to the charge of sectarianism tell us much about the nature of this charge. On the one hand, it may be tempting to try to show that no reasonable person could reject the model of democracy being proposed. But if this seems to be an impossible goal, then the alternative is boldly to admit that this model will not be acceptable to all citizens, whatever their particular ethical values. In this case, one must accept that the advocacy of this model is itself part of the ordinary business of democratic politics. While this latter approach promises much less than the approaches of Honneth and Fraser, I would suggest that it is by far the most realistic approach to the problem of sectarianism. Indeed, I would go as far as to say that it is the approach that most fully embraces the idea of the circularity of democratic justice.

6.6 Conclusions

In light of my critical analysis of these three models of democracy, I want finally to return to the overall theme of this chapter: namely, the relationship between democracy and recognition. As we have seen, Fraser consciously embraces a circular conception of democratic justice. She contends that democratic deliberation is necessary to determine the content of justice, but at the same time that justice is a necessary precondition of democracy. On the one hand, democracy is the arena in which citizens determine the laws, policies and institutions which best promote parity of participation. On the other hand, individuals must be recognized in order for them to be able to play an effective role in democratic deliberation. In short, democracy determines recognition, while recognition constrains democracy. However, in spite of her explicit endorsement of a circular conception of democratic justice, I have argued that closer examination of Fraser's account reveals that she seeks to give the philosophical determination of justice absolute priority over the democratic interpretation of claims for justice. In this final section, I want briefly to consider whether Taylor and Honneth deal any better with this conundrum. Is it possible – or necessary – to square this circle of democratic justice?

In section 6.2, I sketched Taylor's ideal of democracy as 'a free self-governing society' (1995b: 260). I argued that, on close inspection, it is possible to discern a distinction between respect and esteem at work in this ideal. So far as the first type of recognition is concerned, Taylor believes (1) that individuals deserve respect in light of their capacity for autonomy, and (2) that peoples deserve respect for their capacity for collective self-rule. With regard to the second type of recognition, he argues (3) that individuals may enjoy esteem for their distinctive identities, and (4) that they may also enjoy esteem in virtue of their identity as part of the political community. In light of this analysis, it is possible to ask how Taylor thinks that recognition and democracy are related. On the one hand, it could be argued that democracy must precede recognition, since citizens have to deliberate in order to determine what forms of recognition are appropriate. It is only through such deliberation that they can decide (1) what specific rights individuals should enjoy, (2) how far the ability of that community to govern itself should extend, (3) whether particular communities within the polity should be valued, and (4) what the ethical identity of their political community should be. On this reading, it appears that democratic deliberation determines the content of justice. On the other hand, it could be argued that recognition must precede democracy, since, without due recognition, democracy is impossible: (1) without individual rights, citizens could not take part in democratic deliberation; (2) without respect for the *demos*, there would be no democratic polity in the first place; (3) without esteem for particular identities, citizens would not be motivated to take part in democratic deliberation; and (4) without esteem for the collective body, there would be no common good about which citizens could meaningfully deliberate. Given these two rival interpretations of Taylor's model, it is clear that it must confront the same problem of circularity which concerns Fraser. Is democracy necessary in order to determine what recognition is due, or is recognition necessary before democracy can exist? I do not imagine that Taylor has an easy answer to this question, since I do not believe that an easy answer exists. I suspect that he might argue that a properly constituted democratic polity is one which fulfils an obligation to show its citizens due respect and esteem. This is because such recognition is a condition of possibility of democracy itself.

I would argue that Honneth must confront the same problem. He also assumes both that recognition is necessary if democracy is to be possible, and that democracy is necessary to determine what recognition requires. On the one hand, there are aspects of Honneth's model which suggest that democracy has priority over recognition. It is in democratic deliberation that citizens collectively determine which claims for new rights are well grounded and which claims for esteem are justified. On the other hand, there are other aspects of his model which suggest that recognition has priority over democracy. Only if citizens have generalized and de-formalized rights, and equalized and individualized opportunities to win esteem, will they have both the ability and the motivation to take part in democratic deliberation. In light of these considerations, it is clear that Honneth's model of democracy must face up to the same problem of the circularity that confronts both Fraser and Taylor. He argues that recognition is needed to make democracy possible, and that democracy is the essential medium for determining the character of recognition. I suspect that Honneth might respond to this conundrum by invoking his idea that recognition is a dynamic process rather than a static condition. As we shall see in detail in the next chapter, he believes that struggles for recognition – including struggles in democratic assemblies – unleash the developmental potential of recognition. In this way, he could argue that struggles for recognition are what bring democracy about, and that democracy then enables relations of recognition to develop further. In short, Honneth might accept that democratic justice is circular, but then give this idea a dynamic twist. In this case, the circle, like a wheel, rolls forward over time and becomes an upward spiral. I conclude that there is no easy way of facing up to the circularity of the relationship between democracy and recognition. To accept such circularity seems to be to embrace a logical paradox, but to try to reject it involves giving democracy either too much power or too little power relative to justice.

7

Struggles for Recognition

7.1 Introduction

One phrase often heard in debates about recognition is that of the 'struggle for recognition'. This idea that recognition is something that must be struggled for has a long history. It made its first appearance in Hegel's account of the dialectic of master and slave in the *Phenomenology of Spirit* (1807). Here Hegel drew a picture of a struggle in which two individuals battle for domination over one another. As Charles Taylor puts it, 'here we have man as a particular individual . . . who strives to impose himself, to achieve external confirmation'. Hence, when two individuals meet, 'each seeks one-sided recognition', and indeed they 'will risk their lives for it' (1975: 153). A number of later writers took up this theme and developed it in a variety of ways. In *Being and Nothingness* (1943), Jean-Paul Sartre used the idea of the struggle for recognition to illuminate the nature of human relationships. He argued that all such relationships are necessarily conflictual, involving a struggle in which each subject tries to turn the other into an object, and at the same time tries to resist being turned into an object by that other.[1] A little later, Sartre deployed the same idea in a more overtly political context to think about the nature of anti-Semitism (1946). On his account, anti-Semites 'create' the Jews that they despise, seeing them as sinister representatives of a modern world which threatens their fantasy of unified community.[2] At about the same time, Frantz Fanon was employing the idea of struggle in his writings on colonialism. In *Black Skin, White Masks* (1952), he argued that the colonial subject is created by the racist colonial system. Thus the fight against colonialism can be regarded as a struggle for recognition against this system.

The idea of a struggle for recognition is used widely – indeed, one might say indiscriminately – in contemporary literature on the politics of recognition. Detached from its Hegelian origins, this idea is used to characterize the many, various forms of the politics of identity and difference (e.g. Tully 2004: 84). In fact, it seems as if every form of political action which is not exclusively economic or redistributive in character, and which involves issues of identity and difference in however indirect a manner, is considered to be a struggle for recognition. However, while most normative theories of recognition may use the rhetoric of struggles for recognition, they do not in practice take their proper character into account. I would argue that, according to these theories, recognition is a one-way, one-off act which is directed toward a single object. It is a one-way act in the sense that it takes the form of a judgement by one party, according to a particular set of values, of another party.[3] There is no mutuality of recognition, since the party that judges is not affected by the attitude to it of the party that is being judged. The act of recognition assumed by this account is also one-off in the sense that there is no dimension of time involved. The act is not located in a series of such acts; in fact, recognition is regarded more as a condition than a process. Finally, this act of recognition generally focuses on one object. It is assumed that it makes sense to consider whether a particular individual or collectivity should be recognized without inquiring into the status of the party doing the recognizing or the nature of the relationship between the two. Bringing these various points together, this account regards recognition as a state of affairs in which a particular party may be recognized if it measures up to the values in accordance with which recognition is conducted.

There is one contemporary normative theorist who is fully aware of the origin of the idea of the struggle for recognition. As Axel Honneth expounds his normative theory of recognition, he frequently looks to Hegel for inspiration. He believes that, since some parties will resist others' attempts to gain recognition, struggle is inevitable. Moreover, it is only through a series of conflicts that recognition will be achieved. In Honneth's account, then, recognition is not a one-way, one-off judgement of a single object. In marked contrast, he regards recognition as an intersubjective, reciprocal and dynamic process. To begin with, recognition is necessarily intersubjective, since it always involves more than one party. The relationship between these parties must be taken into account in order to understand the significance of their struggle. Moreover, recognition is necessarily reciprocal in the sense that the meaning and worth of recognition depend crucially on the value that each party places on the other. Hegel's most fundamental insight was that an act of recognition is only of benefit to the party being recognized if it values the party which recognizes it. Finally, recognition is dynamic in the sense that it is always possible to discern a sequence of acts of recognition in which the character and significance of each particular act are partly determined by the act (or acts) that preceded it. Thus recognition is a process rather than a state of affairs. Bringing these three points together, I want to suggest that Honneth regards recognition as a reciprocal process in which the judgements of worth of two (or more) parties are dynamically interrelated.

It is because he offers the most nuanced account of struggles for recognition that my investigation in this chapter will focus almost exclusively on Honneth. The discussion is organized in the following way. In the next section, I sketch Honneth's account of struggles for recognition, focusing on the links that he makes between negative emotions, the sense of injustice, and acts of struggle themselves (7.2). In the section after that, I assess a number of criticisms that can be made of this account. I concentrate on the three stages of his argument that I have just mentioned (7.3). In the final section of this chapter, I reach a considered conclusion about the cogency of Honneth's account of struggles for recognition (7.4).

7.2   Axel Honneth: Struggles for Recognition

The idea of struggle is a vitally important part of Honneth's account of recognition. He believes that recognition, by its very nature, is likely to be achieved only through what Joel Anderson, his translator, calls a 'conflict-ridden developmental process' (1995: p. xi). This explains the full title of Honneth's book, *The Struggle for Recognition: The Moral Grammar of Social Conflicts*. Here we can see the strong connection that he makes between normative theory and social theory. Looking at it one way, social conflicts can be explained by using the idea of recognition. Such conflicts occur, Honneth believes, when people demand the recognition that they are presently denied. In order to understand the history of the American civil rights movement, for instance, it would be useful to regard this movement as a series of struggles by African-Americans to obtain due recognition. Looking at it the other way around, Honneth thinks that it is possible to shed light on the idea of recognition by examining social conflicts. Such conflicts tend to move society toward the realization of undistorted relations of recognition. Thus, by looking in the direction in which these conflicts point, we can understand what full recognition would be like. This hints at a third element in Honneth's account. Since he argues that struggles for recognition move society towards an ideal state characterized by undistorted relations of recognition, he believes that the idea of recognition also holds the key to a theory of moral progress. In other words, the moral development of society takes the form of a gradual expansion of relations of recognition. In this way, Honneth combines a normative theory of recognition (which describes the ideal form that a society should take) with a theory of social conflict (which explains why such conflicts occur) and a theory of moral progress (which explains how the ideal society can be achieved through a series of social conflicts). In order to understand how he proposes to justify this ambitious argument, it will be useful to divide it into a number of distinct stages. In the first stage, it is shown that hurt feelings may be understood as evidence of injustice. The second stage suggests that awareness of such injustice can motivate collective struggles. In the final stage, it is argued that such struggles may have the potential to move society towards a state in which there is a complete realization of the idea of recognition.

From Feelings to Injustice

Honneth uses what he calls an 'empirically grounded phenomenology' (1995: 162) in order to found his account of the struggle for recognition. That is to say, he examines the domain of ordinary human experience in order to search for evidence that confirms his hypothesis about the importance of recognition. He believes that he can find such evidence in what he calls the 'hurt feelings' (1995: 163) that characterize some human relationships. Feelings like shame, indignation, rage and anger have cognitive content. In other words, these 'negative emotional reactions' (1995: 135) constitute an 'affective source of knowledge' (1995: 143), giving us insights into our situation. To be specific, having such feelings tells us that the implicit rules of recognition by which we live are being violated. At one point, Honneth suggests that there are in fact three distinctive forms of violation, corresponding to the three forms of recognition themselves (1995: 132–4). If I am maltreated, I will feel humiliated, and my self-confidence will be damaged. If I am excluded from citizenship, and denied the rights to which I am entitled, then my self-respect will suffer. If the way of life with which I associate myself is denigrated, then my self-esteem is at risk. In short, in this first stage of

Honneth's argument, he seeks to demonstrate that hurt feelings may be understood as evidence of injustice. Feelings of shame or rage are triggered by violations of the rules of recognition, and thus these feelings tell me that I am being denied the recognition which is my due.[4]

From Injustice to Struggle

It remains to be seen how the sense of injustice generated by these subjective emotions can motivate collective protest and resistance. How can hurt feelings lead to struggles for recognition? In order for this connection to be made, individuals must come to realize that the private injuries from which they suffer are the result of public injustices. Rather than thinking that my feeling of shame is the result of personal inadequacy, I must instead come to see it as evidence that an injustice is being done, not just to me but to all people who find themselves in a relevantly similar position. In order for this to happen, Honneth argues, there must be a 'semantic bridge' between 'private experiences of injury' and the 'impersonal aspirations of a social movement'. This bridge is provided by an 'intersubjective framework of interpretation' (1995: 163) which can help individuals to see that their hurt feelings are the result of social processes to which a whole set of people are subject.[5] One useful example of such a framework is that provided by second-wave feminism. It has been suggested that, before the emergence of this form of thinking, women in Western societies who experienced anxiety and depression tended to believe (or at least were told) that their problems were caused by personal psychological maladjustment. However, looking through the lens of second-wave feminism enabled these women to see that in reality their problems resulted from an imbalance of power which led *inter alia* to their exclusion from the labour market and their confinement to the domestic sphere. This enabled a new collective identity – the women's movement – to emerge in order to struggle against these unjust conditions. Thus, by using this feminist interpretive framework, it was possible to convert particular subjective feelings into awareness of objective oppression.[6] Honneth argues that it is this realization that we are suffering from collective injustice that can motivate collective struggle against that injustice. As he says, the experience of 'disrespect' – which he uses as a general term for lack of recognition – can provide 'the motivational impetus for social resistance' (1995: 132). Aware that my feelings of shame result from the unjust conditions in which not just I, but many others, find themselves, I have reason to join with these others in order to struggle with them against this injustice.[7]

From Struggle to Recognition

So far I have shown why Honneth believes that it is awareness of the violation of implicit rules of recognition which triggers social protest and resistance. Thus recognition explains conflict. Turning this around, he also believes that the study of social protest can cast light on the nature of recognition. This is because struggles tend to move society towards a full realization of undistorted relations of recognition. Hence, by examining the direction in which these relations are moving, we can better understand the idea of recognition which is emerging. Honneth claims, moreover, that this account of the expansion of recognition is also the story of the moral progress of society. Although they are intimately interrelated, it is worth keeping two issues separate. First, we must ask why Honneth thinks that struggles for recognition push society in a particular direction. Having addressed this question, we can then ask why he believes that this movement constitutes moral progress.

I would suggest that the best way to answer the first question is to look at Honneth's interpretation of T. H. Marshall's well-known account of citizenship (1950). According to this account, the development of citizenship in Britain occurred in a series of historical stages which saw the successive emergence of civil, political and, finally, social rights. By the time Marshall was writing, all adults in Britain had the status of citizens and thus enjoyed an extensive set of rights. Honneth's suggestion is that the evolution of citizenship which Marshall describes was the result of the unfolding of the developmental possibilities inherent in relations of recognition (1995: 118). Thus he suggests that, once the principle of equality was introduced, this created a 'developmental pressure' towards the further expansion of these relations. Indeed, he suggests that 'one is forced to do justice to this demand' for equality (1995: 115). Once all men were acknowledged to be equal, for instance, there was no good argument against considering women to be the equal of men as well. In short, 'the establishment of each new class of basic rights is consistently compelled by arguments' (1995: 116). At some points, Honneth's account sounds almost teleological in character. He suggests, for instance, that the 'normative principle' which guided 'the successive expansion of individual basic rights' was 'there from the start as its guiding idea' (1995: 117). Here it appears that the ideal of recognition is present in embryo in every struggle for recognition, and that this ideal is gradually realized through the process of struggle itself. It is as though human beings bring about by degrees a goal which is independent of their intentions, a goal which is encoded in the very structure of their interactions.

Having explained why Honneth thinks that struggles for recognition move society in a particular direction, we can now turn to our second question and ask why he believes that this movement constitutes a form of moral progress. Here Honneth's key claim is that the 'model of conflict' which I have just outlined provides 'an interpretive framework for a process of moral formation' (1995: 168). That is to say, the study of social struggles enables us to understand how a society makes moral progress. If it is to be able to do so, this 'interpretive framework' must be able to determine whether any particular struggle for recognition is progressive or reactionary. That is to say, does a struggle help or hinder the development of a more just society? Honneth's argument is that a 'normative standard' can be used to mark out a 'developmental direction' by offering a 'hypothetical anticipation of an approximate end state' (1995: 168–9). In other words, if we know what the final destination is, and therefore in which direction it lies, we can determine whether a particular struggle is leading us in the right direction or not. Then, once we have determined the final destination, we can specify the 'idealized sequence of struggles' which would ensure a 'process of moral development' in which the 'normative potential of mutual recognition' is 'unfolded' (1995: 169). It is then possible to determine whether a particular struggle is part of this 'idealized sequence' (1995: 170). Honneth's conclusion is that, if a society experienced this particular series of struggles for recognition, it would have achieved moral progress.

7.3   Criticisms of Honneth

I have suggested that in a discussion of the nature of struggles for recognition it is worth focusing on Honneth since, unlike many of his rivals, he regards recognition as a reciprocal process between two (or more) dynamically interrelated parties. Were his account successful, he could claim to have demonstrated that a society in which relations of recognition are fully developed can be achieved through a series of social conflicts. Such an ambitious account is bound to attract criticisms, and it is to the examination of a range of these criticisms that I now turn. For clarity's sake, I shall divide the discussion into three parts, corresponding to those in the previous section. First, I look at criticisms that can be made of the purported link between hurt feelings and judgements of injustice. Then I examine criticisms of Honneth's assertion that such judgements are capable of motivating protest and resistance. Finally, I consider criticisms of his claim that struggles for recognition are capable of leading to moral progress.

From Feelings to Injustice

According to one criticism of the link between 'negative emotional reactions' (1995: 135) and judgements of injustice, the objective fact that someone is being mistreated may not necessarily be accompanied by awareness of the injustice of this mistreatment. In other words, being unjustly treated does not necessarily lead to consciousness of injustice. There are two possibilities to be considered.

The first of these suggests that what, for the sake of this argument, I shall call *ideology* can block the conversion of the experience of private injury into the consciousness of public injustice.[8] Roger Foster makes an argument of this kind. He begins by suggesting that 'particular structural arrangements' may 'incapacitate cultural resistance' (1999: 7). In this case, in order to determine whether a struggle for recognition is likely to occur, it is necessary to look at the structural conditions in which the people affected find themselves. Foster's argument is that the 'public sphere of late capitalism' is structured in such a way that the possibility of a 'genuine oppositional stance is effectively excluded'. To be specific, the 'liberal individualist ideology' that operates in this sphere deflects attention away from socio-economic inequalities and towards relatively superficial cultural forms. In this way, he suggests, a 'cultural opposition' which demands fundamental changes to social structures is converted into an 'identity politics' which requires only 'cultural affirmation'. Under these conditions, for instance, the politics of gay and lesbian groups are transformed from demands radically to alter material structures and processes into demands merely to have their identities positively acknowledged. According to the same logic, it could perhaps be argued that campaigns for the right of Muslim schoolgirls to wear the hijab distract attention away from the more important need to demand social and economic justice. 'Accounting for the barriers to effective cultural resistance', Foster concludes, 'would . . . mean that we need to recover a concept which is entirely missing from Honneth's account – namely, ideology' (1999: 12).[9]

A second possibility is that awareness of maltreatment can be blocked by what I shall refer to as *trauma*. Here attention is shifted away from the ideological and towards the social-psychological dimension of struggle. Elliot Jurist makes an argument of this kind, suggesting that Honneth fails 'to contend with the painful truth that victims of aggression are often too traumatized to struggle in response' (1994: 176). In this case, the reason why hurt feelings fail to create a sense of injustice capable of motivating social protest is that the victims of that injustice suffer a form of psychological damage that renders them unable clearly to understand their condition and thus unable to struggle against it. The cruel irony is that, in these circumstances, people are too traumatized precisely by the injustice itself to be able to resist it. Jurist's general conclusion is that, if Honneth is to be able to explain 'why some people can endure disrespect and fight back and others do not' (1994: 176), he must take this psychological dimension into account. The specific suggestion being considered here is that trauma might explain why, in some cases, people fail to fight back.[10] Gail Holst-Warhaft's (2000) account of the victims of the Argentinian dictatorship in the 1970s provides a vivid example of this phenomenon in practice. She shows how only some of the Mothers of the Disappeared were able very slowly to overcome the trauma of having their children vanish.

These two possibilities present important challenges to Honneth's optimistic story. If ideology or trauma severs the link between hurt feelings and a sense of injustice, then people who are being treated badly may not be aware of the injustice of this treatment, and they will thus lack an effective motive to struggle for recognition. It would also follow that the absence of a sense of injustice does not necessarily prove absence of mistreatment. To put this more sharply, just because people do not feel an emotion such as rage in particular circumstances, it does not mean that they *should not* feel rage. How might Honneth seek to defend his claim that hurt feelings will lead to a sense of injustice? There are two possibilities which I shall just mention at this point, since I return to them several times later in this section. First, it has been suggested by some of Honneth's critics that his theory rests on the anthropological assumption that human beings have a drive for self-realization (Alexander and Lara 1996; Zurn 2000). In this case, he could argue that this drive is strong enough to be able to overcome ideology or trauma, so that anyone who is frustrated in their attempts at self-realization by being denied recognition could not fail consciously to experience the hurt feelings caused by such a denial. Later on, in a discussion of what has been called Honneth's 'submerged developmental commitment to an anthropological imperative' (Alexander and Lara 1996: 134), I shall consider whether this sort of reply to the current criticism would be effective. Second, in my analysis of other criticisms of Honneth's account of struggles for recognition, I shall suggest that he is aware of the role that social institutions and the ideas associated with them can play in filtering and interpreting emotional experience. In this case, he could argue that, in a public sphere which is not dominated by what Foster calls a 'liberal individualist ideology', hurt feelings would lead to an appropriate sense of injustice. I shall argue, however, that neither of these options that are available to Honneth come without cost.

A second criticism that can be made of this part of Honneth's argument effectively makes the opposite point to the first: rather than suggesting that injustice may not be accompanied by hurt feelings, it suggests instead that hurt feelings may not always be reliable evidence of injustice. This is because negative emotional reactions may sometimes be unjustified: people may feel that they are being mistreated when in fact they are not. Again, I shall consider two distinct possibilities.

First, there may be a problem of *false comparison*. People may feel unfairly treated when they compare themselves to others. Since they believe that these others are doing much better than they are, they feel anger and demand recompense. However, these feelings may result from a misleading or false comparison, and thus the case for compensation may not be justified. One familiar example would be a situation in which there is an influx of immigrants into a particular area. In certain circumstances, the host population may believe that the immigrants receive all sorts of advantages from the state which the 'natives' do not. It may be suggested, for instance, that they enjoy higher levels of state assistance, greater chances of getting public housing, and so on. In general, the existing population may feel that the state looks more kindly on these new arrivals than it does on them. This perception, always accompanied by intense negative emotions, may lead to a demand for this perceived bias to be ended, and for the 'natives' to be treated fairly once more. According to the present criticism, however, these perceptions of unfair discrimination are often false. New arrivals often do not enjoy greater resources than the existing population.[11] The moral of this story is that, although people may feel resentment towards another group with whom they compare themselves, this could be an unfair comparison. To generalize, even when people feel hurt, they do not always do so with good reason.

Another reason for thinking that hurt feelings may not be proof of injustice is that people can feel hurt and think that they are being treated unjustly as the result of a *distorting interpretive framework*. That is to say, they may have a way of looking at the world which causes them to feel shame, rage or anger. A nationalist framework of interpretation, for instance, may tell a group of people that they have been humiliated by rival nations, that their culture is under grave threat, or that their resources are being drained away by a shadowy group of international bankers. In general, their nationalist framework may present them as victims whose aggressive acts are justified self-defence, rather than as revealing them as aggressors whose actions are justified by no more than collective self-deceit. Slobodan Milošević's reinvigoration of Serbian nationalism would be a good

STRUGGLES FOR RECOGNITION **169**

case in point. Following the breakup of Yugoslavia in the early 1990s, Milosevic retained his grip on power by transforming himself from a Communist ideologue into a nationalist ideologue. Portraying Serbia as a nation threatened by its neighbours and misunderstood by the international community, he provided an interpretation of many Serbs' feelings which justified the acts of aggression against its former Yugoslavian partners.[12] In some ways, this idea of a distorting interpretive framework connects back to the notion of ideology discussed above. There I suggested that ideology can block the conversion of hurt feelings into an awareness of injustice. In the present case, I am suggesting that an ideology such as nationalism is capable of generating hurt feelings and a sense of injustice which are in fact products of paranoid fantasy.

In both of the cases just outlined, people may feel hurt, see this experience as evidence of injustice, and thus struggle against this injustice. If, however, these hurt feelings are shaped by a false comparison or a distorting interpretive framework, then they may not accurately indicate the presence of injustice. In neither of these cases do hurt feelings necessarily provide reliable evidence of maltreatment. People may feel hurt without good reason; to put the point at its crudest, sometimes people just whinge.[13] Once again, these possibilities threaten to sever the link that Honneth makes between hurt feelings and judgements of injustice. I would suggest that, in response to this type of criticism, Honneth has two possible lines of defence. First, he could try to defend his assumption that emotions are a reliable source of knowledge about the situations to which they are a response. This assumption can be seen at work in his claim that emotions are 'pretheoretical facts' (1994: 263). They are, in other words, the raw, pristine data on which accounts of social justice and moral progress can be built. Second, Honneth could admit that the right sort of framework of interpretation is vital in order to determine when negative emotions are reliable indicators of injustice. It is important to note, however, that these two lines of defence work against each other. On the one hand, if the first line works, the second is redundant. If it can be shown that emotions are reliable sources of knowledge, then there is no need for the right sort of interpretive framework. On the other hand, if the second line of argument is necessary, the first must have failed. That is to say, if it is conceded that the framework of interpretation does not simply enable the expression of feelings, but rather plays an active role in shaping them, then it follows that emotions in themselves cannot be a reliable source of knowledge about justice. I shall return to this point in my discussion of the role of 'mediation' below.

A third and final criticism that may be made of this part of Honneth's account suggests that the link which he makes between feelings and injustice depends on an illegitimate inference from the 'is' of hurt feelings to the 'ought' of judgements of injustice. As we saw in section 5.4, Christopher Zurn raises a concern about this issue. Commenting on Honneth's use of 'a formal conception of ethical life as a normative standard for social critique', he points to 'the perennial difficulty of drawing an "ought" from an "is"' (2000: 119). In this particular case, Honneth bases his ethical ideal of self-realization on a factual account of the nature of human identity. This slide from the positive to the normative in Honneth's theory is occluded by his shifting semantics. While phrases such as 'hurt feelings' (1995: 163) and 'negative emotional reactions' (1995: 135) appear to denote entirely empirical phenomena, other phrases such as 'moral experiences' (1995: 162) and 'moral feelings' (1995: 168) refer, by contrast, to explicitly normative phenomena. Against this linguistic slippage, it may be argued that no fact about a particular emotional state can in itself justify a normative claim about how one should be treated. The fact that people *feel* hurt – and indeed feel that they are unjustly treated – does not logically imply that they *are* unjustly treated. The structure of Honneth's argument as it stands is logically incoherent and indefensible. It slides from certain facts about states of affairs (experiences of negative emotions) to certain conclusions about what should be done in response to those facts (normative principles of recognition).

In chapter 5, I argued that Honneth could reply to this criticism by explicitly defending the normative principle that a just society is one that creates and maintains the conditions of self-realization. In this case, if hurt feelings were reliable evidence that such self-realization was being frustrated, it would follow that a just society should respond to such feelings by trying to facilitate self-realization. Whilst, as we have seen, the empirical claim about the emotions may be challenged by critics who dispute the link between hurt feelings and a sense of injustice, at least the status of normative principle of recognition would be clear. My suggestion in section 5.4 was that, as a Critical Theorist, Honneth would probably offer a very different response to this criticism. In Fraser's formulation, Critical Theory is distinguished from other ways of understanding the world by 'its distinctive dialectic of immanence and transcendence' (2003: 202). In other words, Critical Theory contends that the perspective from which the world is criticized (and may thus be *transcended*) must be rooted (or *immanent*) in that world itself. In Honneth's case, his critique of the existing social order is grounded in his phenomenology of the emotions. His account of hurt feelings as evidence that relations of recognition are imperfect or damaged provides an immanent perspective from which these relations can be criticized. I would suggest that, by arguing in this way, Honneth seeks to transcend, rather than respect, the fact/value distinction. However, since these remarks on the nature of Critical Theory raise issues far beyond my current concerns, I shall say no more about the matter here.

From Injustice to Struggle

A second set of criticisms that can be made of Honneth's account of struggles for recognition focuses on his assumption that a sense of injustice (to which it is claimed that hurt feelings give rise) provides sufficient motivation for struggle. These criticisms raise doubts about whether Honneth can explain why struggles of recognition occur simply by referring to people's sense that they have been unjustly treated. In other words, they challenge his assumption that a sense of injustice is a sufficient condition of such struggles. There are a number of distinct issues which need to be considered here.

One issue concerns the origin of frameworks of interpretation. It will be recalled that, for Honneth, such frameworks – such as 'moral doctrines and ideas' – provide the necessary semantic bridge between private injury and public injustice. That is to say, a moral doctrine gives people a way of understanding that the hurt they feel is the result of social injustice rather than purely personal circumstances. I have suggested that the idea of Islamophobia is intended to play exactly this sort of role. However, it is necessary to ask how the emergence of such interpretive frameworks can be explained. Before the appearance of such a framework, a series of separate individuals each has a private experience of injury. None of them understands this injury as evidence of an injustice done to them as a collectivity, since *ex hypothesi* they lack the interpretive framework needed to reach this conclusion. In this case, it would appear that none of the victims of this injustice themselves can devise such a framework. If they cannot do so, it seems to follow logically that this framework must be the invention of some person or persons who do not themselves suffer this injustice or who have special insight into this situation. This suggests that there is what might loosely be called a Leninist model at work in Honneth's account. According to such a model, it is those with objective knowledge of social conditions who are able to produce an accurate account of them. This account then enables ordinary subjects to become aware of the conditions that they are in, and thus to make sense of their experiences. Thus, just as Bolshevik revolutionaries offered workers an objective account of their situation, so, it seems, Honneth claims to show people how their negative emotions should be correctly understood.

If this analysis of the logic of Honneth's account is correct, then it could be argued that it contains a serious threat to democracy. This arises from the unacknowledged assumption that the definitive account of a situation must be provided by those with objective knowledge, rather than those with subjective experience, of that situation. The threat to democracy, then, is that citizens' own accounts of their experiences may be discounted in favour of those of the experts.[14] Honneth could try to defend himself against this criticism by resorting to what I have already referred to as his anthropological assumption that people have an innate drive to self-realization. Such a drive, he could argue, is capable of explaining why someone who is suffering a particular injustice, which means that their ability fully to realize themselves is frustrated, is able to devise a framework of interpretation capable of explaining this frustration. Since this feeling will inevitably impinge on their consciousness, and as it were compel them to try to understand their situation, they do not stand in need of external experts telling how to interpret their experience. I have already said that this strategy has been vigorously criticized. Jeffrey Alexander and Maria Pia Lara suggest that 'in trying to explain how . . . a semantic bridge can be constructed, Honneth moves . . . directly from an anthropological emphasis on emotional needs to historical practices of resistance, emancipation, and enlarged participation'. They argue that Honneth neglects the essential mediating role of 'symbolic representation' in getting from negative emotional reactions to an objective understanding of those reactions (1996: 135). Assuming that human beings are so constituted that knowledge of this constitution can enable their political behaviour to be predicted, he overlooks the essential mediating role between human nature and political action played by 'social structures and languages' (1996: 136). I would argue that this criticism is somewhat overstated. As we have seen, Honneth is well aware that interpretive frameworks such as moral doctrines must form a bridge between individual experience and general analysis. In this sense, he does not overlook the role of mediation. However, this partial defence of Honneth does not rebut the criticism that he fails to explain the origins of the interpretive frameworks which are capable of performing this role.

A second criticism which may be made of this part of Honneth's theory draws attention to the likelihood that in modern societies there will be a variety of frameworks of interpretation. In contemporary conditions of value pluralism, it is almost certain that a number of interpretive frameworks will draw on the experience of hurt feelings in order to come to judgements of justice. It seems reasonable to assume that these frameworks will interpret the same emotional experience in very different ways, and will thus reach very different normative conclusions. For instance, one framework might suggest that we feel shame because we have failed to live up to our own high moral standards, whilst another might suggest, by contrast, that we feel shame because others have deliberately humiliated us. For Theodore Kemper, we feel shame when another deprives us of status, when this deprivation is the consequence of our own unworthy actions (2001: 65). The implications for justice will be depend heavily on the particular interpretation of shame which is deployed.[15] Zurn offers a version of this criticism when questioning the priority that Honneth gives to self-realization. There are, he points out, a number of candidates for the role of 'the critical yard-stick for the social conditions of the good life' (2000: 119). These include, for instance, 'pious self-abnegation, or virtuous subservience to communal ends, or righteous obedience to the moral law'. All of these could serve as the standard we use to determine the character of a just society. To put this criticism in the terms of the current argument, whilst the experience of certain negative emotions could be seen as evidence that self-realization is being frustrated, it could also be read as evidence for other ethical theories. It could, for example, be taken to mean that we need to reinvigorate a sense of communal obligation, or that we need to return to the path of righteousness. In this case, Honneth's problem is 'to show that the telos of self-realization through intersubjective recognition itself should be the governing ideal of social organization' (Zurn 2000: 121).

Such considerations prompt the following question: does Honneth believe that one of these frameworks is right and that the rest are wrong? Does he think that one framework offers a correct interpretation of people's hurt feelings, whilst the other frameworks do not? At one level, it seems that the answer to this question must be 'No'. Honneth intends his formal conception of ethical life to be sufficiently abstract to be compatible with a diversity of values. Indeed, as we saw in chapter 4, he imagines that in a society which realizes the formal conception there will be an ongoing competition between different sets of values. In that case, it would seem that he would be reluctant to declare that his own framework of interpretation trumps all others. At another level, however, it appears that Honneth *does* want to privilege one particular framework over the rest. He wants to argue that his own framework correctly demonstrates that hurt feelings are signs that the rules of recognition have been violated. He would reject a rival interpretation which suggested, for instance, that the very same hurt feelings are evidence of our sinful condition. This prompts a second question: namely, on what grounds can he justify the priority of his framework of interpretation over all others? How can he argue that his framework is the best one for interpreting injustice, and that its rivals are mistaken? Why, in particular, is the imperative to realize the conditions of self-realization uniquely justified? Why not the imperative to realize other conditions which people may demand as a result of their negative emotional experiences? There is no doubt that these questions present a significant problem for Honneth, since, if he were to deny the superiority of his interpretive framework, then he would not be able to argue that recognition struggles lead to an expansion of recognition relations, and his entire theory of moral progress would fall. I think it is likely that, in these circumstances, he *would* assert the superiority of his framework.

At this point, the current discussion connects back to my analysis of Fraser's critique of Honneth's theory in section 5.4. It will be recalled that she accuses him of founding his entire theory on a monist social psychology which seeks to deduce normative conclusions directly from facts about the individual psyche. At the end of my discussion there, I suggested that Fraser's charge is well-founded. For Honneth, a psychology of recognition supports a sociology of recognition which determines an ethics of recognition. In this case, if one is persuaded by Honneth's foundationalist thesis, then one will also be persuaded by his argument for the superiority of his framework of interpretation. If one is not persuaded, however, then other ways of interpreting the raw data of emotional experience may well appear more plausible.

If the previous criticism is right in suggesting that a variety of interpretive frameworks is likely to flourish in modern societies, is it possible to predict which of these rivals will become dominant? A third criticism focuses on Honneth's assumption that, at least under all normal conditions, his framework of interpretation will win out over all others. He needs to make this assumption in order to demonstrate that, as a result of political struggles, relations of recognition will expand rather than remain static, become distorted, or even contract. Without such a demonstration, the link that he wishes to make between recognition struggles and moral progress will fail. To bring this problem into focus, let us consider the status of what, for the sake of this argument, I shall call the neo-Nazi interpretive framework. This is grounded in the same emotions of anger and humiliation that catch Honneth's attention. However, in contrast to his account, the neo-Nazi world-view assumes that the protection of its members' collective self-esteem necessitates despising all those outside its own narrow community of value. As Alexander and Lara put it, 'esteem is, in fact, often provided within the particularistic, self-affirming boundaries of segmented communities which experience themselves as downwardly mobile'. 'Based on deep resentments', they suggest, the demands for recognition made by such groups 'can easily become demands for domination' (1996: 134). They conclude that, 'as the history of reactionary social movements that have marked the twentieth century indicates, grasping a moral content in response to feeling publicly and privately shamed is not particularly likely in an empirical sense' (1996: 135). Indeed, it is more likely that the experience of shame will lead a group to adopt values which, for instance, extol its virtue and purity whilst condemning the viciousness and dirtiness of all outsiders. In short, this criticism suggests that there is no certainty that emotional experience will be interpreted in the way necessary if relations of recognition are to develop as Honneth hopes.

At one point, Honneth discusses the neo-Nazi case himself. In an article written at about the same time as *Struggle for Recognition*, he acknowledges the danger that Alexander and Lara describe: 'the experience of social disrespect' can lead to a search for 'social esteem . . . in small militaristic groups, whose code of honor is dominated by the practice of violence' (Honneth 1994: 268). For him, this presents 'the question of how a moral culture could be so constituted as to give those affected, disrespected and ostracized, the individual strength to articulate their experiences in the democratic public sphere, rather than living them out in the countercultures of violence' (1994: 269). The implication of this remark is that if a 'democratic public sphere' were in place, then those who might otherwise become neo-Nazis would have the chance to voice their disquiet in the public sphere. Honneth's assumption appears to be that, since they will therefore feel included in public debate, it is less likely that these alienated citizens will become neo-Nazis in the first place. Here he endorses the idea that the structure of the public sphere can have a crucial influence on the interpretation of particular negative emotional reactions, and therefore on the motives that are generated by this interpretation. To put this in the terms he deploys in *Struggle for Recognition*, it follows that the sort of 'moral-political conviction' generated depends on the 'cultural-political environment' in question (1995: 138–9). It is possible, in other words, deliberately to create the conditions in which hurt feelings will move a group in one direction rather than another. Since each particular environment is more likely to produce certain convictions, rather than others, frameworks of interpretation are not neutral: different frameworks will push a particular group in different directions. Hence it is possible to create an environment in which the reaction to shame is to adopt the 'right' rather than the 'wrong' ethical values. It should be noted, once more, that this acknowledgement of the role of mediating institutions is in tension with Honneth's account of emotions as 'pretheoretical facts'.

As we have seen, Honneth concedes that an interpretive framework is necessary to convert private feelings into public judgements of injustice. He assumes that such judgements are then capable of providing sufficient motivation for people to engage in collective resistance against the unjust conditions which cause those feelings. I feel hurt, realize that I am not the only one who feels hurt, and hence join with those others collectively to struggle against the conditions that are causing this hurt. However, according to a fourth criticism of this stage of Honneth's argument, this is a very narrow and partial account of the factors which are likely to determine the probability of social resistance. It is an account which relies exclusively on the idea that such resistance will be triggered by an interpretation of negative emotions. It is because people feel as they do, and give their feelings a particular ethical interpretation, that they will struggle to escape their situation. It could be argued that this account overlooks a wide range of other factors which determine whether or not struggle will occur (and whether that struggle is likely to be successful). The extensive body of empirical research on social movements identifies a number of other factors which will be important in determining whether struggles take place. Let me mention five distinct – although clearly interrelated – categories: available resources, rational incentives, strategic choices, cultural factors, and the prevailing political opportunity structure. First, what money and other resources does a group have at its disposal? Poor social movements may face particular difficulties in struggling against the injustice they suffer (Piven and Cloward 1988). Second, are there reasons of rational self-interest for this group to engage in struggle? That is, can it calculate that certain advantages will be gained by such struggle (Chong 1991)? Third, what strategic options does the group have available to it? For example, has the group adopted particular forms of political action over time? And what sort of established repertoire of action can it draw on? Fourth, does the dominant culture or the group's own subaltern culture provide motivation for resistance? Fifth, is the structure of the state conducive to struggle or not (Tarrow 1989)?

All these questions will need to be answered in order to determine whether a struggle for recognition will break out in particular circumstances. Turning back to Honneth, I would argue that it is not enough simply to think that the collective interpretation of emotional experiences will necessarily trigger collective action. Absent resources, incentives, opportunities and so on, negative emotional reactions may very well not be converted into positive struggle. If the state is too repressive, or the group too poor, or the likelihood of success low, then shame and rage, and the sense of injustice which they fuel, may not lead to active struggle against such injustice. It could be argued, furthermore, that these various factors will also need to be taken into account in order to determine the chances of a struggle being successful. When will a struggle achieve its aims, and when will it simply be crushed? To answer this question, it will be necessary to look beyond hurt feelings and moral experience to consider resources, strategy, culture and so on. I do not think that there is any way that Honneth could deny this. At best, he could argue that, while his account of recognition struggles does not provide an exhaustive analysis of all the factors involved in such struggles, it does help to rectify the existing balance by giving due consideration to the hitherto neglected role of emotions.

From Struggle to Recognition

A third and final set of criticisms focuses on Honneth's claim that struggles for recognition lead to moral progress. His contention is that, through a series of such struggles, a society's relations of recognition are expanded, and that this process of expansion can be understood as moral development for this society. Once more, there are several distinct issues which need to be considered.

Towards the end of section 7.2, I suggested that there are points at which Honneth appears to be committed to a form of teleology. He remarks, for instance, that the 'inherent potential' of each pattern of recognition is unleashed by a 'moral learning process' (1995: 169). Here Honneth suggests that the two patterns of recognition which are capable of expansion – law and solidarity – each have an inner potential which can be realized through struggle. In the case of law, for instance, the 'normative principle' which guided 'the successive expansion of individual basic rights' was 'there from the start as its guiding idea' (1995: 117). Since the ideal of complete mutual recognition is present in embryo in all struggles, the effect of these struggles is progressively to unfold this ideal. At its strongest, Honneth's teleological argument may suggest that even history itself has a rational direction: rather than being, as Macbeth says of life, 'a tale / Told by an idiot, full of sound and fury/ Signifying nothing', it displays a logical and predictable pattern as it moves towards its final destination. On this reading, recognition struggles help to realize history's hidden *telos*, or final purpose, which is to bring about a state of perfect mutual recognition, and so end conflict between the warring parties.[16]

One criticism of this part of Honneth's thesis contends that in practice he offers no justification for this teleology. Thus Peter Osborne argues that, although Honneth 'takes over the early Hegel's identification of struggles for recognition as the dynamic of historical development', in practice 'this thesis is not discursively redeemed' (1996: 35). In other words, Honneth offers no reasons in support of his assertion that recognition struggles are the motor of history. Other critics focus on what they see as Honneth's assumption that history is always progressive, and never regressive. There is, in other words, a ratchet effect at work which means that only moral progress – and not moral regress – is possible. These critics then present counterexamples to this purported effect in which historical reversals see moral gains overturned by later events. Thus Alexander and Lara point out that '[a]partheid laws were imposed during South African modernity; the Nuremburg laws emerged in the midst of what had been considered an expansion of German modernity in the 1920s and early 1930s' (1996: 133). Their conclusion is that Honneth is 'overly confident that the struggle for recognition will lead to progressive social change' (1996: 134). Using the most dramatic example imaginable, Jurist argues that '[a]fter the Holocaust, it is no longer possible to have the illusion that a modern society cannot regress to barbarism' (1994: 177). All of these examples, the critics believe, undermine Honneth's claim that struggles for recognition lead to constant, irreversible moral progress.

What can Honneth say in response to these criticisms? I would argue that, as it stands, Osborne's criticism is too quick. As I said in section 7.2, Honneth does offer reasons to support his claim that struggles for recognition promote historical progress. I suggested that, with regard to his remarks on Marshall's history of British citizenship, Honneth believes that each stage of the expansion of the relations of recognition is caused by the force of the arguments which are unleashed by the previous stage. Thus, once civil rights are won, it becomes hard to resist the idea that political rights should also be enjoyed by all. Osborne may want to argue that this case for historical progress is inadequate, but at least it cannot be denied that Honneth makes it. With regard to the criticism of the claim that moral progress is irreversible, does Honneth have an adequate defence? If he really means to deny that there can be historical phases in which the moral gains of the past are halted or even reversed, then I believe that his position is indefensible. Whether it be the rise of Nazism or just the New Right's attack on the welfare state in the 1980s, it would be foolish to deny that past moral achievements can never be completely protected against future events. Indeed, such a position looks so implausible that I cannot believe that it can be correctly ascribed to Honneth. It may be that one of his friendly critics gets his position about right. Zurn, asking how Honneth might defend his 'implicit claim' that 'uncoerced, full self-realization' should be the standard by which all existing social arrangements are criticized, considers several possibilities (2000: 119). He concludes that the 'most promising' approach is 'to see the telos of non-coerced self-realization as the result of a Hegelian-style rational reconstruction of the immanent progress of history' (2000: 120).[17] In the current context, the important thing to note is that such an approach does not necessarily require one to deny the possibility of reverses in the process of moral development. Rather, it commits one only to look at the broader picture in order to find evidence that, at least in the long run, progress does occur. Thus the resistance to and defeat of Nazism can be adduced as evidence for this view. Of course, this way of reading Honneth's account will still be too strong for many to stomach. But at least it does not require a commitment to a thesis so strong that the invocation of the Holocaust would stand as decisive evidence against it.

In addition to a commitment to teleology, it could be argued that Honneth is also committed to the idea that there is one, and only one, path towards the ideal of complete mutual recognition. There is some evidence for this commitment in his comments on Marshall's account of the development of citizenship. As we saw in section 4.3, Honneth extends and generalizes this account by suggesting that, in modern societies, two distinct forms of recognition have emerged, and that each of these has developed along two distinct dimensions. In the case of recognition as respect, he identifies processes of 'universalization' (as more individuals enjoy the status of citizenship) and 'de-formalization' (as this status comes with an increasing range of rights). In the case of recognition as esteem, he suggests that there are processes of 'individualization' (as individuals, rather than status groups, become the objects of esteem) and 'equalization' (as fixed hierarchies of esteem are replaced by horizontal competition for esteem) (1995: 170). This account of the development of the relations of recognition prompts the following questions. First, is it necessarily the case that these relations expand in just the way described? Second, if they do not, does it necessarily follow that moral progress has been stalled? In order to answer these questions, let us consider each of these four processes in turn.

Honneth contends that the first axis along which legal recognition develops is that of universalization. With regard to this axis, moral development occurs when increasing numbers of people come to be included within the sphere of citizenship. But does Honneth assume that universalization requires the same rights and duties to be applied uniformly to increasing numbers of individuals? Or does he think that this process is compatible with inclusion on a differentiated basis, according to which rights and duties may vary from individual to individual? Commentators from a number of political perspectives argue that, in some circumstances, justice requires the law to be applied differentially. Some argue, for instance, that cultural membership can provide a legitimate reason for exemption from a particular law. One famous example is that of Sikhs enjoying legal exemption from the requirement to wear crash-helmets when riding motor-cycles. From this point of view, it is argued that some laws need to be more particular – rather than more universal – in order to be fair. The second axis along which relations of legal recognition can expand is that of de-formalization. This is a process in which the status of citizenship comes with increasingly substantive rights. Here Honneth makes the familiar social democratic argument that formal rights alone cannot secure justice. If individuals experience unequal levels of resources, then equal formal rights cannot compensate for this inequality. Hence there is a need for substantive social rights, which, by guaranteeing a minimal level of resources, make it possible for all citizens effectively to exercise their formal rights of citizenship. As we know, however, over the last several decades, social rights have come under vigorous and sustained attack. Since the late 1970s, wherever the New Right has had influence, the set of social rights associated with the welfare state has been whittled away. For those associated with the New Right, the reduction of these rights is essential to protect and enhance personal liberty.

Honneth believes that relations of solidarity – like those of law – are also capable of undergoing expansion along two distinct axes. First, such relations can undergo a process of individualization as the object of esteem gradually becomes the individual rather than the group. As we saw in section 4.3, according to Honneth's formal conception of ethical life, individuals should have equal opportunities to earn esteem by using their distinctive traits and abilities to make a contribution to societal goals. In making this claim, Honneth sets himself against a number of theorists of recognition who believe that there are circumstances in which esteem can be appropriately shown not to the individual but to the group as a whole. Thus, in section 4.2, I showed that Taylor believes that it is possible to show esteem for a culture by including its works in the canon. It may be argued, for instance, that in this way due acknowledgement may be given to women's culture or to Islam, rather than to individual women or Muslims. The second axis along which relations of solidarity can expand is that of equalization. For Honneth, moral progress also occurs when fixed hierarchies of esteem are eroded as increasing numbers of individuals come to enjoy equal opportunities to earn esteem. It must be emphasized that, according to Honneth's ideal, individuals should enjoy equal *opportunities* to earn esteem, rather than a guaranteed *level* of esteem. The implication is that in practice some people will enjoy more esteem than others. In this respect, Honneth is opposed to accounts of recognition which insist that esteem should be enjoyed equally by all.[18]

It is not my intention to assess the merits of each of these arguments. Rather than seek to determine whether Honneth's or his critics' accounts of the development of recognition are more satisfactory, I want instead to consider the status of the debate. Honneth contends that recognition struggles lead to moral progress, and that they do so by moving society along the four axes just described. In each case, however, I have shown that there are critics who would question whether each of these processes should really be considered progressive. Against Honneth, it has been argued that moral progress occurs when individual rights become more differentiated, when social rights are removed, when collectivities gain the chance to be esteemed, and when all individuals are offered a guaranteed level of esteem. How should Honneth respond to these dissenting views? Should he instead offer a grand theory of moral progress which seeks to show that his critics are mistaken? Or should he try to offer specific arguments which aim to show, for instance, why it is better that individuals rather than collectivities have the opportunity to be esteemed? I have very little sympathy for the first option, according to which Honneth would airily declare that his critics have failed to understand the nature of recognition. I have much more sympathy for the second option. I think that, if Honneth is to make good his claims about moral progress, he will need to demonstrate in specific terms why his account of the various aspects of this phenomenon is right. Whichever option Honneth chooses, it is clear that his assumption that there is a unique path of moral progress must be discursively redeemed.

A third and final criticism which may be made of this final stage of Honneth's theory focuses on his account of the end-point of the process of moral development. In section 7.2, I showed why he believes that struggles for recognition lead to the expansion of relations of recognition towards a condition in which there is complete mutual recognition. My question is this: does Honneth believe that in this final condition there will be an end to struggles for recognition? There are general theoretical reasons for thinking that he does. It will be recalled that he identifies an 'idealized sequence' of struggles which will lead to his formal conception of ethical life being realized. It seems unlikely that there could be further stages of conflict after this sequence is complete. There are also more particular and concrete reasons for thinking that Honneth envisages an end to recognition struggles. In earlier chapters, I described how a society regulated by the formal conception of ethical life is characterized by two principal features. First, there is a single horizon of value within which individual citizens have an equal opportunity to earn esteem. It would seem to follow that there would be only interpretive battles within this single horizon, rather than any radical challenges to it. Second, all citizens enjoy respect under a legal system which protects their universal rights. Again, it would seem to follow that individuals have no reason to struggle for inclusion within that system, since they are already included. To bring these two points together, it would appear that, within a polity in which the formal conception of ethical life has been realized, there will be no further need for individuals or groups to struggle for recognition.

Against this interpretation, it could be argued that there are points at which Honneth implies that moral progress towards his ethical ideal does not mean that struggles for recognition will cease. Even if his formal conception of ethical life is realized, he suggests, struggles will still continue. Given the argument of the previous paragraph, I do not think that such struggles could take the dramatic form that they do prior to the realization of the formal conception. It may be, however, that struggles could continue in a rather attenuated form. For instance, struggles for respect may continue as the citizens of Honneth's ideal polity dispute the particular interpretation, and thus the method of implementation, of a particular right. They may argue, for instance, about whether social rights should include a guarantee of employment or not. Similarly, struggles for esteem may also persist, albeit in a rather etiolated way, in Honneth's ideal polity. There may be ongoing debates – I hesitate to call them struggles – about the significance of particular values within the general horizon of value. As Honneth himself suggests, society's value horizon will be 'permanently subject to cultural conflict' (1995: 126) as a result of an ongoing struggle over the interpretation of society's goals (1995: 127). While domestic labour is valued, is it given sufficient recognition? Although African-Americans now enjoy formal legal equality with other Americans, do the forms of depreciation from which they continue to suffer damage their chances of self-realization? Do laws to protect people against those who incite racial hatred give sufficient protection to those singled out on specifically religious grounds? In this sense, Honneth might claim that struggles for recognition will continue without cease, although I think it must be conceded that they will be only a shadow of their former selves.

Is it plausible to think that in the future, recognition struggles will significantly diminish in significance, or even entirely cease? I believe that there are reasons for thinking, to the contrary, that struggles for recognition cannot be either ended or limited in the ways just postulated. Instead, I would argue, such struggles will continue to pose radical challenges to the political *status quo*. For the purposes of the current argument, I shall draw on James Tully's analysis of struggles for recognition. He gives a series of reasons for thinking that such struggles should not be regarded as a temporary phase which precedes a final, stable state of complete mutual recognition (1999: 175; 2000: 472, 477; 2001: 20). He invokes in particular the following considerations. First, such struggles are complex and unpredictable. For instance, they nearly always involve more than two parties; hence they are not simply dialogical but multilogical (2000: 474; 2001: 5, 20). Second, one demand for recognition provokes another (2000: 474). Thus a never-ending series of demands is made over time, each sparked off by previous demands. Third, there are always asymmetries of recognition, so misrecognition will always exist (2000: 474–5, 477; 2001: 7). It follows that, since all sets of rules of recognition harbour some elements of misrecognition, new demands will be made, and so struggles will continue. There will always be grounds for making new demands for recognition. Fourth, all rules of recognition are necessarily compromises (2000: 475). It is impossible finally to satisfy all parties' demands. Fifth, discussions about recognition take place in real time under real constraints (2000: 476; 2001: 28). Since a decision has to be made and enacted, it is impossible for people to talk until all are agreed. Sixth, there can always be reasonable disagreement about, for instance, how to implement the decisions taken (2000: 476; 2001: 28). People can disagree about how particular rules of recognition should be operationalized in practice. Seventh, identities change in the course of negotiations (2000: 476; 2001: 29). Our identities as citizens are formed by our participation in politics. Hence, as we demand, disclose, acknowledge and accommodate, our sense of who we are changes, and with this our sense of what we want and deserve to struggle for.[19] Tully's conclusion is that struggles for recognition will go on without end. Indeed, he believes that they *should* not cease. This is because such struggles are an endless battle against injustice, and an incessant practice of freedom (2001: 22). It is clear that Tully's analysis presents a serious challenge to both interpretations of Honneth's account. In other words, it gives us reason to think that recognition struggles will not lessen or end.

7.4 Conclusions

In this chapter, I have conducted a critical examination of Honneth's account of struggles for recognition. I suggested that it is worth focusing on this account, since Honneth, to a much greater extent than either Taylor or Fraser, seeks to develop an account of such struggles that draws strongly on Hegelian ideas. Indeed, his highly ambitious thesis is that an understanding of the nature of recognition struggles can help to forge a link between an account of 'everyday suffering' and a theory of moral progress. As he says, 'the moral force within lived social reality is a struggle for recognition' (1995: 143). It came as no surprise to find that this highly ambitious account of struggles for recognition has attracted its critics. Focusing on the link that Honneth makes between the experience of hurt feelings and a sense of injustice, I considered various ways in which this link could fail. What this discussion has suggested is that his account of the nature of emotions needs more work if it is to be able to serve as the foundation of this theory. Moving on to the relationship which Honneth believes exists between a sense of injustice and the outbreak of struggle, I highlighted the vital role that frameworks of interpretation play in mediating that relationship. I also suggested that a range of other factors – such as resources, incentives and opportunities – have a vital role to play. Finally, with regard to the last link in the argument between recognition struggles and moral progress, I considered various challenges to the teleological assumptions underlying Honneth's argument. Here I drew in particular on Tully's argument that recognition struggles cannot, and should not, cease.

If there is a single argument which emerges from this discussion, it is that Honneth, in his account of struggles for recognition, finds himself pulled in two different directions. On the one hand, he wants to claim that emotions constitute a source of knowledge about social conditions which is in a sense uncorrupted by those conditions. More than this, he wants to say that the knowledge they provide is of an especially reliable kind. In this way, he aligns himself with those philosophers who defend an epistemic account of the emotions (e.g. Nussbaum 2003). On the other hand, Honneth tries to allow that various mediating institutions and the ideas with which they are associated can play a key role in determining the significance of the emotions. We see this in his references to the role of 'moral doctrines or ideas' and 'moral culture', and in his insistence on the importance of an appropriately constituted 'democratic public sphere' within which emotions can be adequately expressed. The problem is that these two impulses are in tension with one other. In order to show that hurt feelings are the raw, untainted data which can be used as the basis for a normative critique of society, Honneth must play down the role of mediation. Without taking mediation properly into account, however, he is vulnerable to the criticism that his theory depends on an anthropological or social psychological foundationalism. I can see no easy way in which Honneth could square this circle.

8

Conclusion

My purpose in this book has been to conduct a critical analysis of three well-known political theories of recognition. Charles Taylor, Axel Honneth and Nancy Fraser all believe that a just society is one in which everyone receives due recognition. I wanted to assess the strengths and weaknesses of each of these theories, in order to determine which one of them – or which combination of elements from different theories – is the most coherent and convincing. While I concentrated on the debate between these three theorists, I also considered alternative ways of thinking about recognition, and I assessed a range of criticisms made of the very idea of a politics of recognition. In chapter 1 I said that, if Taylor, Honneth and Fraser are right about the importance of recognition, then an examination of their theories could provide important insights into the shape of the contemporary political landscape, and also provide invaluable guidance in matters of social justice. Having studied these theories in detail, I can now remove the conditional 'if' from the previous sentence. I think that the political theory of recognition *does* have important things to say about the nature of contemporary politics. For instance, it can help us to understand the significance of the politics of identity and difference, and the importance of the ongoing debate between multiculturalists and their critics. It also enables us take a principled stance with respect to these developments. For instance, it can help us to decide which individual rights should be protected, whether cultures ought to be valued, and whether a case can be made for group representation. Of course, I would not claim that the political theory of recognition will always have an answer to all questions of this kind. In any case, I have shown that there are a number of different theories, each of which is likely to offer a different answer. Nor would I claim for a moment that the answer that a political theory of recognition came up with would necessarily be the right one. As I have shown, there are a number of serious criticisms which all of these theories must face. Nevertheless, I do think that it is always worth listening to what political theorists of recognition have to say.

My analysis of the debate between Taylor, Honneth, Fraser and their critics has led me to a number of conclusions about the form that a political theory of recognition should take. To begin with, it could incorporate a psychological account of identity formation based on an idea of recognition, so long as this account does not take the form of a foundationalism, accepts that experiences of recognition and misrecognition are rooted in material conditions and mediated by social institutions, and is prepared to defend the empirical basis on which it depends. In addition, it should be based on a clear distinction between respect and esteem, so that arguments for protecting individual rights and for protecting collective cultures are kept separate. This would make it possible to argue both that justifying special provision for members of particular cultures does not need to invoke claims about cultural value, and that it is legitimate to allow groups to defend their cultures so long as they are not offered guarantees of survival. Moreover, it must synthesize the best of Fraser's and Honneth's accounts of the relationship between recognition and distribution, so that the resulting tripartite theory incorporates cultural, economic and political dimensions. It should also take seriously Fraser's analysis of the circularity of democratic justice. As she says, while recognition is a necessary condition of democracy, democratic deliberation determines the content of justice. In specific circumstances, the theory I favour would also support systems for the special representation of particular groups. Finally, it should seek to understand the character of struggles for recognition by developing a framework of analysis in which both emotions themselves and their forms of social mediation have an important role to play. It should also accept Tully's argument that struggles for recognition will continue without cease. Of course, I have not tried to offer a complete justification for these claims. My aim in this book has been to present a critical analysis of a range of existing political theories of recognition. The defence of my own particular theory of recognition which would incorporate all of these claims must wait for another day.

Notes

Chapter 1 Introduction

1 At <http://www.elysee.fr/ang/rech/rech_.htm>, accessed 29 September 2005.

2 At <http://www.guardian.co.uk/usa/story/0,12271,1167874,00.html,> accessed 29 September 2005.

3 At <http://www.whitehouse.gov/news/releases/2004/01/20040120-7. html,> accessed 29 September 2005.

4 This is also referred to as the dialectic of master and slave. See O'Neill 1996 for Hegel's original text and a series of very useful commentaries.

5 For excellent recent studies of the Frankfurt School, see Bottomore 2002 and Jay 1996.

6 I could have looked at other features of such theories. For example, a number of them include justifications for innovative forms of political representation, collective self-determination and historical restitution. In this case, my decision to focus on redistribution, democracy and struggle may look arbitrary. In defence of this selection, I would argue that these three themes are of importance to all political theories of recognition. Furthermore, each of them figures as a major theme in at least one of the theories of particular interest to me here.

Chapter 2 Recognition as Love

1 Patchen Markell (2003: ch. 2) argues that, since Taylor carries this idea of authenticity over into his political theory, his political ideal of recognition harbours an ontological form of misrecognition.

2 For an implicit acknowledgement of the role of a 'philosophical anthropology' in his theory of recognition, see Honneth 2002: 500.

3 In the next two chapters, I shall argue that Honneth's conceptions of respect and esteem can be correlated with the two forms of public recognition that Taylor distinguishes. To be specific, Taylor's politics of universalism and politics of difference map on to Honneth's conceptions of recognition as respect and recognition as esteem, respectively.

4 It may be noted that this characteristic is not unique to love. Honneth also draws attention to the affective quality of esteem. By contrast, he refers to 'cognitive respect' (1995: 129; and see 110), which suggests that he thinks that this mode of recognition is without affect.

5 This emphasis on the positive character of affect accords with the idea that recognition is always a matter of positive acknowledgement. See, for instance, Abbey 2000: 138; Anderson, in Honneth 1995: p. viii; Inwood 1992: 245.

6 In his strong reading of Honneth, Arto Laitinen uses the idea of 'singularity' to emphasize that this mode of recognition is directed to unique individuals (2002: 470–2).

7 There are, of course, other accounts of love which appear to place no such restriction on it. For example, the Christian doctrine of brotherly love – seen in the injunction to love one's neighbour – suggests that love should not be limited to our significant others. It is worth reiterating that in the present context 'love' is being used in a very specific sense to refer to a person's strong emotional connection to their significant others. For this reason, it is almost true by definition that love – as the term is understood here – is necessarily restricted in scope.

8 This idea of bodily self-confidence corresponds to R. D. Laing's conception of 'ontological security' (1965) and Erik Erikson's conception of 'trust' (1959). Building on these ideas, Anthony Giddens contends that what he calls 'trust' is 'the main emotional support or *protective cocoon* which all normal individuals carry around with them as the means whereby they are able to get on with the affairs of day-to-day life' (1991: 40).

9 In an essay from 2002, Honneth develops this idea further. Here he argues that 'the early childhood experiences of symbiosis have life-long influences, in that they compel the subject to rebel again and again against the experience of not having the other at our disposal' (2002: 504).

10 In his theory of recognition, James Tully takes this sort of account even further. Following Jacques Derrida in particular, he endorses an idea of 'non-self identity'. By this he means that identity is always different from itself as well as from others (1995: 45). Tully defends such a conception of identity because he wants to claim that recognition is a process rather than a condition, and therefore struggles for recognition will go on without end.

11 I discuss different aspects of this case in chapters 3 and 4 in particular.

12 Taylor's remarks echo Anthony Appiah's distinction between the 'two major dimensions' of 'individual identity': 'a collective dimension' and 'a personal dimension' (1994: 151). Perhaps he would also share Appiah's worry that the politics of recognition may seek to regulate aspects of identity that should be kept personal, where 'personal means not secret, but not too tightly scripted' (1994: 163).

13 This is an allusion to John Locke's *Letter Concerning Toleration* (1689), in which he argues that, in matters of religious faith, coercion – as the only alternative to toleration – cannot work since faith cannot be compelled.

14 For more details, see section 4.4.

15 In a personal communication, Christopher Zurn has suggested to me that, if Fraser herself were to take this route, her model of recognition would effectively cease to be a form of critical theory.

16 I return briefly to this issue in section 5.4.

17 For example, if Fraser can show that Honneth is wrong to claim that the acquisition of bodily self-confidence is necessary for the development of self-respect and self-esteem, then she will have made an effective criticism of Honneth's position.

Chapter 3 Recognition as Respect

1 Cécile Laborde's subtle analysis (2002) of the idea of *laïcité* suggests that Raffarin's argument depends on a very partial account of this idea.

2 It could be argued that Taylor identifies a third form which the politics of recognition can take. He suggests that civic humanism is a political tradition which is centred on the importance of 'participatory self-rule'. Such self-rule, he suggests, is essential to the dignity of a people (1995b: 199). On this account, civic humanism could be seen as a form of the politics of respect in which it is not individual citizens but 'the people' itself which is the object of respect. For further discussion of this idea, see chapter 6.

3 The final category of rights are defended by those universalists who believe that excessive inequality of resources creates a distinction between first- and second-class citizens.

4 At <http://www.un.org/Overview/rights.html>, accessed 11 August 2005.

5 It may be noted that here my reading of Taylor is opposed to those accounts which assume that he rejects the politics of universalism in its entirety.

6 It must be admitted that this model of procedural liberalism fails to capture many of the subtleties of the theories of justice articulated by Dworkin, Rawls and others. This does not matter for my current purposes, however, since this is the model against which Taylor defines his own position.

7 As we shall see in the next chapter, Barry responds robustly to Taylor's point by arguing that 'it is "difference-blind" liberalism that gets the right answers and the "politics of difference" that should be rejected' (2001: 65).

8 Others who defend a line close to Taylor's include Will Kymlicka 1998 and Kenneth McRoberts 1997. It should be noted, however, that other commentators contend that this way of regarding the relationship between Quebec and the rest of Canada through the lens of recognition severely misrepresents the case. They argue, by contrast, that since Quebec is a nation in all but name, it wants independence from – rather than recognition by – the rest of Canada.

9 It is in this light that struggles for respect can be understood as practical attempts to realize current expectations about the necessary conditions of rational agency – where these expectations exceed existing reality. I discuss this idea further in chapter 7 in an analysis of Honneth's account of struggles for recognition.

10 I return to the issue of social rights in chapter 5 when discussing the relationship between recognition and redistribution.

11 In a conversation with the author, Fraser suggested that universalist recognition may be appropriate at a variety of levels. Thus, in so far as we share a biosphere, we should be recognized as equal beings; and, in so far as we share a common polity, we should be recognized as equal citizens.

12 I would suggest that, if she made her commitment to this form of recognition more explicit, she would answer critics like Barry who contends that she (and Iris Young) reject 'the liberal contention that it makes sense to talk about equal rights, and that the case for equal rights can be made on the basis of an appeal to justice' (2001: 278).

13 They may also suffer 'exclusion or marginalization from public spheres and deliberative bodies' (2003: 21). I shall return to this point in chapter 6.

14 As I shall argue in section 3.5, this last point may tell against Honneth's close association of respect and rights. It suggests that equal respect can be shown not just by providing equal rights, but by removing existing rights as well.

15 It could be that with this comment Fraser answers Barry's charge that she 'gets everything back to front' by suggesting that 'permissive legislation' follows '[m]ore liberal attitudes' (2001: 275). Here she implies, rather, that changing marriage laws would 'foster parity of participation'.

16 Here Fraser's account steps over some important complications. In theory, the French law places a ban on all conspicuous religious symbols – be they headscarves or crosses. In practice, however, since crosses are much less likely to be considered conspicuous, the ban effectively discriminates against the wearers of headscarves. In this context, Anna Galeotti remarks that, for the dominant majority in society, their habits and customs are considered normal: they can 'be "normally" present and "quietly" visible in the public space' (2002: 73). For her earlier debate with Norma Moruzzi, see Galeotti 1993, 1994; and Moruzzi 1994a, 1994b. I shall return to this issue in the next chapter.

17 Fraser herself believes that allowing the *foulard* would not erect new boundaries to participatory parity since in fact it is 'a symbol of Muslim identity in transition' (2003: 42). She emphasizes, however, that the authoritative answer to this question can be decided only in a democratic debate in which all citizens take part (2003: 42). I discuss this idea further in chapter 6 below.

18 For a useful overview, see Larrivee 2003.

19 In an essay in response to criticism from Heikki Ikäheimo (2002), Honneth appears to loosen somewhat the connection between particular modes of recognition and particular political mechanisms. Thus he suggests that 'we can often demonstrate to children that we care by confirming their autonomy through the attribution of non-juridical rights, or we can grant persons formal rights that protect them exclusively with regard to their singularity' (2002: 511). Notice, however, that these concessions do not allow that respect can be shown to adults through means other than juridical rights.

Chapter 4 Recognition as Esteem

1 At <http://www.arts.ulst.ac.uk/ulsterscots/>, accessed 29 September 2005.

2 Her Majesty's Stationery Office 1998.

3 For further analysis of this particular case of the politics of recognition in action, see Thompson 2002, 2003.

4 It should be noted that, for some commentators, this interpretation of the Canadian situation in terms of the politics of recognition is highly tendentious. They argue that, since Quebec is a distinct polity in all but name, the objective should not be to win acknowledgement of its identity from the rest of Canada, but to secure its sovereignty as an independent nation-state.

5 For the Runnymede Trust, Islamophobia 'refers to unfounded hostility towards Islam. It refers also to the practical consequences of such

hostility in unfair discrimination against Muslim individuals and communities, and to the exclusion of Muslims from mainstream political and social affairs' (1997).

6 For useful overviews of communitarianism, see Kymlicka 2002: ch. 6; Mulhall and Swift 1996.

7 It may be worth noting that there are two distinct arguments at work here, one based on a principle of equality, the other on an account of human psychology. It is important not to conflate the two, since it would be possible to argue for equal cultural value using either argument on its own.

8 In his essay on 'Comparison, History, Truth' (1995a), Taylor suggests that magic has been misunderstood in this way, first regarded as a method of control to be compared with science and technology, and later understood as a way of making sense of the world. Although the latter may be less explicitly ethnocentric than the former, both understand magic in the terms in which we understand the world. Since we value both control of the environment and sense-making, we assume that they do too.

9 I shall say more in defence of this claim in section 4.5.

10 I return to this theme in chapter 7 when considering Honneth's analysis of struggles for recognition.

11 Note that, in the first of these two quotations, Fraser appears to define status in such a way that its very existence is sufficient evidence of injustice. Where there is status, there is injustice. In the second quotation, by contrast, she emphasizes that it is status *hierarchy* that is unjust. This may leave open the possibility that there could be a just status order, one compatible with parity of participation.

12 It might be possible to align this second form of recognition with Honneth's conception of a pluralized value horizon. In the previous section, I showed why he believes that, the wider the range of values encompassed within a particular value horizon, the greater the chance that all individuals can be esteemed.

13 Several phrases in the paragraph are adapted from Thompson 1998: 198.

14 I shall discuss both of these possibilities in more detail below.

15 With reference to 'French culture in Quebec', Barry asks why this should be defined first and foremost in terms of the French language rather than in terms, say, of 'adherence to the Roman Catholic Church' (2001: 66).

16 Compare Smith 2002: 158–9 and Wolf 1994: 77–85.

17 As Barry argues, 'justice demands that under some conditions state services should be offered in more than one language' (2001: 65; and see 103–4, 215–20).

18 On 10 June 2004, a group of Muslim academics and educationalists issued a report claiming that the British school system is presently failing to meet the needs of Muslim students. The report calls amongst other things for the introduction of a school qualification in Islamic Studies. It should be noted that the case for such a qualification rests neither on a crude assumption of equal cultural value nor on an account of psychological damage, but on an argument about the need for cultural inclusion to guarantee equal educational opportunity.

19 *Zakat*, or alms-giving, is one of the five pillars of Islam. Muslims are obliged to give 2.5 per cent of their income to the needy.

20 Smith considers the similar charge – which he then goes on to refute – that the guarantee of cultural survival will lead to the forced assimilation of those who do not presently subscribe to that culture (2002: 161–4). Abbey considers a different potential problem for Taylor's account. She points out that guaranteeing cultural survival may be possible only by abandoning a commitment to state neutrality. A government which wishes to ensure the survival of a particular culture may have to treat this culture differently from others. She concludes, however, that Taylor is not vulnerable to this criticism, since he is not committed to a strong version of neutrality (2000: 142–8).

21 In the analysis that follows, I try to avoid formulations, such as that used by Taylor, which anthropomorphize culture. Culture is not an agent which is able to defend itself. Rather, there are human groups who associate themselves with particular cultures, and it is these groups that may take action to defend their cultures.

22 Patchen Markell (2003: 20) reaches the same conclusion by a slightly different route.

Chapter 5 Recognition and Redistribution

1 At <http://www.guardian.co.uk/print/0,3858,4863437-110592,00.html> accessed 17 August 2005.

2 The way Fraser puts this point suggests that we have a choice: we can use *either* perspective to understand *either* social domain. However, since she insists that all injustices contain both cultural and economic elements, it would make more sense to recommend the adoption of a standpoint in which both perspectives were united. She should, in other words, recommend the adoption of a single 'binocular' vision, rather than a choice of one of two 'monocles' at a time.

3 On this point, recall Richard Sennett's remarks about 'shameful' dependence in section 3.5.

4 These various aspects of Fraser's theory were explicated in detail in sections 3.4 and 4.4 above.

5 Chapter 7 focuses on the role of such a phenomenology in Honneth's analysis of struggles for recognition.

6 Confusingly, Honneth uses the word 'disrespect' (*Mißachtung*) to refer to all forms of misrecognition (e.g. 2003: 135). I use the word 'misrecognition' to refer generally to all cases of withheld recognition, and reserve 'disrespect' for those cases where it is respect that is withheld.

7 It should be noted that this particular interpretation of esteem in terms of a principle of achievement is one that Honneth himself rejects. See section 4.3 for further discussion.

8 In chapters 3 and 4, I assessed the relative merits of Fraser's and Honneth's accounts of recognition. In the following discussion, therefore, I focus almost exclusively on the implications of these two theorists' arguments for the relationship between recognition and redistribution.

9 For a parallel argument, see Zurn 2005: 108–10.

10 In a similar vein, James Tully argues that 'identity-related struggles have effects in the realm of distribution of power and resources . . . and, conversely, struggles over distribution are also always struggles over recognition' (2004: 87).

11 For a well-known example of this sort of argument, see Kymlicka 1995.

12 In light of these remarks, it is interesting to note Fraser's observation that Kymlicka's theory suits multinational rather than what he calls 'polyethnic' cases (2003: 100 n.35). Turning this around, I would say that Fraser's theory – at least as it stands – does not cope well with multinational cases.

13 In an as yet unpublished lecture entitled 'Re-framing Justice in a Globalizing World', Fraser now accepts that her 'two-dimensional understanding of justice . . . does not go far enough'. There is, she concedes, a 'third dimension of justice' – namely, '*the political*'. This 'concerns the constitution of the state's jurisdiction and the decision rules by which it structures contestation'.

14 In the case of global capitalism, one useful starting point would be Harvey 2004.

15 See, e.g., Hodgson 2001: ch. 19 for a thesis about the limited but still significant role of culture in the classification of economic systems.

16 As I mentioned in n. 13 above, Fraser now admits that there is a third, political dimension to justice. In this case, she must presumably also agree that social theory must incorporate a third analytical perspective.

17 It may be noted that Fraser presents a picture of Honneth's social theory which appears to be at odds with the interpretation that I offered in section 5.3. There I suggested that Honneth endorses a hermeneutic form of social theory that centres on the interpretation of cultural values. By contrast, Fraser argues that his social theory takes the form of

a foundationalist social psychology. I accept that Fraser is right to emphasize that Honneth's normative lodestone is self-realization. He believes that a just society is one in which relations of recognition make such self-realization possible. These two different interpretations of Honneth's theory are nevertheless compatible. For Honneth, the *activity* of social theory consists of cultural interpretation. However, the *point* of this activity is to determine whether the cultural values prevalent in the existing social order help or hinder individual self-realization.

18 With regard to this aspect of Fraser's theory, Zurn argues that it is 'certainly an improvement over Taylor's attempt to develop a non-procedural liberalism on the basis of a specific, substantive account of the good life' (2003: 527–8).

19 Zurn thinks that he takes the sectarian option: 'Honneth's project in fact presupposes a delimited range of available forms of the good, precisely because it attempts to focus on a perfectionist model of self-realization' (2003: 528).

20 In chapter 7, this theme is pursued further in an analysis of Honneth's account of struggles for recognition. I argue there that this account attempts to reconcile a foundationalist psychology with a social theory which seeks to acknowledge the mediating role of social institutions.

Chapter 6 Recognition and Democracy

1 For an up-to-date account of the New Zealand political system, see Mulgan 2004.

2 Compare Roger Maaka and Augie Fleras's remark that it 'reflects an integrationist (or "institutional") model of tino rangatiratanga that revolves around participation in the established parliamentary system' (2000: 104).

3 At <http://onenews.nzoom.com/onenews_detail/0,1227,251436-1-8,00.html>, accessed 19 August 2005.

4 This is a slight simplification, since, as I argued in section 4.5, it is necessary to draw a distinction between Taylor's arguments about cultural value and cultural survival.

5 In the next section, I shall ask if this criticism applies to Taylor's republican model of democracy.

6 Compare Hilary Putnam's account of democracy as 'the precondition for the full application of intelligence to the solution of social problems' (1995: 180); and John Keane's description of Karl Popper's case for democracy as 'a unique type of polity that contributes to evolutionary learning by enabling the public refutation of nonsense through public conjectures linked to truth claims' (2004–5: 2).

7 For further discussion of this idea, see section 4.3.

8 In section 4.5, I proposed an extension to Honneth's argument. I suggested that the grounds for esteem should be broadened to include not just individual traits and abilities, but also aspects of cultural identity. In this case, esteem may be given in light of the contribution which a distinctive culture makes to society as a whole.

9 In what follows, I follow Owen's analysis of Honneth's model very closely.

10 See sections 3.3 and 4.3 for more detailed accounts of the developmental potential of respect and esteem, respectively.

11 In spite of this injunction, Fraser does on occasion go beyond this limited role to put forward her own substantive arguments about the justice of particular public policies (2003: 72). She offers, for instance, her own opinion about the justice of banning of the *foulard* in French public schools (2003: 42).

12 It should be noted that in section 5.4 I argued that parity of participation does not pass Fraser's own test of nonsectarianism. I shall return to this point in section 6.5.

13 Another criticism concerns the sectarianism of Taylor's and Honneth's accounts. From Fraser's perspective, any justification of democracy which makes reference to common purposes or societal goals should be avoided, since it invokes, or at least presumes, particular ethical values which are not endorsed by all citizens. I shall defer further discussion of this issue until later on in this section.

14 It may be noted that this conclusion echoes Taylor's own concern – mentioned in section 6.2 – about the dynamics of exclusion in contemporary democracies.

15 For further details, see section 4.3.

16 It may be noted that my proposal about how to respond to the first part of this criticism has made it harder to deal with the second part. If, in order to avoid an unrealistic account of the possibility of political harmony, it is argued that a democracy needs only a weak sense of common fate, this could worsen the problem of motivation by giving citizens less reason to participate in democratic deliberation.

17 This way of putting it alludes to Richard Wollheim's (1962) analysis of what he calls a 'paradox in the theory of democracy'.

Chapter 7 Struggles for Recognition

1 See especially Sartre 1943: pt III, ch. 3. As Fanon puts it, Sartre offers 'a description of love as frustration' (1952: 41). In Honneth's rather more wordy formulation, Sartre deploys the idea of a struggle for

recognition to show 'that the prospect of a state of interpersonal reconciliation is, as it were, ontologically excluded' (1995: 156).

2 Here I paraphrase Michael Walzer's 1995 introduction to Sartre
1946: p. ix.

3 On this account, even if the second party also judged the first according to the same set of values, this would simply be a separate act of
one-way recognition.

4 Compare Judith Shklar's suggestion that our sense of injustice arises
'when we do not get what we believe to be our due' (1990: 83).

5 Here Honneth's account closely resembles David Snow and Robert
Benford's work on 'frame alignment' (Snow and Benford 1988;
Benford and Snow 2000). In particular, by placing the idea of 'motivational framing' alongside 'diagnostic framing' ('What's the problem?')
and 'prognostic framing' ('Who is to blame?'), they open up a space in
which to understand the role of the emotions in social mobilization.

6 It could be argued that the development of the concept of
Islamophobia is an attempt to achieve the same goal: to provide a
framework for interpreting experience which demonstrates the existence of a pattern of anti-Muslim prejudice and behaviour.

7 Patchen Markell makes the very interesting point that, while
Honneth says a great deal about the motivating power of misrecognition, he says very little about the motives of those who benefit from
such misrecognition (2003: 21).

8 On this subject, Christopher Zurn claims that one advantage of Nancy
Fraser's status model of recognition is that it can 'handle instances of
unjust subordination due to misrecognition that are nevertheless not
noticed by some or all of its victims' (2003: 533).

9 At its strongest, Foster's thesis implies that the very idea of cultural
recognition is a form of ideological mystification which distracts people from the real problem of socio-economic inequality. In Fraser's
terms, it would thus be an instance of 'culturalism'. See section 5.2
for further discussion of this idea.

10 Jurist also suggests that 'specific phenomena like learned helplessness
and identification with the aggressor, and . . . the whole problem of
masochism' may help to explain whether people will engage in resistance or not (1994: 176).

11 Indeed, even if the immigrants do enjoy greater resources, this may
well be justifiable on the good egalitarian grounds that it is necessary
to concentrate greater resources on those who are more needy.

12 For an insightful account of Serbian nationalism, see Anzulovic 1999.

13 Another possibility is worth mentioning. In some circumstances,
people may argue that they are victims of some injustice in order to
claim compensation. They may, for instance, claim that their cultural

identity has been unduly neglected in order to try to obtain certain resources. In some cases, of course, this claim may be quite genuine. But it is also possible that there may be a strategic choice deliberately to exaggerate or deceive in order to gain particular advantages. I do not consider this possibility in the main body of my argument since, strictly speaking, it is not a case of hurt feelings without just cause, but rather a case of *falsely asserting* that one's feelings are hurt.

14 This criticism echoes Fraser's concerns about the 'Platonic' approach to determining the 'requirements of justice' (2003: 70).

15 A stronger version of this thesis would argue that, rather than simply offering an explanation of pre-existing emotions, frameworks of interpretation actually bring those emotions into existence.

16 I would suggest that G. A. Cohen's idea of 'third-grade potentiality', which he uses in his analysis of Hegel's philosophy of history, describes Honneth's position well: 'If y is third-grade potentiality of x, then x becomes y unless its natural development is impeded'; 'in third-grade potentiality x would become y under *all normal* conditions' (1978: 15). In stark contrast, consider Thomas Hardy's diary entry from 1882 in which he describes 'living in a world where nothing bears out in practice what it promises incipiently' (cited in Irving 1989: 594).

17 Note that, for Zurn, even this way of justifying the ideal of self-realization must still confront the is/ought problem discussed earlier on in this section. As he says: 'The problem is . . . to show that the telos of self-realization through intersubjective recognition itself should be the governing ideal of social organization' (2000: 121).

18 As we saw in section 4.2, Taylor also criticizes such accounts of esteem.

19 At one point, Tully describes these last three reasons as 'factors of plurality' (2001: 29).

References

Abbey, Ruth (2000) *Charles Taylor*, London: Acumen.

Alexander, J. C. and Pia Lara, Maria (1996) 'Honneth's New Critical Theory of Recognition', *New Left Review*, no. 220, 126–36.

Anzulovic, Branimir (1999) *Heavenly Serbia: From Myth to Genocide*, London: Hurst & Co.

Appiah, K. Anthony (1994) 'Identity, Authenticity, Survival: Multicultural Societies and Social Reproduction', in Amy Gutmann (ed.), *Multiculturalism: Examining the Politics of Recognition*, Princeton: Princeton University Press.

Barry, Brian (2001) *Culture and Equality: An Egalitarian Critique of Multiculturalism*, Cambridge: Polity.

Benford, Robert and Snow, David (2000) 'Framing Processes and Social Movements: An Overview and Assessment', *Annual Review of Sociology*, 26, 11–39.

Benjamin, Jessica (1988) *The Bonds of Love: Psychoanalysis, Feminism and the Problem of Domination*, New York: Pantheon.

Blum, Lawrence (1998) 'Recognition, Value and Equality: A Critique of Charles Taylor's and Nancy Fraser's Accounts of Multiculturalism', *Constellations*, 5 (1), 51–68.

Bottomore, Tom (2002) *The Frankfurt School and its Critics*, London: Routledge.

Butler, Judith (1998) 'Merely Cultural', *New Left Review*, no. 227, 33–44.

Chong, Dennis (1991) *Collective Action and the Civil Rights Movement*, Chicago: University of Chicago Press.

Cohen, G. A. (1978) *Karl Marx's Theory of History: A Defence*, Princeton: Princeton University Press.

Cook, Robert (1998) *Sweet Land of Liberty? The African-American Struggle for Civil Rights in the Twentieth Century*, Harlow: Longman.

Dworkin, Ronald (1978) 'Liberalism', in Stuart Hampshire (ed.), *Public and Private Morality*, Cambridge: Cambridge University Press.
—— (1986) *Law's Empire*, London: Fontana.
Eisenberg, Avigail (1994) 'The Politics of Individual and Group Difference in Canadian Jurisprudence', *Canadian Journal of Political Science*, 27 (1), 3–21.
Erikson, Erik (1959) *Identity and the Life Cycle*, repr. New York: W. W. Norton, 1994.
Fairclough, Adam (2002) *Better Day Coming: Blacks and Equality 1980–2000*, Harmondsworth: Penguin.
Fanon, Frantz (1952) *Black Skin, White Masks*, repr. New York: Grove Press, 1967.
—— (1967) *The Wretched of the Earth*, repr. London: Penguin, 1990.
Feinberg, Joel (1980) 'The Nature and Value of Rights', in his *Rights, Justice, and the Bounds of Liberty: Essays in Social Philosophy*, Princeton: Princeton University Press.
Feldman, Leonard (2002) 'Redistribution, Recognition, and the State: The Irreducibly Political Dimension of Injustice', *Political Theory*, 30 (3), 410–40.
Finlayson, Alan (1997) 'The Problem of Culture in Northern Ireland: A Critique of the Cultural Traditions Group of the Community Relations Council', *Irish Review*, 20, 76–88.
Foster, R. (1999) 'Recognition and Resistance: Axel Honneth's Critical Social Theory', *Radical Philosophy*, no. 94 (March/April), 6–18.
Foucault, Michel (1976) *The History of Sexuality*, vol. 1: *An Introduction*, New York: Vintage Press.
Fraser, Nancy (1995) 'From Redistribution to Recognition? Dilemmas of Justice in a "Postsocialist" Age', *New Left Review*, no. 212, 68–93.
—— (1997) *Justice Interruptus: Critical Reflections on the "Postsocialist" Condition*, London: Routledge.
—— (2000) 'Rethinking Recognition', *New Left Review*, no. 3, 107–120.
—— (2001) 'Recognition without Ethics?', *Theory, Culture and Society*, 18 (2–3), 21–42.
—— (2003) Contributions to *idem* and Axel Honneth, *Redistribution or Recognition? A Political-Philosophical Exchange*, London: Verso.
Galeotti, Anna Elisabetta (1993) 'Citizenship and Equality: The Place for Toleration', *Political Theory*, 21 (4), 585–605.
—— (1994) 'A Problem with Theory: A Rejoinder to Moruzzi', *Political Theory*, 22 (4), 673–7.
—— (2002) *Toleration as Recognition*, Cambridge: Cambridge University Press.
Gamble, Andrew and Wright, Tony (eds) (1999) *The New Social Democracy*, Oxford: Blackwell.
Giddens, Anthony (1991) *Modernity and Self-Identity: Self and Society in the Late Modern Age*, Cambridge: Polity.
Habermas, Jürgen (1994) 'Struggles for Recognition in the Democratic Constitutional State', in Amy Gutmann (ed.), *Multiculturalism: Examining the Politics of Recognition*, Princeton: Princeton University Press.

Harvey, David (2004) *The New Imperialism*, Oxford: Oxford University Press.

Hegel, G. W. F. (1807) *The Phenomenology of Mind*, ed. James Baillie, London: George Allen & Unwin, revised 2nd edn, 1949.

Held, David et al. (1999) *Global Transformations: Politics, Economics, and Culture*, Stanford, Calif.: Stanford University Press.

Her Majesty's Stationery Office (1998) *The Agreement Reached in the Multi-Party Negotiations*, London: HMSO.

Hodgson, Geoffrey (2001) *How Economics Forgot History: The Problem of Historical Specificity in Social Science*, London: Routledge.

Holst-Warhaft, Gail (2000) *The Cue for Passion: Grief and its Political Uses*, Cambridge, Mass.: Harvard University Press.

Honneth, Axel (1992) 'Integrity and Disrespect: Principles of a Conception of Morality Based on the Theory of Recognition', *Political Theory*, 20 (2), 187–201.

—— (1994) 'The Social Dynamics of Disrespect: On the Location of Critical Theory Today', *Constellations*, 1 (2), 255–69.

—— (1995) *The Struggle for Recognition: The Moral Grammar of Social Conflicts*, Cambridge: Polity.

—— (1998) 'Democracy as Reflexive Cooperation: John Dewey and the Theory of Democracy Today', *Political Theory*, 26 (6), 763–83.

—— (2002) 'Grounding Recognition: A Rejoinder to Critical Questions', *Inquiry*, 45 (4), 499–520.

—— (2003) Contributions to Nancy Fraser and Axel Honneth, *Redistribution or Recognition? A Political–Philosophical Exchange*, London: Verso.

Ikäheimo, Heikki (2002) 'On the Genus and Species of Recognition', *Inquiry*, 45, 447–62.

Inwood, Michael (1992) *A Hegel Dictionary*, Oxford: Blackwell.

Irving, John (1989) *A Prayer for Owen Meany*, London: Corgi.

Jay, Martin (1996) *The Dialectical Imagination: History of the Frankfurt School and the Institute of Social Research, 1923–50*, Berkeley: University of California Press.

Jones, Peter (1998) 'Political Theory and Cultural Diversity', *Critical Review of International Social and Political Philosophy*, 1, 28–62.

Jurist, Elliot (1994) 'Review of Axel Honneth, *Kampf um Anerkennung*', *Constellations*, 1 (1), 177–80.

Keane, John (2004–5) 'Humble Democracy?', *The CSD Bulletin*, 11 (2)–12 (1), 1–2.

Kemper, Theodore (2001) 'A Structural Approach to Social Movement Emotions', in Jeff Goodwin et al. (eds), *Passionate Politics: Emotions and Social Movements*, Chicago: University of Chicago Press.

Klatch, Rebecca (1999) *A Generation Divided: The New Left, the New Right and the 1960s*, Berkeley: University of California Press.

Kymlicka, Will (1995) *Multicultural Citizenship*, Oxford: Oxford University Press.

—— (1998) *Finding Our Way: Rethinking Ethnocultural Relations in Canada*, Toronto: Oxford University Press.

—— (2002) *Contemporary Political Philosophy: An Introduction*, 2nd edn, Oxford: Oxford University Press.

Laborde, Cécile (2002) 'On Republican Toleration', *Constellations*, 9, (2), 167–83.

Laing, R. D. (1965) *The Divided Self: An Existential Study in Sanity and Madness*, Harmondsworth: Penguin.

Laitinen, Arto (2002) 'Interpersonal Recognition: A Response to Value or a Precondition of Personhood?', *Inquiry*, 45 (4), 463–78.

Larrivee, Pierre (ed.) (2003) *Linguistic Conflict and Language Laws: Understanding the Quebec Question*, London: Palgrave Macmillan.

Locke, John (1689) *A Letter Concerning Toleration*, repr. Indianapolis: Hackett Publishing Co., 1983.

Lyons, Paul (1996) *New Left, New Right and the Legacy of the Sixties*, Philadelphia: Temple University Press.

Maaka, Roger and Fleras, Augie (2000) 'Engaging with Indigeneity: Tino Rangatiratanga in Aotearoa', in Duncan Ivison, Paul Patton and Will Sanders (eds), *Political Theory and the Rights of Indigenous Peoples*, Cambridge: Cambridge University Press.

Malos, Eileen (ed.) (1995) *The Politics of Housework*, Cheltenham: New Clarion Press.

Markell, Patchen (2003) *Bound by Recognition*, Princeton: Princeton University Press.

—— (2006) 'Recognition and Redistribution', in John Dryzek, Bonnie Honig and Anne Phillips (eds), *The Oxford Handbook of Political Theory*, Oxford: Oxford University Press.

Marshall, T. H. (1950) *Citizenship and Social Class*, repr. London: Pluto Press, 1991.

McRoberts, Kenneth (1997) *Misconceiving Canada: The Struggle for National Unity*, Toronto: Oxford University Press.

Modood, Tariq (2005) *Multicultural Politics: Racism, Ethnicity and Muslims in Britain*, Edinburgh: Edinburgh University Press.

Moruzzi, Norma Claire (1994a) 'A Problem with Headscarves: Contemporary Complexity of Political and Social Identity', *Political Theory*, 22 (4), 653–72.

—— (1994b) 'A Response to Galeotti', *Political Theory*, 22 (4), 678–9.

Mulgan, Richard (2004) *Politics in New Zealand*, Auckland: Auckland University Press.

Mulhall, Stephen and Swift, Adam (1996) *Liberals and Communitarians: An Introduction*, 2nd edn, Oxford: Blackwell.

Nussbaum, Martha (2003) *Upheavals of Thought: The Intelligence of Emotions*, Cambridge: Cambridge University Press.

Oakeshott, Michael (1975) *On Human Conduct*, Oxford: Clarendon Press.

O'Day, Alan (ed.) (1997) *Political Violence in Northern Ireland: Conflict and Conflict Resolution*, London: Greenwood.

O'Leary, Brendan (1999) 'The Nature of the British–Irish Agreement', *New Left Review*, no. 233, 66–96.

Olson, Kevin (2003) 'Reflexive Citizenship and the Paradoxes of Participation', paper presented at APSA Annual Meeting, Philadelphia.

O'Neill, John (ed.) (1996) *Hegel's Dialectic of Desire and Recognition: Texts and Commentary*, Albany, NY: State University of New York Press.

Osborne, Peter (1996) 'Review of Axel Honneth, *Struggle for Recognition*', *Radical Philosophy*, no. 80 (November/December), 34–7.

Owen, David (Forthcoming) 'Self-government and "Democracy as Reflexive Co-operation": On Honneth's Social and Political Ideal', in Bert van den Brink and David Owen (eds), *Recognition and Power*, Cambridge: Cambridge University Press.

Parekh, Bhikhu (2000) *Rethinking Multiculturalism: Cultural Diversity and Political Theory*, London: Macmillan.

Parkin, Frank (1971) *Class Inequality and Political Order*, London: MacGibbon and Kee.

Phillips, Anne (1997) 'From Inequality to Difference: A Severe Case of Displacement?', *New Left Review*, no. 224, 143–53.

Piven, Frances and Cloward, Richard (1988) *Poor People's Movements: Why They Succeed, How They Fail*, New York: Random House USA Inc.

Porter, Norman (1998) *Rethinking Unionism: An Alternative Vision for Northern Ireland*, revised edn, Belfast: Blackstaff Press.

Putnam, Hilary (1995) *Renewing Philosophy*, Cambridge, Mass.: Harvard University Press.

Rockefeller, Stephen (1994) 'Comment', in Amy Gutmann (ed.), *Multiculturalism: Examining the Politics of Recognition*, Princeton: Princeton University Press.

Rorty, Amelie (1994) 'The Hidden Politics of Cultural Identification', *Political Theory*, 22 (1), 152–66.

Rorty, Richard (2000) 'Is "Cultural Recognition" a Useful Notion for Leftist Politics?', *Critical Horizons*, 1 (1), 7–20.

The Runnymede Trust (1997) *Islamophobia: A Challenge for Us All*.

Sartre, Jean-Paul (1943) *Being and Nothingness*, trans. Hazel E. Barnes, repr. London: Routledge, 2002.

—— (1946) *Anti-Semite and Jew*, trans. George Becker, repr. New York: Schocken Books, 1995.

Sassoon, Donald (1997) *One Hundred Years of Socialism: The West European Left in the Twentieth Century*, London: Fontana.

Schlesinger, Arthur (1992) *The Disuniting of America*, New York: Norton.

Schumpeter, Joseph (1942) *Capitalism, Socialism and Democracy*, repr. London: Routledge, 1994.

Sennett, Richard (2003) *Respect*, London: Allen Lane.

Shapiro, Ian (1999) *Democratic Justice*, New Haven: Yale University Press.

Shklar, Judith (1990) *The Faces of Injustice*, New Haven: Yale University Press.

Smith, Nicolas (1994) 'Charles Taylor, Strong Hermeneutics and the Politics of Difference', *Radical Philosophy*, no. 68 (Autumn), 19–27.

—— (2002) *Charles Taylor: Meaning, Morals and Modernity*, Cambridge: Polity.

Snow, David and Benford, Robert (1988) 'Ideology, Frame Resonance and Participant Mobilization', *International Social Movement Research*, (1), 197–219.

Sullivan, Harry Stack (1953) *The Interpersonal Theory of Psychiatry*, New York: Norton.

Tarrow, Sidney (1989) *Democracy and Disorder: Protest and Politics in Italy, 1965–1975*, Oxford: Oxford University Press.

Taylor, Charles (1975) *Hegel*, Cambridge: Cambridge University Press.

—— (1985) 'What's Wrong with Negative Liberty?', in his *Philosophical Papers*, vol. 2: *Philosophy and the Human Sciences*, Cambridge: Cambridge University Press.

—— (1989) *Sources of the Self: The Making of Modern Identity*, Cambridge: Cambridge University Press.

—— (1993) *Reconciling the Solitudes: Essays on Canadian Federalism and Nationalism*, Montreal and Kingston: McGill-Queens University Press.

—— (1995a) 'Comparison, History, Truth', in his *Philosophical Arguments*, Cambridge, Mass.: Harvard University Press.

—— (1995b) 'The Politics of Recognition', in his *Philosophical Arguments*, Cambridge, Mass.: Harvard University Press.

—— (1998) 'The Dynamics of Democratic Exclusion', *Journal of Democracy*, 9 (4), 143–56.

—— (1999) 'Democratic Exclusion (and its Remedies?)', in Alan Cairns et al. (eds), *Citizenship, Diversity and Pluralism*, Montreal and Kingston: McGill Queen's University Press.

—— (2002) 'The Politics of Recognition Today: An Interview with Charles Taylor', conducted by Simon Thompson, in *Bulletin of the Centre for Critical Theory*, University of the West of England.

Thompson, Simon (1998) 'Recognizing Multiculturalism', in B. Brecher, J. Halliday and E. Kolinska (eds), *Nationalism and Racism in the Liberal Order*, Aldershot: Ashgate.

—— (2002) 'Parity of Esteem and the Politics of Recognition', *Contemporary Political Theory*, 1 (2), 203–20.

—— (2003) 'The Politics of Culture in Northern Ireland', *Constellations*, 10 (1), 53–74.

Tregenza, Ian (2004) 'Oakeshott on Freedom and Civil Association', paper presented to the Collingwood and Oakeshott symposium, Macquarie University, Sydney, 19 March 2004, <http://www.michael-oakeshott-association.org/pdfs/papers_tregenza_freedom.pdf>, consulted 23 February 2005.

Treiman, Donald, and Hartmann, Heidi (eds) (1981) *Women, Work and Wages: Equal Pay for Jobs of Equal Value*, Washington: National Academy Press.

Tucker, Robert (1972) *The Marx–Engels Reader*, London: W. W. Norton.

Tully, James (1995) *Strange Multiplicity: Constitutionalism in an Age of Diversity*, Cambridge: Cambridge University Press.

—— (1999) 'The Agonic Freedom of Citizens', *Economy and Society*, 28 (2), 161–82.

—— (2000) 'Struggles over Recognition and Distribution', *Constellations*, 7 (4), 469–82.

—— (2001) 'Introduction', in Alain Gagnon and James Tully (eds), *Multinational Democracies*, Cambridge: Cambridge University Press.

—— (2004) 'Recognition and Dialogue: The Emergence of a New Field', *Critical Review of International Social and Political Philosophy*, 7 (3), 84–106.

Walzer, Michael (1994) 'Comment', in Amy Gutmann (ed.), *Multiculturalism: Examining the Politics of Recognition*, Princeton: Princeton University Press.

Weber, Max (1958) 'Class, Status, Party', repr. in *From Max Weber: Essays in Sociology*, London: Routledge, 1991.

Winnicott, Donald (1965) *The Maturational Process and the Facilitating Environment: Studies in the Theory of Emotional Development*, London: Hogarth Press.

Wolf, Susan (1994) 'Comment', in Amy Gutmann (ed.), *Multiculturalism: Examining the Politics of Recognition*, Princeton: Princeton University Press.

Wollheim, Richard (1962) 'A Paradox in the Theory of Democracy', in Peter Laslett and W. G. Runciman (eds), *Philosophy, Politics and Society*, 2nd series, Oxford: Blackwell.

Yar, Majid (2001) 'Beyond Nancy Fraser's "Perspectival Dualism"', *Economy and Society*, 30 (3), 288–303.

Young, Iris Marion (1989) 'Polity and Group Difference: A Critique of the Ideal of Universal Citizenship', *Ethics*, 99 (2), 250–74.

—— (1990) *Justice and the Politics of Difference*, Princeton: Princeton University Press.

—— (1997) 'Unruly Categories: A Critique of Nancy Fraser's Dual Systems Theory', *New Left Review*, no. 222, 147–60.

—— (2000) *Inclusion and Democracy*, Oxford: Oxford University Press.

Zurn, Christopher (2000) 'Anthropology and Normativity: A Critique of Axel Honneth's "Formal Conception of Ethical Life"', *Philosophy and Social Criticism*, 26 (1), 115–24.

—— (2003) 'Identity or Status? Struggles over "Recognition" in Fraser, Honneth, and Taylor', *Constellations*, 10 (4), 519–37.

—— (2005) 'Recognition, Redistribution, and Democracy: Dilemmas of Honneth's Critical Social Theory', *European Journal of Philosophy*, 13 (1), 89–126.

Other documents
The Canadian Charter of Rights and Freedoms (1982), on the world-wide web at <http://laws.justice.gc.ca/en/charter/>
The Charlottetown Accord (1992), on the world-wide web at <http://www.ola.bc.ca/online/cf/documents/1992CHARLOTTE-TOWN.html>
The Meech Lake Accord (1987)), on the world-wide web at <http://www.solon.org/Constitutions/Canada/English/Proposals/Meech Lake.html>
The *Guardian*, 13 March 2004.

Internet sources
<http://www.arts.ulst.ac.uk/ulsterscots/>, accessed 15 December 2005.
<http://www.elysee.fr/ang/rech/rech_.htm>
<http://www.guardian.co.uk/usa/story/0,12271,1167874,00.html>
<http://www.un.org/Overview/rights.html>, accessed 11 August 2005.
<http://www.guardian.co.uk/print/0,3858,4863437-110592,00.html>, accessed 17 August 2005.
<http://onenews.nzoom.com/onenews_detail/0,1227,251436-1-8,00.html>, accessed 19 August 2005.
<http://www.whitehouse.gov/news/releases/2004/01/20040120-7.html>

Index

18242
9878